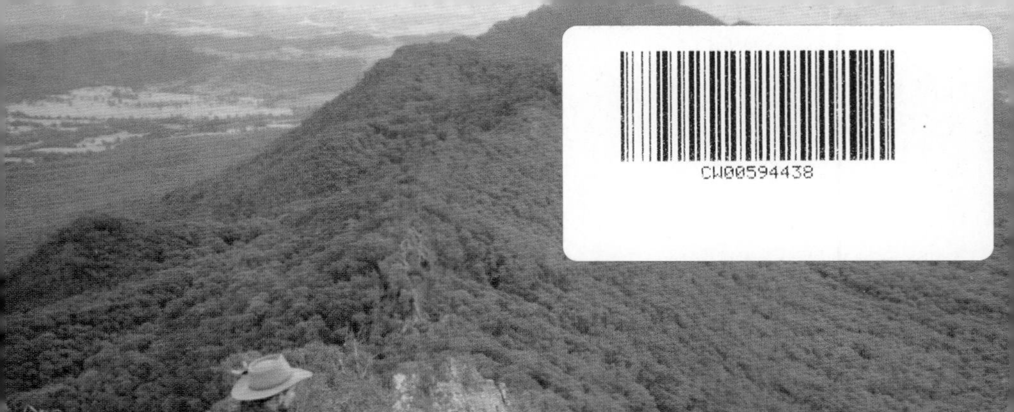

Australia's Best Walks

Tyrone Thomas and
Andrew Close

EXPLORE
AUSTRALIA

Contents

Introduction		vii
Map legend		ix
Walks locations map		x
Index to walk/hike suggestions		1
New South Wales		2
Walk 1	Valley of the Waters, Blue Mountains	5
Walk 2	Grand Canyon, Blue Mountains	9
Walk 3	Mount Gower, Lord Howe Island	12
Walk 4	The Breadknife, Warrumbungles	18
Walk 5	Mount Warning, Northern Rivers	22
Queensland		26
Walk 6	Mount Cordeaux, Main Range	29
Walk 7	Green Mountains, South-East Rim	33

Victoria		38
Walk 8	Mount Feathertop, Alps	41
Walk 9	Point Addis, Surf Coast	47
Walk 10	Briggs Bluff, Grampians	51
Walk 11	Mount Stapylton, Grampians	54
Walk 12	Sealers Cove, Wilsons Promontory	58
South Australia		62
Walk 13	St Mary Peak, Flinders Ranges	65
Walk 14	Bunyeroo Gorge, Flinders Ranges	71
Walk 15	Mount Gambier, South-East	74

Tasmania 78

Walk 16 Dove Lake, Cradle Mountain 81

Walk 17 Tarn Shelf, Lake Webster 85

Walk 18 Freycinet Peninsula, East Coast 89

Western Australia 93

Walk 19 Pinnacles Desert, Cervantes 96

Walk 20 Murchison Gorge, Kalbarri 99

Overview of Australia 104

Climate of Australia 105

Geology of Australia 106

Flora of Australia 110

Australian Biomes 113

Human impact on the natural world 118

Fauna of Australia 120

Safety and commonsense in the bush 122

Equipment and food suggestions for walks 130

Mapping and navigation 131

Glossary 132

Australian road atlas 134

Introduction

This book contains information about twenty walks in Australia that, in our opinion, are among the best walks (hikes) in the country. Australia is the oldest, driest, flattest and smallest continent on earth. It therefore follows that by world standards, the terrain is very ancient, eroded fantastically and geologically interesting. Many primitive plant and animal species are evidence of the country's uniqueness, created by isolation, from other land masses. Even the most famous of Australian animals, the kangaroo, is in effect a living fossil. Classification as the smallest continent gives perhaps some impression of the vastness of the landscape to be explored, yet conveniently, the huge area is all just one country, with no problems of political boundaries to be crossed.

For safety reasons, some very remote, spectacular places have been omitted. The Bungle Bungles of north-west Western Australia for instance are very remote. Australia's most challenging mountain ascent of Federation Peak in Tasmania, is probably best left to skilled rock climbers. The twenty selected walks are a good representation of what exists and the walks chosen are easily accessed by road from nearby towns. The representation includes the best of rainforest, desert, coast, volcanic features, inland gorges and mountain scenery. The selected walks are in southern parts of Australia as northern Australia tends often to be too hot for comfortable walking. Additionally, most suggested walks have a longer seasonal window during which you can enjoy walks.

Walks are graded as easy, medium, or hard. In all walks, time taken will vary greatly, depending upon the experience of individuals. Track notes are therefore provided with references that give both exact distances and variable times, excluding lunch or other significant breaks. As a rough guide, we have doubled the walking time it took us to do the walk. Weather conditions will influence times greatly. The direction of the walk, clockwise or anti-clockwise, is intended for ease of navigation or effort.

A word of warning to all: do not underestimate the distances involved in traveling overland and the subsequent time necessary to undertake the travel. Australia is as big as continental USA without Alaska and as big as Europe without Russia.

Australia naturally lends itself to air travel over the longer hauls. Hitch hiking is to be discouraged. Towns are hundreds of kilometres apart and day time temperatures soar. We recommend that you use coach, air or train services. When driving, avoid fatigue by taking frequent breaks (every two hours) and try not to drive between dusk and dawn as native animals are more active at night.

Tyrone Thomas

Our intention is to introduce you to a wide variety of environments in which you can immerse yourselves fully with respect for flora and fauna and for your own safety. Special sections deal with safety, mapping and navigation.

We have walked all routes in the book as near to publication date as possible. All track notes and the complete map coverage were simultaneously compiled. The maps show all walking and four-wheel-drive tracks on the entire map coverage so that you have an option to create your own walk routes or short cuts or vary the described walks. We are fully aware that government and other maps often fail to show vast numbers of tracks and other information relative to bushwalkers. The aim is to provide accurate maps with information that is generally not available elsewhere.

Andrew Close

It is our policy to walk all routes fully to ensure correctness. However, it must be expected that changes will occur in some places with the passing of time. Likewise, it is impossible to know in advance of particular and unusual problems such as bushfires, bridge washouts and landslides. Every care has been taken in compiling notes and maps, but no responsibility will be accepted for any inaccuracies or for any mishap that might arise out of the use of this book. You should take account of your medical condition, your elementary navigation ability and bush craft skills, your equipment and your safety. Please read pages 122–131 for more information. Most walks in this book are unsuitable for children unless the children are accompanied by an adult. The authors and publisher welcome advice of any errors or desirable amendments to bring future editions of the book up to date.

Tyrone Thomas
Andrew Close
Mount Macedon Victoria

Map legend

Symbol	Meaning	Symbol	Meaning
START	Walk Start		Walk Route with Direction Arrow
	Information		Other Track
	Ranger	Falls	Stream with Waterfall
P	Carpark		Stream with Flow Direrction
	Toilet		Cliffline
	Lookout		Lake, Reservoir or Sea
	Picnic Area		Swamp or Intermittent Lake
	Picnic Area with Shelter	][	Bridge / Track Crossing
	Car Camp	Mount Mayson	Trig point / Named Peak
	Bush Camp	+	Mountain Apex / Named Peak
	Caravan Park	250	Contour Elevation
HUT	Hut or Enclosed Shelter		Place of Interest
31	Highway Sealed		National Park
	Main Road Sealed		Park Other
	Road Unsealed		Private Land
	Four-Wheel-Drive		Residential Area
			Sand / Beach

N

0 500m

Scale

Walks locations map

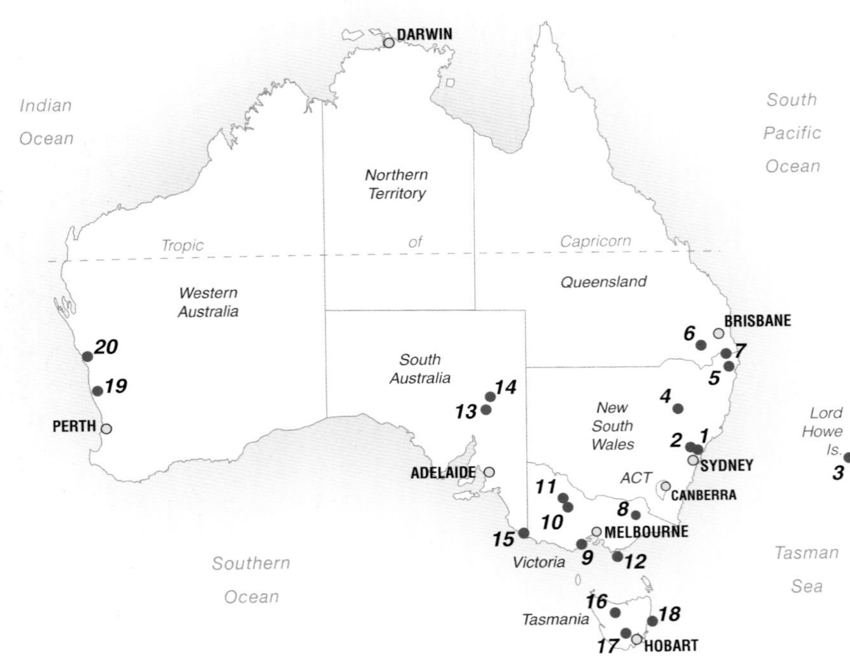

1 Valley of the Waters, Blue Mountains, NSW
2 Grand Canyon, Blue Mountains, NSW
3 Mount Gower, Lord Howe Island, NSW
4 The Breadknife, Warrumbungles, NSW
5 Mount Warning, Northern Rivers, NSW
6 Mount Cordeaux, Main Range, QLD
7 Green Mountains, South-East Rim, QLD
8 Mount Feathertop, Alps, VIC
9 Point Addis, Surf Coast, VIC
10 Briggs Bluff, Grampians, VIC
11 Mount Stapylton, Grampians, VIC
12 Sealers Cove, Wilsons Promontory, VIC
13 St Mary Peak, Flinders Ranges, SA
14 Bunyeroo Gorge, Flinders Ranges, SA
15 Mount Gambier, South-East, SA
16 Dove Lake, Cradle Mountain, TAS
17 Tarn Shelf, Lake Webster, TAS
18 Freycinet Peninsula, East Coast, TAS
19 Pinnacles Desert, Cervantes, WA
20 Murchison Gorge, Kalbarri, WA

Index to walk/hike suggestions

Walk no.	Walk area	Walk km	Walk hours	Walk grade	Page
1	Valley of the Waters, Blue Mountains, NSW	5.5	2.5	easy	5
2	Grand Canyon, Blue Mountains, NSW	5.2	3	medium	9
3	Mount Gower, Lord Howe Island, NSW	8.5	7	hard	12
4	The Breadknife, Warrumbungles, NSW	13.7	6	medium	18
5	Mount Warning, Northern Rivers, NSW	8.8	4.5	medium	22
6	Mount Cordeaux, Main Range, QLD	12.6	5	medium	29
7	Green Mountains, South-East Rim, QLD	18.8	8	hard	33
8	Mount Feathertop, Alps, VIC	29	Two day	medium	41
9	Point Addis, Surf Coast, VIC	11.5	4	medium	47
10	Briggs Bluff, Grampians, VIC	10.8	4.5	medium	51
11	Mount Stapylton, Grampians, VIC	5.6	3	medium	54
12	Sealers Cove, Wilsons Promontory, VIC	19	Two day	easy	58
13	St Mary Peak, Flinders Ranges, SA	21.2	9	hard	65
14	Bunyeroo Gorge, Flinders Ranges, SA	8	2.5	easy	71
15	Mount Gambier, South-East, SA	5	2	easy	74
16	Dove Lake, Cradle Mountain, TAS	5.6	2	easy	81
17	Tarn Shelf, Lake Webster, TAS	13	6	medium	85
18	Freycinet Peninsula, East Coast, TAS	13	4.5	medium	89
19	Pinnacles Desert, Cervantes, WA	5	2	easy	96
20	Murchison Gorge, Kalbarri, WA	8	3.5	medium	99

Walk hours indicated exclude lunch or other significant breaks. As a rough guide the actual walking time taken by the authors is doubled.

NEW SOUTH WALES

1	**Valley of the Waters**	Blue Mountains National Park
2	**Grand Canyon**	Blue Mountains National Park
3	**Mount Gower**	Lord Howe Island National Park
4	**The Breadknife**	Warrumbungle National Park
5	**Mount Warning**	Mount Warning National Park

Walking, Lord Howe Island

New South Wales at its southern end boasts Australia's highest peak, Mount Kosciusko, part of the Great Dividing Range that continues north through the state to Queensland. Northern New South Wales has a subtropical climate limited to the eastern slopes of the range. Inland the 'outback' is famous for the red dust and hard-working farming communities that exist through seemingly endless droughts.

The Warrumbungle National Park, located in the north-east of the state, has spectacular volcanic features, which are a real attraction for walkers. An ascent to the Breadknife and Grand High Tops offers commanding views here.

Sydney has many fine walking tracks within easy reach of the city, and many of these are located in the fantastically eroded sandstone Blue Mountains. This area is of breathtaking beauty, often dusted with snow in the winter. The sandstone plateaus have been eroded into valleys and canyons. Wentworth Falls and the Grand Canyon are featured walks in this book. The Sydney Harbour–Hawkesbury River long-distance walking track is recommended, as is the Great North walk. These walks can be undertaken in sections. The Manly to Spit Bridge section traverses Sydney National Park and offers commanding views of the harbour area. Sydney lies in a basin of sandstone and is surrounded by very rugged sandstone national parks such as Ku-ring-gai Chase and Royal National Park.

Off the east coast, Lord Howe Island is a green, volcanic jewel in the Tasman Sea, with the world's most southerly coral reef. It is home to many rare species of plants and animals due to its isolation from the mainland.

New South Wales' floral emblem: Waratah (Telopea speciosissima)

Australian Capital Territory

Canberra, in the Australian Capital Territory, is in the southern Great Dividing Range of New South Wales.

Canberra is renowned for its many parks and Lake Burley Griffin, named after the American architect who designed the layout of the city. These parklands provide many opportunities for walks.

The long distance Alpine Walking Track went from Canberra south, through the alps to Walhalla in Victoria, but unfortunately recent fires have ravaged most of this area.

New South Wales' fauna emblem: Platypus (Ornithorhynchus anatinus)

1 VALLEY OF THE WATERS

Blue Mountains, New South Wales

Walk:	5.5 km circuit
Time required:	Including minimal breaks, 2 hours 30 minutes
Grade:	One day, easy but with many steps to negotiate
Environment:	Sandstone cliffs, forest and waterfalls
Last review date:	July 2007
Map reference:	New South Wales Lands, 1:25 000 Katoomba and Map 1
Best time to visit:	Suited to any season but may be cold and slippery in winter from June to August

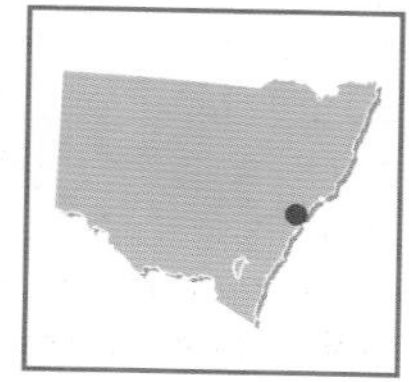

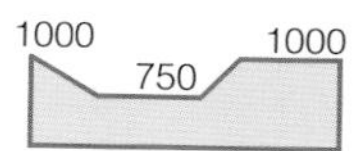

The small township of Wentworth Falls may be overlooked by most visitors to the Blue Mountains region, as they make their way to better-known Katoomba. However, here can be found magnificent areas of natural beauty and superb walk opportunities. This is essentially a cliff-side walk, which takes in many fine waterfalls

Sandstone cliffs at Queen Elizabeth Lookout, Blue Mountains

1-1 VALLEY OF THE WATERS

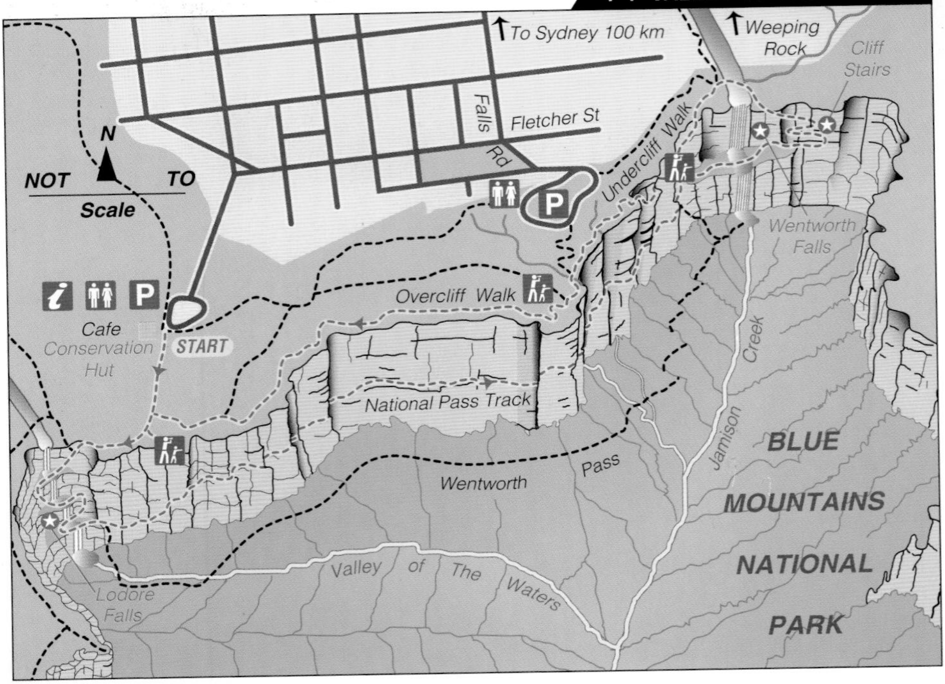

Mt Victoria	J	F	M	A	M	J	J	A	S	O	N	D	Year
Rain av. mm	110	97	80	76	45	58	42	50	47	63	70	72	810
Temp av. max. °C	22	22	20	17	12	10	9	10	13	16	19	21	15
Temp av. min. °C	12	12	11	8	5	3	2	3	4	7	9	11	7

and cascades, dramatic changes of vegetation and many great viewpoints.

Access is along the Great Western Highway to Wentworth Falls village, which is about 100 km from Sydney. Rail travel is available from Sydney to Wentworth Falls station, some 2 km from the walk start. Coaches operate along the highway too. There are plenty of options for accommodation in the Blue Mountains, especially around Katoomba.

Turn off the Great Western Highway on to Falls Road at Wentworth Falls, take the third turn on the right into Fletcher Street, then after 500 m veer left to Conservation Hut and cafe carpark. The walk starts here where there is limited tourist information, toilets and perhaps the opportunity for a cafe snack after the walk.

Head off west from the hut, down many steps for 400 m to Queen Victoria Lookout for your first amazing view of the incredible Jamison Valley and its very high sandstone cliffs. Next, retrace a few metres and turn left to nearby Empress Lookout for a second vantage point. Continue down a little further. Here you turn left on to National Pass beside the Valley of the Waters stream. Empress Falls are then the first of some seven waterfalls as the stream plunges through the high cliffs. The track

descends a steep set of historic steps to Lodore Falls. These are the major falls. They must surely be some of the most perfectly formed and picturesque falls that you are likely to find anywhere in the region. There are magnificent rock overhangs, swimming holes and ferny glades. Just below the falls, take the left-fork track rather than the lower alternative Wentworth Pass track. Here it is apparent how far you have descended, with the cliffs towering above you.

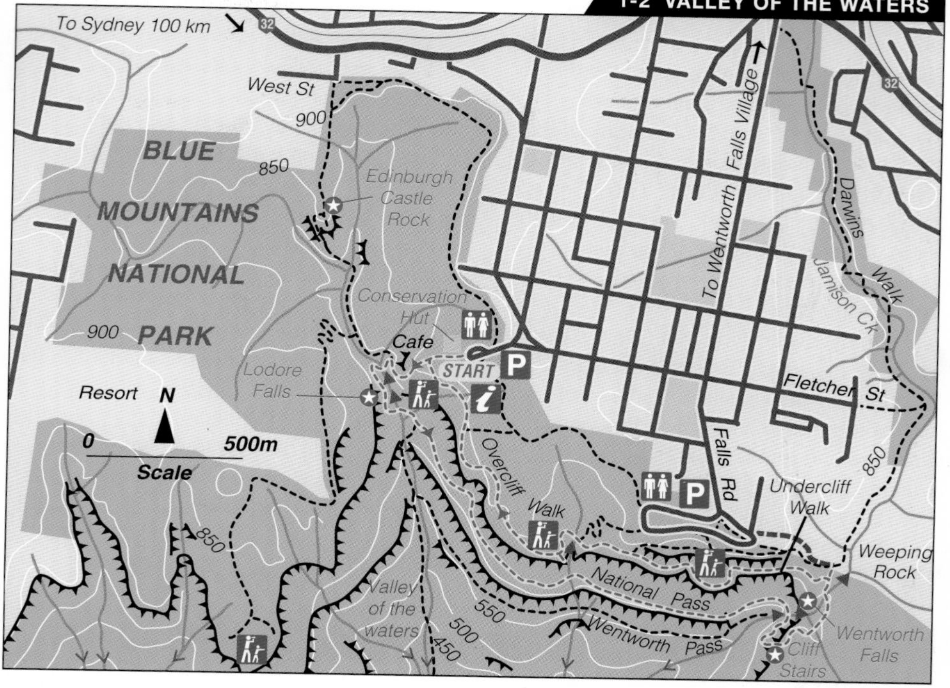

National Pass Track, the one you should follow, then rises a little via steps and you get glimpses back at the previous falls. The track continues for some 2 km on what surely is the most spectacular cliff walk in Australia and about the best overall walk in the Blue Mountains. The sandstone cliffs are in horizontal beds and this remarkable track follows around the contour of the bedding on a tiny ledge. In places the cliffs have been carved out to permit a through route and for most of the way you are under cliff overhangs. You even pass behind waterfalls. The views of the Jamison Valley are often uninterrupted as there is little foreground vegetation to block the view. Eventually, after passing Slacks Steps, you should arrive at Wentworth Falls, which plunge in two stages. National Pass crosses the stream, amid spray, between the two drops. If there has been recent heavy rain, a raincoat would be advisable. Cut stone blocks form a footbridge across Jamison Creek with falls both above and below you. Quite often the wind, being channelled up the valley, will blow the water upwards as it spills over the top. This walk is, therefore, better undertaken following rain.

From here, begin the climb up the well-defined and precipitous steps to the cliff rim. It is interesting to note that these historic steps have been hewn from the cliff-face and must have involved an unimaginable amount of time of quite dangerous work. Once at the brink of the falls, a small creek is crossed prior to the main flow of Jamison Creek. Cross more fine stepping stonework to a track junction. Here you may wish to take the quite short side trip upstream to lovely Weeping Rock on Darwins Walk.

It may interest you that Charles Darwin, while on his way to Bathurst, passed through this area, visited Wentworth Falls and noted that in his opinion the region was desolate and untidy. With due respect to Mr Darwin's descendants (if any), we believe he was wrong.

To continue, climb steps on to Undercliff Walk to begin the return trip westwards. Stay as close to the cliff rim as possible, veering left at each junction. The aim is to follow the Undercliff and Overcliff walking tracks that, like National Pass, follow cliff overhangs and rim along sandstone bedding, but well above National Pass.

Keep heading west. At two points, tracks lead off left. At the first, the side track leads to a small waterfall then on to a lookout. In the second case, the track leads to a minor lookout. Take both these side trips. Many minor tracks lead off to the right from the cliff rim area as you progress and all should be bypassed in favour of the cliff edge route. Always keep left at each junction. After crossing some boggy areas, and when at the fifth branch off to the right, turn right and retrace the track up to the Conservation Hut cafe.

Wentworth Falls, Blue Mountains

GRAND CANYON

Blue Mountains, New South Wales

Walk:	5.2 km circuit
Time required:	Including minimal breaks, 3 hours
Grade:	One day, medium with many steps to negotiate
Environment:	Sandstone cliffs, forest and waterfalls
Last review date:	July 2007
Map reference:	New South Wales Lands, 1:25 000 Katoomba and Map 2
Best time to visit:	Suited to any season but may be cold and slippery in winter from June to August

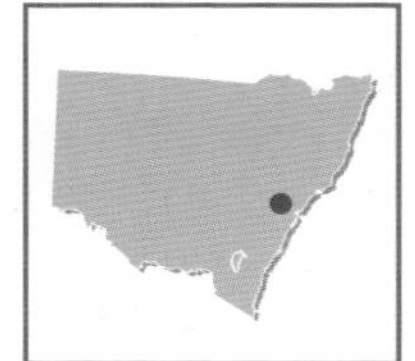

Evans Lookout and the Grand Canyon are undoubtedly major attractions of the Blackheath district in the Blue Mountains. Both result from tremendous erosion of sandstone. The valleys north-east of the two points reach depths of some 600 m. Grand Canyon is really a contorted hanging valley that is rapidly being eroded by

Greaves Creek as it plunges into the main valley at Beauchamp Falls. The main deep valley of the district is Grose River Valley. Deep chasms and plunging waterfalls will leave no one disappointed.

Grand Canyon ferns, Blue Mountains

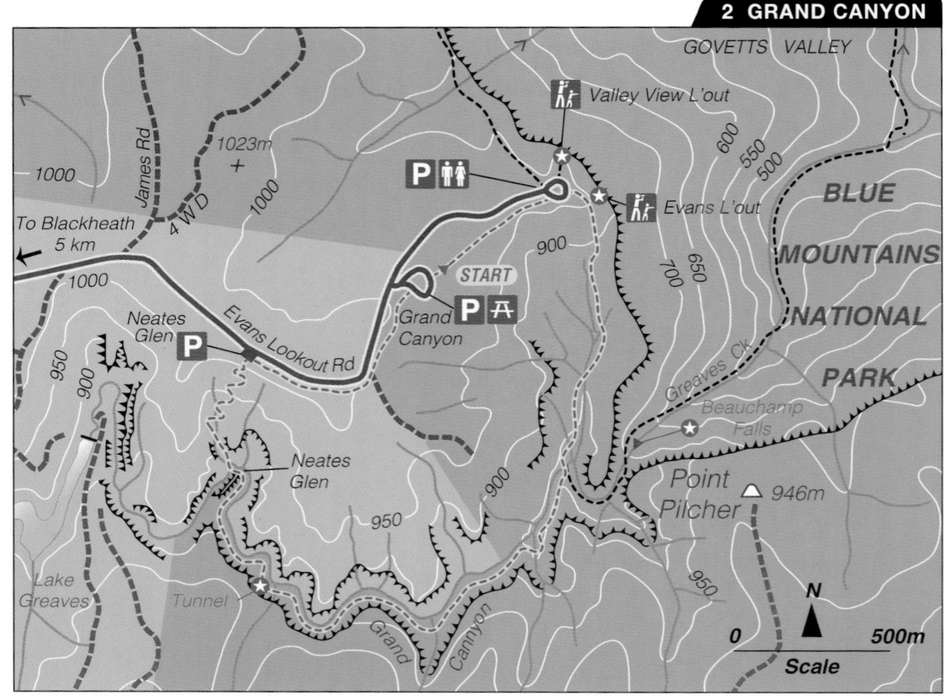

Mt Victoria	J	F	M	A	M	J	J	A	S	O	N	D	Year
Rain av. mm	110	97	80	76	45	58	42	50	47	63	70	72	810
Temp av. max. °C	22	22	20	17	12	10	9	10	13	16	19	21	15
Temp av. min. °C	12	12	11	8	5	3	2	3	4	7	9	11	7

Access is along the Great Western Highway to Blackheath, which is about 116 km from Sydney. Trains are available for access to Blackheath. There are plenty of options for accommodation in the Blue Mountains at Blackheath and especially around nearby Katoomba. The walk start is at the large Grand Canyon carpark and picnic ground 3.7 km east of the Great Western Highway via Evans Lookout Road. This is not to be confused with the lesser Neates Glen carpark, which you encounter first.

This walk takes in the views at Evans Lookout before descending into the Grand Canyon and is considered to be of a medium grade and although suited to any season is perhaps best enjoyed after rainy periods when the waterfalls are at their most spectacular phase.

At the far end of this carpark, a walking track leads north-east, roughly parallel to the road, 400 m towards Evans Lookout. This lookout gives spectacular views through the Grose Valley. From here deviate north 150 m to Valley View Lookout, which gives commanding vistas north towards Govetts Leap and Pulpit Rock. Return to Evans Lookout and locate the Grand Canyon access track heading south.

This soon descends steeply into a very pleasant gully and creek with abundant ferns. At 1.2 km from Evans Lookout,

A view of the escarpment from Govetts Leap, Blue Mountains

this gully meets Greaves Creek. Here you should turn right and head upstream from this confluence and on to the floor of the canyon. During the 2 km walk through the canyon, the sandstone walls become deeper and closer together, with numerous crossings of the creek required as you progress. After some 500 m it will be necessary to climb away from the creek up a number of well-formed steps to a walkway skirting the cliff-face. Here the sedimentary layering of sandstone is clearly evident with variations of colour due to various impurities. The track gradually turns north with many rock overhangs and the creek is now far below you in the narrowest part of the canyon. Once through a 10 m long tunnel, the canyon floor becomes quite flat with the stream temporarily disappearing underground, on its way through the canyon.

You may wish to stop for lunch or a rest here before starting the ascent out. Approximately 30 m from the tunnel, a number of steps formed on the eastern rock face must be climbed, the track then continues for 700 m to eventually climb to Neates Glen carpark. From here a well-defined track heads east, parallel to the road for 1 km, back to the walk start at Grand Canyon carpark.

MOUNT GOWER
Lord Howe Island, New South Wales

Walk:	8.5 km retrace
Time required:	Including minimal breaks, 7 hours
Grade:	One day, hard (875 m elevation rise)
Environment:	Coastal cliffs and mountain ascent
Last review date:	September 2001
Map reference:	New South Wales Lands, 1:15 000 Lord Howe Island and Map 3
Best time to visit:	September to May; winter can be windy and misty

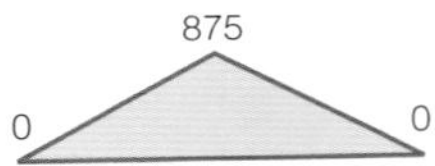

Tahiti, Moorea, Bora Bora and Lord Howe Island are all South Pacific sub-tropical islands of incredible beauty. Their magnificence has resulted from the combination of high island volcanic plug topography with surrounding tropical seas and coral reefs. Lord Howe Island is equal in scenic and natural attractions to any of the better-known tourist venues of Polynesia. Furthermore, Lord Howe Island is part of New South Wales and unlike the others destinations is relatively close to the Australian east coast. It is also, perhaps, one of the world's best

View to Mt Eliza, Lord Howe Island

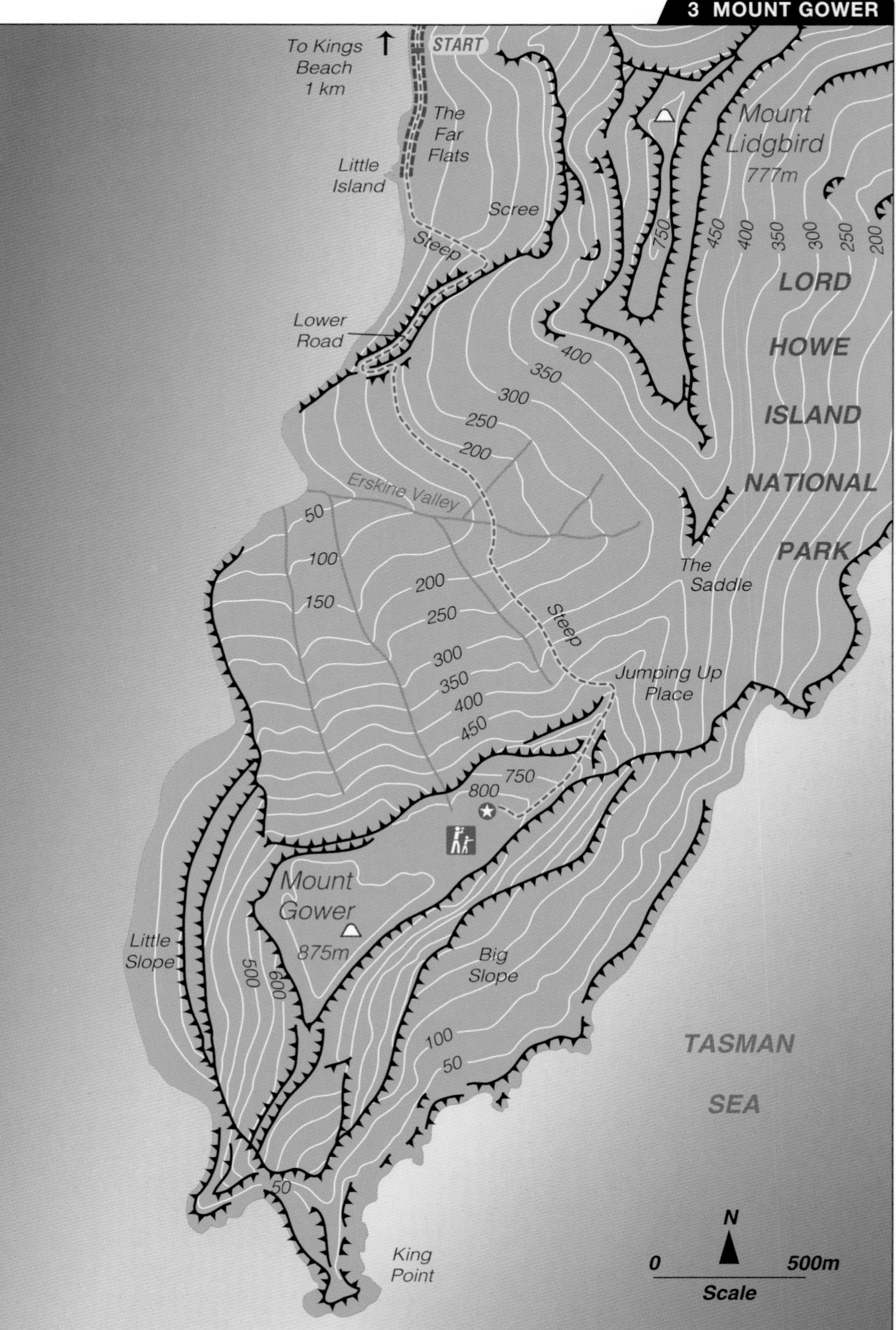
To Kings Beach 1 km
START
The Far Flats
Little Island
Scree
Steep
Lower Road
Mount Lidgbird
777m
LORD HOWE ISLAND NATIONAL PARK
Erskine Valley
The Saddle
Steep
Jumping Up Place
Mount Gower
875m
Little Slope
Big Slope
TASMAN SEA
King Point
N
0 500m
Scale

Lord Howe Is.	J	F	M	A	M	J	J	A	S	O	N	D	Year
Rain av. mm	121	117	138	114	153	176	143	105	106	114	111	104	1505
Temp av. max. °C	25	25	24	23	21	19	18	18	19	20	22	23	22
Temp av. min. °C	20	20	19	17	16	14	14	13	14	15	17	19	17

kept tourist secrets. It does not have the luxury resorts and trappings of mass tourism and therefore represents a truly natural paradise. In fact, a special Act of Parliament protects the people and environment from commercial exploitation and large scale development. Clearly the aim is to limit the tourist industry and one gathers that the islanders are intent on keeping their island low key. Lord Howe Island, named after an eighteenth-century admiral in the British navy, was discovered on 17 February 1788, less than a month after settlement at Sydney Cove.

There are at least 219 native plant species on Lord Howe Island. Some 79 of these occur nowhere else in the world. There are 400 fish species and 60 coral species living in the lagoon, reef and surrounding sea. There are 120 species of birds, ranging from large gannets to terns, and they include the rare Lord Howe Island woodhen. Boobies, mutton birds and wideawakes nest in large numbers on isolated parts of the coast. There is total protection of all plant life, bird life and marine life and the island has United Nations World Heritage classification.

Lord Howe Island lies about 800 km north-east of Sydney and 800 km south-east of Brisbane; it is roughly east of Port Macquarie. It is the centrepiece of 28 islands, islets and rock stacks set on a submarine ridge between Australia and New Zealand. The warm East Australian sea current ensures that the ocean water temperature remains warm and thereby enables the world's most southerly living coral to flourish. The island is about 11 km long, crescent shaped and aligned north–south. Its narrowest point, between Old Gulch and North Bay beach, is only about 250 m wide. Its widest point is 2 km. The northern and southern ends of the island are both declared permanent parkland to preserve flora and fauna. The eastern coastline consists mostly of rugged ocean cliffs with small surf beaches and the west coast is mainly lagoon and coral reef. The coastline is readily accessible for only about 8 km. The lagoon is 6 km long and generally just 1–2 m deep.

The volcanic activity that created the island occurred earlier in the north than in the south where there are massive vertical-sided peaks known as Mount Gower (875 m) and Mount Lidgbird (777 m). These two peaks, especially, create the appearance of a typical South Pacific 'Bali Hai'.

Lord Howe Island's walks, unlike most in this publication, entail a good deal of expense for transport and accommodation. For the enthusiastic walker, the outlay is certainly warranted. Airlines operate from Sydney and Brisbane. The air fares are expensive by Australian standards. It should be appreciated that the short island runway prevents larger planes operating; therefore each flight can only transport a few people.

Accommodation cost is high due to isolation and high transportation cost of supplies. Full-board guesthouse accommodation or self-contained apartments have to be used. In effect, camping is not permitted. It is limited to islanders and only at North Beach and on the eastern slopes of Mount Gower with the view to facilitating the collection of palm seeds for export. In special cases, permission to camp may be granted to visitors if an island guide is hired to accompany the campers. In such cases North Beach is the venue.

There are three general stores on the island, but merchandise, again, is costly. Several restaurants are available. The usual mode of transport is by hired bicycle with just a few vehicles being available for hire. Some accommodation operators run minibuses for their guests. Walkers can in fact reach most parts of the island and return in a day. There is an extensive walking track network. The island has a small hospital but limited search and rescue services and walkers should take extra safety measures.

Lord Howe Island has a maritime climate and frosts do not occur. The seas are warm and there is a moderately heavy rainfall spread throughout the year, but heavier in winter. Winter rain and winds cause a definite tourist off season and some accommodation closes during June, July and August. February is the driest month and has a minimum monthly average temperature of 23 °C.

Some special points to remember include:

- the need for a torch as there is very little street lighting
- glass bottom boat trips are available to see the reef and its life
- snorkelling gear can be hired
- coral is sharp so do not walk barefoot near it
- the island has a very interesting museum
- dress at restaurants is smart casual
- airways luggage limits are very small
- there is an airport departure tax included in the cost of tickets
- there are no snakes on the island.

As mentioned, the twin peaks that form the southern end of Lord Howe Island are Mount Gower and Mount Lidgbird.

Lower road access to Mount Gower

The ascent of Mount Gower should only be attempted by experienced walkers prepared for a difficult hard climb. Mount Lidgbird, which is 777 m, is rarely climbed. It is a rock climbers' peak and they too are discouraged due to lack of full search and rescue facilities on the island. The grey-black volcanic rock of both peaks conveys an awesome, eerie impression, especially near the cliff bases.

Official island advice is that intending climbers of Mount Gower should use an island guide. This is said to be because of an awkward section known as the Lower Road that involves negotiating a 500 m long ledge with about a 150 m sheer drop to the sea. Clearly there is an advantage in using a guide on any walk in an unfamiliar location to ensure the most interesting spots are visited and to have flora and fauna described.

The island board ranger's advice is that although walkers cannot be forced to use a guide, there is a preference that island-registered guides be used. They are islanders and not island board staff and they are sometimes very selective about the times when they may be available to lead walks. On several past preview walks, a guide has not been used and the route was well defined with a broad pad and track markers.

However, the Lower Road and 'The Getting Up Place' near the summit both involve very exposed climbing and it would be unwise for most people to climb without a guide. As well, the rare Lord Howe Island woodhen has the Mount Gower summit as one of its main habitats. Providence petrels nest there too so that there is also a need to prevent undue intrusion.

The small summit plateau is covered with luxuriant, dripping, mossy rainforest. The tops are often shrouded in mist and on rainy days the whole area appears most forbidding, with waterfalls plunging over huge cliffs into the sea.

There are excellent views to be had from the peak, especially from the knife-edge northern approach spur. The island appears dwarfed in a vast expanse of ocean. The colours of the lagoon waters and the coral reef, together with the line of breakers along the outer reef edge, are simply magnificent. Mount Lidgbird's huge bulk dominates the foreground.

Closer at hand is an impressive display of unusual plants and there is a big range of birds, most of them sea birds. Sea birds are a special feature of Lord Howe Island. They visit each summer in hundreds of thousands for breeding.

The rare woodhen is a flightless bird and displays no fear of man. By 1978, there were said to be just 30 birds in existence, so in 1980 three pairs were taken into captivity and used for raising chicks. By 1984, 79 birds were released and now over 200 birds live there.

To start the walk to the peak named after John Gower, Rear Admiral and First Captain to the British Admiral, Lord Howe, it is best to use bicycle or other transport to reach the south end of sealed Lagoon Road. Rather than walking the road, the time would be better spent on the mountain.

The distance from the end of Lagoon Road to Little Island, then up to the peak, is only 4.25 km (8.5 km return), but progress will be slow and it is best to allow about 7 hours or more. Island advice is to allow 8 hours.

From the south end of Lagoon Road and a road barrier, a four-wheel-drive track needs to be walked for 1.2 km to Little Island. The track remains close by the sea. The guides, of course, need to be booked well in advance and poor weather can see your guide advising against tackling the ascent as rocks can be slippery.

After the initial 1.2 km coast walk to Little Island, rock hop the boulder-strewn beach southwards for about 130 m to locate the indistinct start of the peak's ascent track. The pad leads off immediately adjacent to the southern edge of an old scree. The scree is now partly covered by vines. Palms on the slopes stretch right to the rocky beach immediately north of the scree, causing the scree to be more obvious through lack of trees. Once located, the pad is easy to discern. The track rises very quickly, and about 50 m from the beach there are ropes as an aid to the steep climb. About 150 m elevation is gained in about 300 m distance from the beach to the base of the cliffs and an overhang.

These cliffs are part of the western buttress of Mount Lidgbird. It is then necessary to begin a contouring walk south at the cliff base. Shortly afterwards, ropes are again provided as the pad leads on to a distinct narrow ledge. This ledge (Lower Road) gets quite breathtaking with a 150 m sheer drop to the sea below. Some inexperienced people could become nervous at this point. Ropes stretch along the side of the track for about 400 m of the 500 m long Lower Road. The pad then turns east around the end of the cliff-face and there is a climb up a rocky slope for about 150 m. The way is then via a basically contouring track east into the Erskine Valley for about 600 m to where the creek is forded on flat rocks. The volume of water in the creek varies greatly, depending upon the weather. There is always adequate water for a good drink and at times there can be a real torrent. The whole area is deep within damp forest and a great place for a rest. Next, the track swings south-east and climbs steadily for 700 m, gaining 350 m elevation up the crest of a spur to a high ridge linking Mount Lidgbird and Mount Gower. Dense forest, including the usual palms, extends right up to the ridge. The ridge is attained well above and south of the 400 m Lidgbird–Gower saddle. From this point on, there is a very steep ascent of a knife-edge spur. Ropes are again provided in a particularly steep section. There is a rise in elevation of about 350 m over about 600 m, so exposure becomes acute as the summit plateau is neared. Sea birds are often seen soaring in the updraughts. Views become spectacular. The vegetation is heavily wind pruned and stunted and the prevailing misty conditions usually mean that great care is needed on slippery rocks.

At the top, the main attraction is the view just past a knob. The large collection of unusual plants, many of which grow nowhere else in the world, is a great draw-card. Orchids are abundant.

The rest of the walk involves a retrace with much care being exercised in slippery places.

After the walk seems an ideal opportunity to take the tourist boat trip that circumnavigates the island. The boat passes right alongside both the east and west cliff-faces of Mount Gower and really highlights how very steep and huge the cliffs are. The eastern face gives an impression of having been subjected to an enormous prehistoric landslide into the sea. Also, as you round the southern tip of the island, the famous rock spire, Balls Pyramid, can be seen 23 km to the south. It rises sheer from the sea in a 548 m high spire.

THE BREADKNIFE

Warrumbungles, New South Wales

Walk:	13.7 km circuit
Time required:	Including minimal breaks, 6 hours
Grade:	One day, medium
Environment:	Volcanic lava plugs, forest and mountain ascent
Last review date:	August 2007
Map reference:	New South Wales Lands, 1:30 000 Warrumbungle National Park and Map 4
Best time to visit:	Suited to any season, but avoid hot summer days and carry water

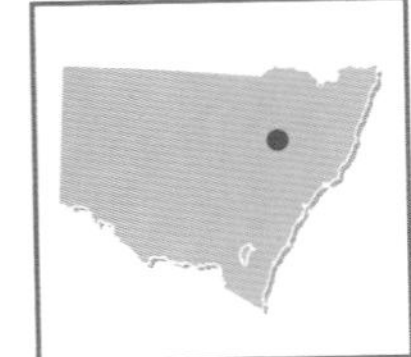

Some 400 km inland and west of Coonabarabran is Warrumbungle National Park. This area contains many significant igneous rock columns, plugs, domes and mesas, which are the remains of composite volcanic activity occurring some 13 million years ago. Much erosion of softer ash and other ejected material has since occurred with a radiating stream flow pattern emerging. These streams link to be part of the present Castlereagh River system. In stark contrast to the now exposed

The Breadknife panorama

4 THE BREADKNIFE

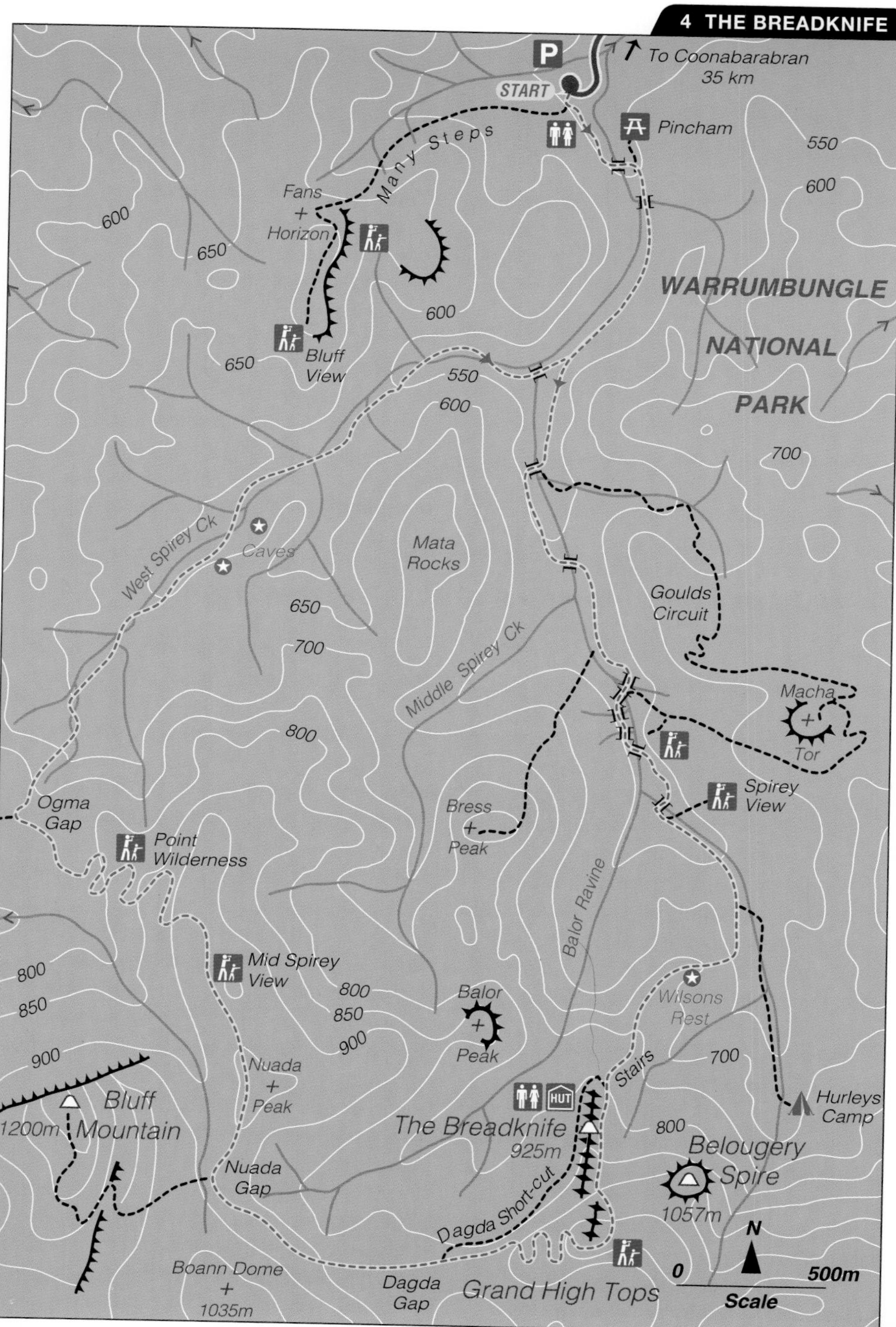

Coonabarabran	J	F	M	A	M	J	J	A	S	O	N	D	Year
Rain av. mm	90	80	62	53	54	57	55	53	49	59	63	66	745
Temp av. max. °C	31	30	28	23	19	15	14	16	20	24	27	30	23
Temp av. min. °C	15	14	11	7	3	1	0	1	3	7	10	13	7

plugs and domes, formations such as the Breadknife occur when cracks in the side of the volcano allowed magma to well up from below. Rapid cooling formed stronger rock. The lava was a viscous, trachyte type, rich in silica. In many cases, this process blocked the throat of volcanic vents and this often led to explosive discharges, which can blow large quantities of rock great distances. Such features as Belougery Spire and Crater Bluff are excellent examples of plugs.

The park is noted for a wide variety of flora and fauna. White cypress pines (*Callitris glaucophylla*), and black cypress pines (*Callitris endlicheri*), rough-barked apple (*Angophora floribunda*), grass trees (*Xanthorrhoea glauca*) and 17 different species of eucalyptus are present. Up to 35 varieties of orchid proliferate. Of note is the shiny leaved hopbush (*Dodonea viscosa*). You will most likely encounter grey kangaroos, echidnas, wedge-tailed eagles, emus and galahs along the way.

Generally speaking, the park is quite dry and lack of water is often a problem. Hot summer days are better avoided by walkers and it is essential to carry plenty of drinking water during walks. You are advised to bring in water from a treated source.

Climbing the rock faces of the Breadknife is not allowed by park authorities, but rock climbing is popular at designated sites in the park; a permit is required. The park has an extensive system of walking tracks and the climb to the Breadknife and the Grand High Tops are among the most popular.

This walk goes to the Breadknife and beyond to Spirey View beginning at Camp Pincham. The land in this area was donated by a grazier Alfred Pincham. Camp Pincham carpark is at the end of a side road, 800 m south from the main park road. The spot also services a side trip to Fans Horizon just 1.6 km each way.

The remote area of the park means private transport is needed for access. The town of Coonabarabran has good facilities for accommodation, and coach services operate along the highway through the town. Excellent camping with full facilities are within the park. Local wildlife has become tame to the presence of humans and may prove troublesome near food.

From the carpark at Camp Pincham head off south, past a bush camp area, via Pincham Track in the valley of Spirey Creek for 1.2 km. Avoid the right fork, West Spirey Creek track, as this is your return route, returning across the creek at this point. Some 500 m later, avoid the left fork Macha Tor track, so as to continue in the wooded valley on the main track. Three other lesser side pads are also passed.

At 3.7 km from the walk start, you begin to leave the valley at the Hurleys Camp turnoff. Start a steady climb up past a seat at Wilsons Rest. Excellent views of Belougery Spire and western cliffs help to make this climb more pleasant. It is a 1 km climb mostly by paved path and stairway to a track junction. Here you are at the lower end of the Breadknife. On hot days, the cypress pines provide some shade. The right fork leads within 70 m to locked Balor Hut (bookings required for use), toilet and viewpoint, where a welcome rest is afforded. You may well consider lunch here, as it is less exposed than 700 m further ahead, atop the summit.

Next, retrace your steps and take the left fork uphill, climbing alongside the eastern base of the blade formation. After 400 m you will reach the upper end of the Breadknife. However, you need to climb a little further for spectacular views. Follow the track east around the base of another blade, Lugh's Wall, parallel to, and south-east of, the Breadknife. As you reach its top end, walk 10 m west on to the blade for the view over the Breadknife and beyond.

Climbing under Breadknife Blade

Next, continue up the rocky slopes, following orange reflective track markers. Within 300 m you will reach the Grand High Tops, offering commanding views of Belougery Spire, Crater Bluff and surrounds. It is probably the best panorama in the park and is especially good towards the now familiar Breadknife.

From the tops, head 600 m west, at first along the tops, then steeply downwards to Dagda Gap. Keep heading west from the track junction at the gap. You pass through sparse forest amid some cypress pines to reach Nuada Gap after another 1.2 km. Avoid the left fork to Bluff Mountain and continue along the tops, past Nuada Peak to Mid Spirey View. Take time here to appreciate the view of Bluff Mountain and its cliffs, which dominate the scene to your west. Evident are the basalt columns that form the core of the bluff with expansive scree slopes near the base. When 1.7 km from Nuada Gap you reach Point Wilderness. Continue down zigzags for 600 m past Ogma Rocks to Ogma Gap and Ogma bush camp site. A small clearing here is most suitable for a rest.

Next, turn down the right-fork track, north-east towards Camp Pincham. The track is steep and somewhat rough at first. It then flattens out to follow the West Spirey Creek valley through cool woodlands with abundant plant species. This sheltered somewhat cooler gully forms a great microclimate for a wide variety of ferns and orchids alike. At two points there are small caves to the right of the track. The bushland here is tranquil compared to the exposed high places visited earlier. After 3 km rejoin your outward route and retrace the 1.2 km along Spirey Creek path back to Camp Pincham carpark.

5 MOUNT WARNING
Northern Rivers, New South Wales

Walk:	8.8 km retrace
Time required:	Including minimal breaks, 4 hours 30 minutes
Grade:	One day, medium
Environment:	Mountain ascent in rainforest
Last review date:	August 2007
Map reference:	New South Wales Lands, 1:25 000 Burringbar and Map 5
Best time to visit:	April to October, summer from December to March can be hot and humid; avoid the summit during storms

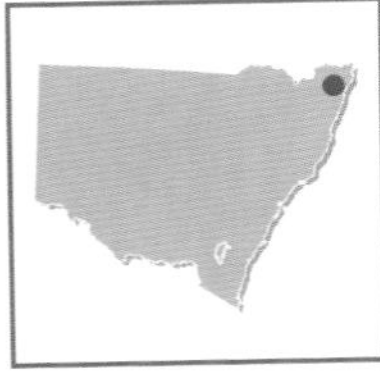

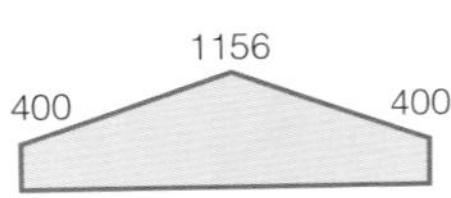

The Gold Coast in Queensland has developed as Australia's main tourist beachside centre with the best that Australia offers in facilities including extensive air services to and from the rest of Australia and from New Zealand. The attractions are not only associated with the beaches along the coast but also inland, where the Border Ranges contain superb rainforests, waterfalls and national parks.

Bangalow Palms (Archontophoenix cunninghamiana)

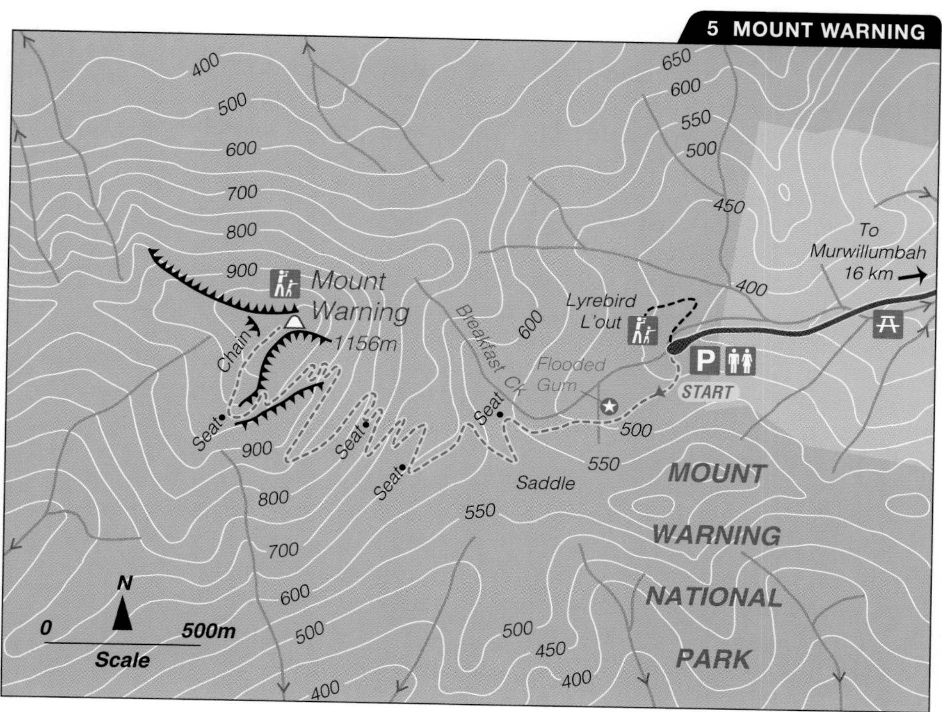

Byron Bay	J	F	M	A	M	J	J	A	S	O	N	D	Year
Rain av. mm	164	184	208	183	179	164	107	92	66	102	120	143	1720
Temp av. max. °C	27	27	26	24	22	19	19	20	22	23	24	26	23
Temp av. min. °C	20	20	19	17	15	12	11	12	14	16	17	19	16

Surfers Paradise has the most tourist development but the tourist area extends from Southport in Queensland to Tweed Heads in New South Wales, and beyond.

A glance at the 1:250 000 scale Tweed Heads map sheet reveals the immensity of a vast ancient (early tertiary) volcano, which we are told, last erupted about 23 million years ago. It is adjacent to the Gold Coast, on the border of northern New South Wales and southern Queensland. The Tweed River and other streams have eroded and enlarged the central explosion crater, but left an 'island' of harder, more acid lava rock dome, called Mount Warning. It was named by Captain Cook as he discovered the east coast of Australia. The mountain once attained about 2000 m, nearly double the present 1157 m height. The flanks of the former, huge mountain's basaltic dome remain along the state's border in the form of the McPherson and Tweed Ranges, but erosion has created great low angle spurs (or Planeze) with deep gorges between them. Such dramatic features as the Pinnacle mark the rim of the eroded crater where the harder surface rocks have given way. The erosion caldera is about 30 km in diameter.

A most informative and enjoyable day ascent of Mount Warning can be taken from the Breakfast Creek carpark serving the national park, which encompasses the peak. Access is via Murwillumbah in New South Wales and the south arm of the Tweed River valley, then up the valley of Karrumbyn Creek. Many Gold Coast visitors find the walk to be an excellent day's outing during their stay.

Murwillumbah has a good range of accommodation options and there are also places to stay close to Mount Warning, but not in the national park. Be aware that the mountain (Wollumbin) is considered sacred to Aboriginal people and they prefer its summit not be climbed. Despite this fact, thousands of people ascend the peak each year. You should remain on the provided walking track if you choose to climb. There is no public transport towards the mountain beyond Murwillumbah. You should not leave valuables in vehicles in the carpark at the trackhead as thieves evidently operate in the area. Carry drinking water and do not start the walk late in the day. Keep off the summit during thunderstorms as lightning frequently strikes the top. There is a pleasant picnic area on more level ground down the road from the carpark if needed. There is also a table, seats and toilet at the carpark.

A 4.4 km foot track leads from the carpark to the summit. It starts off well graded with many steps and zigzags, but for the last short steep ascent above about 1000 m elevation it has a long chain hand-hold to assist with scaling the sloping rocks. Seats along the way, plant label on some trees and distance markers also help make the walk more enjoyable. The rocks near the summit can be slippery when wet.

The rainforests in the area are part of the much larger, World Heritage classified Gondwana Rainforests of Australia. Rainforest is therefore abundant and is most dense on the igneous rock areas of the main peak and associated peaks where soil depth and moisture is deeper. White Booyong and palms are especially prevalent on the sheltered, lower reaches. These are called bangalow palms by Aboriginals in New South Wales and piccabeen palms by the Aboriginals of Queensland. Brush box trees (*Lophostemon confertus*) are common and some 400 m from the walk outset you pass an enormous flooded gum (*Eucalyptus grandis*). Buttressed trees such as the huge strangler figs are present. Daughwood, tamarind and glossy laurel are also seen. The mid-level forest includes numerous tree species such as lilly pilly, rosewood, corkwood, cedar, coachwood and beech. There are also many epiphytes such as orchids, elkhorn, staghorn climbing ferns and birds-nest ferns plus many vines. Lawyer vines (*Calamus muelleri*) with their nasty tendril barbs are also present. Vines are characteristic of rainforest environments. High cliff-faces have many giant spear or gymea lily (*Doryanthus palmeri*), which are noted for their giant red flower heads late each spring and early summer. The exposed, summit rock faces feature shrubby montane heath and grassy plants such as tussock grass, grass tree, blunt-leaf mountain wattle, yellow tea tree, bottlebrush and broad-leaved cassinia.

You are sure to see and hear lyrebirds, scrub turkeys, green catbird, whipbird and quail but most wildlife tends to be nocturnal. Numerous species of bats, spiders, possums, pademelons, lizards and frogs are common. Leeches can be a problem in wet weather.

Four viewing decks on the summit provide the best possible panoramas and plaques illustrate and name the features to be seen. Views occur only on the upper reaches and at the summit where there is a spectacular outlook to the erosion crater walls, which on average are 15 km

Mount Warning Summit

distant. On the top, the north coast of New South Wales and the high-rise buildings of Queensland's Gold Coast are within view as is the Tweed River, distant Cape Byron and the nearby towns of Murwillumbah, Tyalgum and Uki.

The top of Mount Warning, by reason of elevation and easterly aspect, is the first part of the Australian mainland to receive sun rays at dawn. There are no branch tracks along the route of the climb, so you need simply ascend and descend via the same route. Lunch is suggested on the top before you retrace the way down the mountain.

Flooded gum at base of Mount Warning

QUEENSLAND

6	Mount Cordeaux	Main Range National Park
7	Green Mountains	Lamington National Park

Cunninghams Gap, Main Range National Park

Queensland has most of its area in the tropics and as such is a favourite destination for travellers. Among its most famous natural features is the Great Barrier Reef, the world's largest living organism. Vast areas of rainforest exist along the seaward side of the Great Dividing Range. At Cape Tribulation, the rainforest meets the coast at the reef.

The Brisbane region has some of the state's best geological formations, notably precipitous cliffs and lava 'plugs' at such places as the Glasshouse Mountains. Those who take time to explore away from the more popular beach attractions will find an amazing array of plant and animal life. Main Range National Park includes a great walk to Mount Cordeaux, which features rainforest at lower levels and the more exposed tops are colonised by the spear lilly (*Dorianthus palmerii*). Near Lamington National Park, Green Mountains section has extensive rainforest featuring numerous waterfalls. Queensland is home to many spectacular orchids.

As with much of coastal northern Australia, crocodiles can await the unwary in Queensland! Visitors unfamiliar with humidity should plan walks and other activities with care, as heat exhaustion can lead to poor judgement with unhappy consequences.

One of the main crops grown is sugar cane. Hinchinbrook Island off the coast of Cardwell features the magnificent Thorsborne Trail long distance walk through tropical rainforest and coast scenery. It is Australia's largest island National Park. Those wanting to get away from it all can catch a boat from Cardwell through mangrove forests to the remote Ramsay Bay, which offers commanding views of Mount Bowen. Travelling further on to Macushla, one may camp in isolation. The Cape Richards walking track crosses the Island into rich littoral coastal forest with giant buttressed trees, solitaire palms, vines and orchids. In the state's northern rainforests, the lawyer vine is one to watch out for as its barbs can cause injury; also stinging trees known as the gympie gympie have a multitude of needle-like poison-filled hairs on their heart-shaped leaves. Skin contact should be avoided.

Far north Queensland's wet tropics are a living museum containing many endemic plants and animals. The sunbird and the Ulysses butterfly are notable species found here. This world heritage bio-region contains some of the most genetically diverse breathtakingly beautiful scenery with Australia's highest concentration of ferns.

Queensland's floral emblem:
Cooktown Orchid (Dendrobium bigibbum)
Photo courtesy of Greg Campbell

Queensland's fauna emblem:
Koala (Phascolarctos cinereus)

6

MOUNT CORDEAUX

Main Range, Queensland

Walk:	12.6 km retrace
Time required:	Including minimal breaks, 5 hours
Grade:	One day, medium
Environment:	Mountain ascent in sub-tropical area
Last review date:	August 2007
Map reference:	Queensland Sunmap, 1:25 000 Cunninghams Gap and Map 6
Best time to visit:	Suited to any season but December to March can be hot and humid

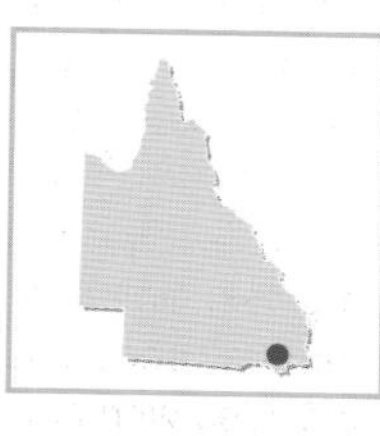

QLD

This walk on the Great Dividing Range in the Main Range National Park is the best of several walk alternatives at Cunninghams Gap. The gap is 755 m high, and the busy Cunningham Highway passes through it, 115 km south-west of Brisbane. The pass was discovered by explorer Allan Cunningham in 1828 and he named the two abrupt peaks astride the gap, Mount Mitchell 1168 m and Mount Cordeaux 1144 m, after surveyor Major Mitchell and Mitchell's assistant, Cordeaux. The Great Dividing Range in this vicinity is very rugged. The dramatic terrain ensured the gap was used only as a pass for a bridle track until 1927.

Strangler fig tree (Ficus watkinsiana)

The range is mainly of heavily eroded basalt from a huge shield volcano some 23 million years old, but unlike Mount Warning in New South Wales, there is no known specific eruption point. Erosion of the volcanic material has been more pronounced on the eastern flanks leaving massive east-facing cliffs.

Rainforest covers the sheltered moister parts of the range, while grass trees and low wind-pruned shrubs are predominant on the rocky tops. On exposed cliffs and steep slopes, the giant spear lily (*Doryanthus palmeri*) thrives. It has huge flax-like leaves and up to a 4 m flower stalk with a brilliant red flower head. It blooms in late spring and early summer. Because the whole area has rich volcanic soils, farms occupy all possible surrounding land, leaving only

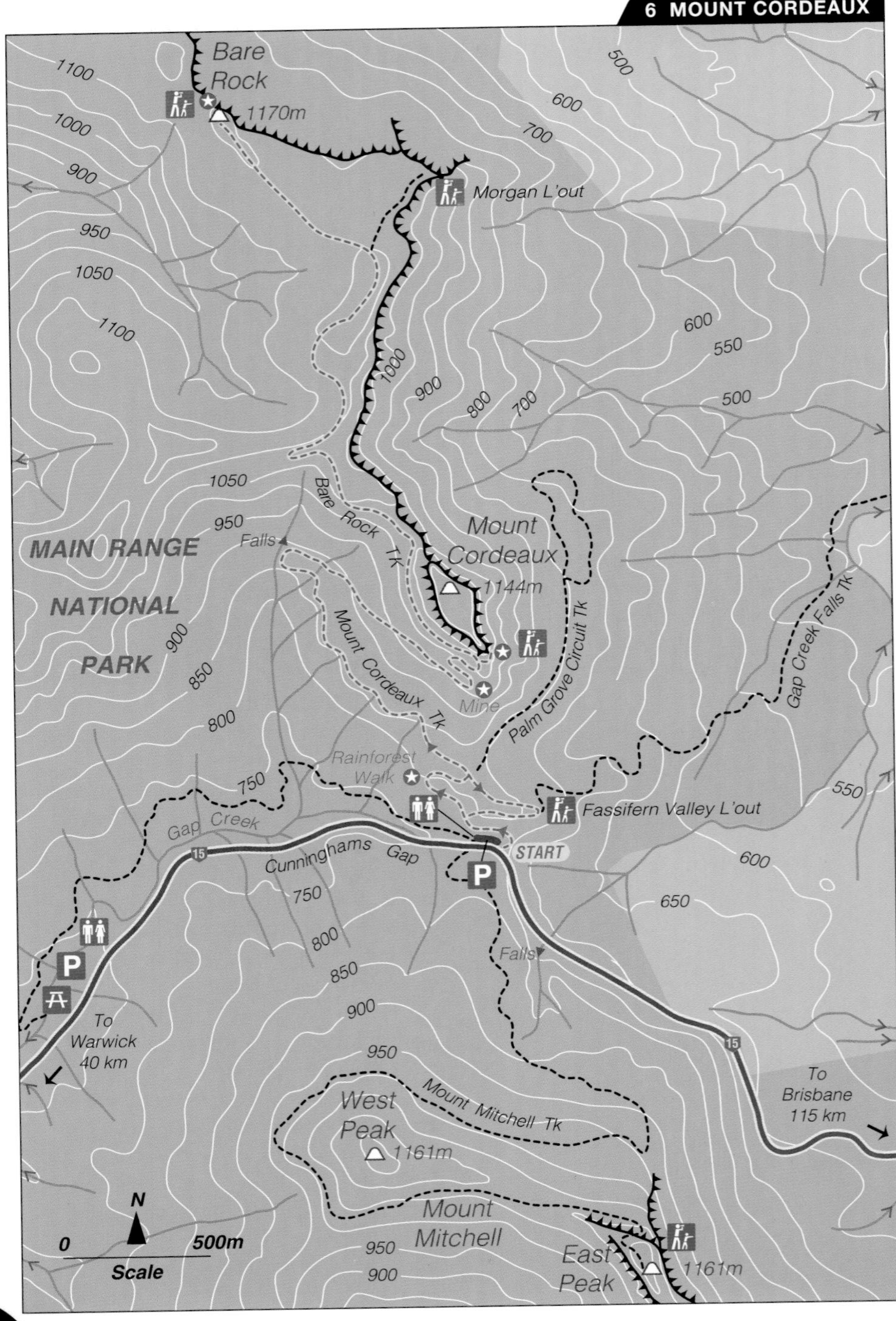
Bare Rock
1170m
Morgan L'out
MAIN RANGE NATIONAL PARK
Falls
Bare Rock Tk
Mount Cordeaux
1144m
Mount Cordeaux Tk
Mine
Palm Grove Circuit Tk
Gap Creek Falls Tk
Rainforest Walk
Fassifern Valley L'out
Gap Creek
Cunninghams Gap
START
Falls
To Warwick 40 km
To Brisbane 115 km
West Peak
1161m
Mount Mitchell Tk
Mount Mitchell
East Peak
1161m
N
0
500m
Scale

Brisbane	J	F	M	A	M	J	J	A	S	O	N	D	Year
Rain av. mm	159	158	140	92	73	67	56	45	45	75	97	133	1149
Temp av. max. °C	29	29	28	26	23	20	20	21	24	26	27	29	25
Temp av. min. °C	20	20	19	16	13	10	9	10	12	15	18	19	1

those places too steep to farm for the heavily forested park. This forest is part of the much larger World Heritage classified Gondwana Rainforests of Australia.

The suggested walk is north from Cunninghams Gap and includes what is known as the Rainforest Circuit. The track is very well graded via many zigzags, so the climb to the range crest is moderately easy. Some 415 m elevation has to be gained to reach the destination at Bare Rock, but this rise is all but completed after the first 4 km. The rock has a commanding view of the massive cliffs along the escarpment and to the city skyline of Brisbane, 115 km away. Mount Cordeaux Lookout is included in the walk, being only 65 m off the main track.

Private transport is best used for access to Cunninghams Gap and there is little accommodation in the immediate area. The small town of Aratula, north-east of the gap, has limited accommodation. The nearest large town facilities are at Boonah and Warwick both some 40 km distant.

The track to follow leaves from the east end of the carpark at the gap. Do not leave valuables in vehicles at the gap as thieves evidently operate in the area. Also carparking spaces are limited especially at weekends. Carry water for lunch as the tops are usually dry. A toilet is available at the gap. Shortly after setting off, you pass a monument to Allan Cunningham.

Set off up past the monument to a division of tracks, which mark the two sides of the Rainforest Circuit. Go left so as to climb to a second track junction 700 m from the walk start. Some plants here are labelled. The tracks at the junction lead to Palm Grove, back down to the carpark, and up to Mount Cordeaux. The latter is your route. It climbs gradually in and out of steep gullies, amid sheltered rainforest and soon you are away from the noise of trucks on the highway. Look up to the tree canopy to see the birds-nest ferns, orchids, epiphytes, vines, and mosses.

After 1.4 km, near a grove of piccabeen palms (*Archontophoenix cunninghamiana*), the track doubles back south-east at a small intermittent waterfall, but remains on the south-west slopes of Mount Cordeaux. These palms are known as bangalow palms in New South Wales. The track continues to rise gradually, until reaching the area of the main southern spur of Mount Cordeaux. At this point the track zigzags upwards several times and provides excellent views across the gap to Mount Mitchell as it rises above the rainforest canopy. There is an old open-cut gold mine at the zigzags. It has both a deep horizontal cutting and a vertical shaft. Just after the turns, take the 65 m long side track to Mount Cordeaux Lookout. This rocky platform is adjacent to the sheer cliffs that ring the mountain summit. The actual top is dangerous to climb. We find the platform area a great place to sit and enjoy the surrounds and broad views. Significant grass trees (*Xanthorrhoea*) and giant spear lilies (*Doryanthus*) are a feature here.

Continue up the track along the south-west side of Mount Cordeaux. Soon a saddle is reached just north of the peak. Look back at the north-east side of the cliffs of the mountain to see the giant spear lilies and to better appreciate this rugged knob on the tops. Many orchids and grass trees up to 4 m tall (some with multi-trunks), grow beside the track in this locality. Hoop pines (*Araucaria cunninghamii*) protrude above the tree canopy on the slopes westwards. These are one of the tree species that existed at the times of Gondwana.

On again north-west along the range, the track re-enters rainforest with tree ferns present and climbs a little further. When some 2.1 km from Mount Cordeaux Lookout, the 350 m long, right-fork track to Morgan Lookout has a disappointing view so you could bypass it, although it is a peaceful spot in the bush. It is best to keep left and go another 680 m to reach Bare Rock. Its rocky summit is just above the rainforest, from which can be seen one of the better views in south-east Queensland. This makes it an ideal lunch spot. The variations in green of the forest below attract the eye, although the principal focus is along the Scenic Rim cliffs and north-eastwards. There is a 50 m long pad amid the scrub to rock on the south-west side of the summit from which you get great views.

To return, retrace 5.5 km then complete the descent of 900 m via the alternative left-fork part of the Rainforest Circuit. It passes the Gap Falls Track and Fassifern Valley Lookout. The route has been re-aligned adding 200 m to its former length.

Mount Cordeaux

GREEN MOUNTAINS
South-East Rim, Queensland

Walk:	18.8 km circuit
Time required:	Including minimal breaks, 8 hours
Grade:	One day, hard
Environment:	Sub-tropical forest with many waterfalls
Last review date:	August 2007
Map reference:	Queensland Sunmap, Beechmont and Tyalgum 1:25 000 and Map 7
Best time to visit:	Suited to any season, but December to March can be hot and humid

This longer walk in the Lamington National Park Green Mountains section, includes numerous waterfalls along Canungra Creek West Branch and Toolona Creek. Rainforest covers most of the

Elabana Falls, Green Mountains

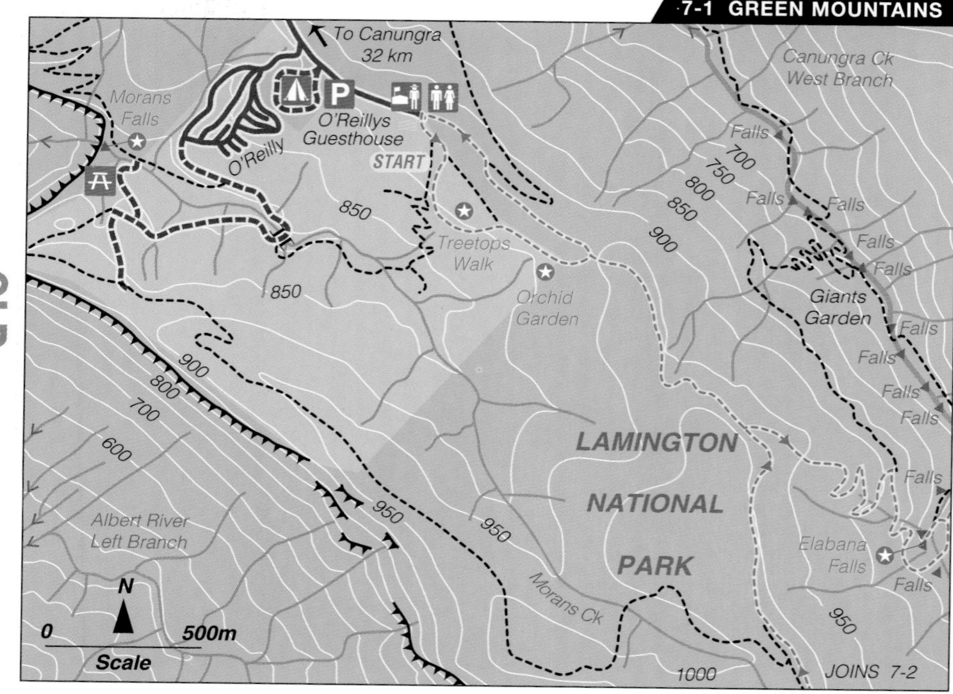

Tamborine Mt	J	F	M	A	M	J	J	A	S	O	N	D	Year
Rain av. mm	228	221	199	118	110	101	90	55	58	95	119	152	1546
Temp av. max. °C	26	26	25	23	20	19	18	18	20	23	25	26	22
Temp av. min. °C	16	16	15	13	10	9	8	8	10	13	15	16	12

distance, including areas of cliff rim on the Queensland–New South Wales state border. It is based from historic O'Reilly's Guesthouse and the national park Green Mountains visitor centre across the road at 950 m elevation. The region is part of the large World Heritage classified Gondwana Rainforest of Australia and rainforest is the prime attraction for this walk.

The outward route of the clockwise circuit of this walk has numerous stream crossings and waterfalls in the Toolona Gorge. Being a high rainfall belt, especially from December to March, these creek crossings could sometimes be awkward after prolonged rain. Slippery conditions occur at any time especially at the creek crossings. At any time you also need to carry a waterproof item upon which to sit during lunch and other breaks because of a lack of dry places to rest. It is essential to start this walk early in the day. You do best to check yourself for possible ticks and leaches during the walk.

Private transport is needed for access to this walk start, which is an hour's drive beyond Canungra by very narrow, winding road. Canungra is south of Brisbane and has numerous town facilities plus accommodation. There is a park-operated basic, fuel stove only, camp area with levelled gravelled sites

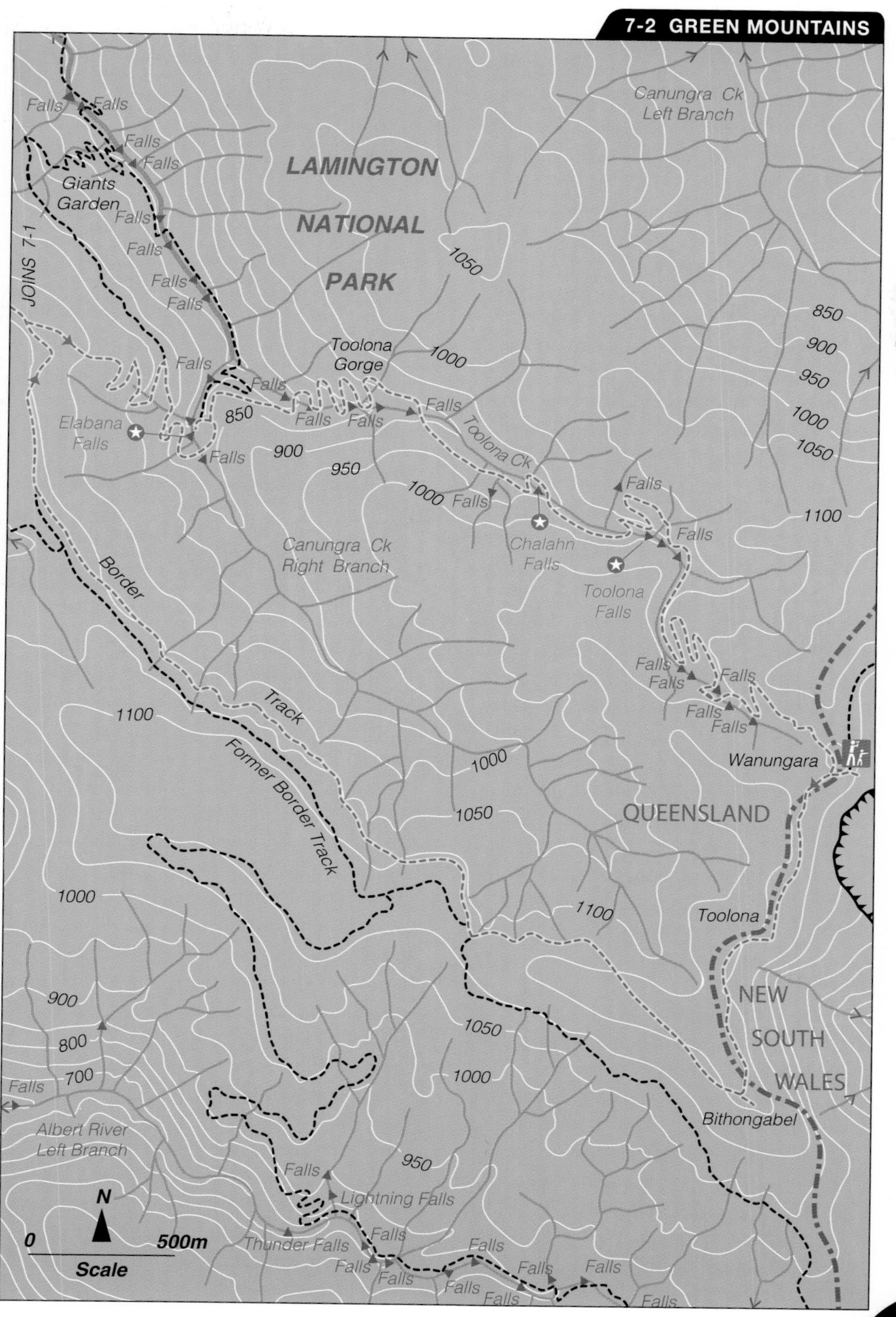
LAMINGTON
NATIONAL
PARK
Canungra Ck
Left Branch
Falls
Falls
Falls
Falls
Giants
Garden
Falls
Falls
Falls
Falls
JOINS 7-1
1050
850
900
950
1000
1050
Toolona
Gorge
1000
Falls
Falls
Falls
Falls
Elabana
Falls
850
Falls
Falls
Toolona Ck
900
950
1000
Falls
Falls
Chalahn
Falls
Falls
1100
Toolona
Falls
Canungra Ck
Right Branch
Border
Track
Former Border Track
1100
Falls
Falls
Falls
Falls
Falls
Wanungara
1000
1050
QUEENSLAND
1000
1100
Toolona
NEW
SOUTH
WALES
900
800
700
Falls
1050
1000
Bithongabel
Albert River
Left Branch
950
Falls
Lightning Falls
Thunder Falls
Falls
Falls
Falls
Falls
Falls
Falls
Falls
Falls
Falls
N
0
500m
Scale

QLD

to combat erosion. Somewhat up-market guesthouse accommodation is available at O'Reilly. You should be aware that the former Pensioners Track shown on many maps has now been re-named as part of the Border Track and a parallel section of the Border Track has been downgraded to be an un-maintained route.

The guesthouse is heavily tourist-orientated on a tract of private land surrounded by park. It has a cafe, gift shop, its own network of walking tracks, garden for orchids and tropical plants, and a tree-tops walk. It encourages bird feeding of colourful rosellas, lorikeets, brush turkeys, satin bower birds and regent bower birds for tourist viewing. This is despite park signs across the road requesting that birds not be fed.

The border rim escarpment is the eroded perimeter of the crater of the huge extinct Mount Warning shield volcano that stands alone 15 km away in the centre of the crater as a volcanic plug of resistant igneous rock. The volcano is said to have been active about 23 million years ago. Essentially for this walk you climb to the rim of the caldera, follow the rim, then descend again. The basaltic rock present has been heavily eroded by Toolona Creek and other streams. However, the greatest erosion has been on the southern (New South Wales) side, which is subject to prevailing weather and highest rainfall.

Set off up past the guesthouse and on to the treetops boardwalk, view the orchid garden briefly perhaps from across the fence. There is a long way to go so do not spend too much time in the garden. When 700 m from the walk start, you join the main Border Track. Some of the trees are labelled. These trees are representative of those to be seen ahead in the nearby rainforest. However, they are subtropical types often with large buttresses like the strangler fig

Regent bowerbird

trees (*Ficus watkinsiana*). Further into the forest there is a cool temperate type forest. Antarctic beech trees (*Nothofagus mooreii*) are typically seen. Only Nothofagus trees support a fungi called beech orange that is also only found in Australia and South America. Both are evidence of Gondwana. As you walk you will see colourful bracket fungi too. It is one of many types of fungi seen in such damp places.

After another 1.1 km, you veer left and start a descent into the rugged Canungra Creek West Branch valley. The way is down via zigzags into a cascading world of water and ferns. After 900 m you keep right to avoid the Box Forest Track and 600 m further down you reach Canungra Creek West Branch. Cross the creek above the first of some seventeen waterfalls to be seen ahead. Just ahead you should take a side trip to see beautiful two-tiered Elabana Falls. It is 400 m return. The other end of the Box Forest Track is near these falls and needs to be avoided.

After the detour, you go 400 m and reach Toolona Creek and from this creek crossing you climb the track for 5.7 km. There are many zigzags to negotiate and some falls drop more than 30 m. Chalahn Falls and Toolona Falls are particularly attractive. Millions of ferns are passed and there are aerial gardens of epiphytes, mosses, vines, ferns and other plants in the canopy. The track zigzags to visit many waterfalls as you ascend further and further into damp forest. There are thousands of stream lilies growing in this mist-drenched area of gullies and cliffs. They flower in September and October and have a large flower stalk. The forest is most beautiful here at their flowering time. Eventually you arrive at the Mount Warning caldera rim and meet a track junction.

Before you turn right, take the 70 m long side trip to Wanungara Lookout for its reasonably good view. Some of the area is closed for revegetation. Next, follow the Border Track south close to the cliff rim and within 1.3 km you reach Boolamoola where you leave the caldera rim. Antarctic beech trees, many mosses and ferns, plus lyrebirds are seen on this section. The beeches are up to 5000 years old and prefer the damp, mist-laden prevailing, south-easterly weather of the escarpment. The limbs are mostly draped with eerie mosses. There is no significant view to the caldera on the way because of the dense forest.

Turn back north-west away from the cliffs and soon you start descending. Within 1.1 km you reach the Albert River circuit track that links on the left. Just 50 m later the return junction of the circuit needs to be bypassed. The former Pensioner Track section (2.8 km long) takes you downhill gradually back into the subtropical rainforest. Another 600 m on you rejoin your outward route. You retrace 1.1 km then keep right on to sealed path that leads directly back to the park visitor centre. The Canungra Creek West Branch Circuit Track links from the right just short of the walk end.

Cycad

VICTORIA

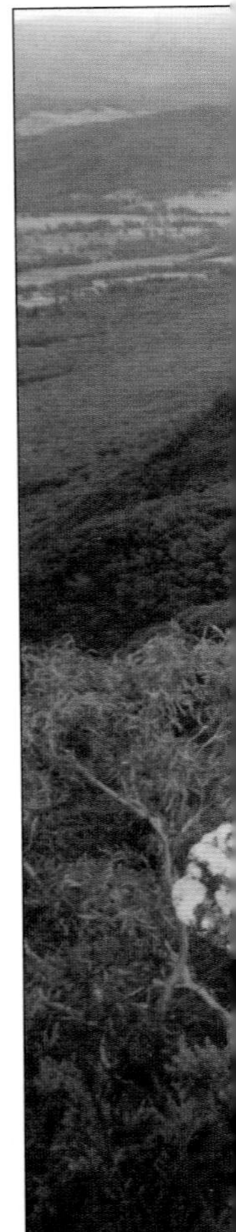

8	**Mount Feathertop**	Alpine National Park
9	**Point Addis**	Point Addis Marine National Park
10	**Briggs Bluff**	Grampians National Park
11	**Mount Stapylton**	Grampians National Park
12	**Sealers Cove**	Wilsons Promontory National Park

Razorback Ridge

Victoria has a wide variety of regions. To the east, the Great Dividing Range dominates, with opportunities for high-country walking over many days, through sparsely populated areas and deep, almost impenetrable valleys. Many of Australia's tallest peaks are located in Victoria, therefore in winter they are snow bound and often inaccessible to walkers. Cross country (Nordic) skiing is an option. A walk above the tree-line along the Razorback to Mount Feathertop in summer is an exceptional alpine experience.

The most southerly extent of the mainland is at Wilsons Promontory. A land bridge once connected Tasmania to the mainland at this point at a time when the sea levels were lower. Here you find rugged granite hills and beautiful white sand beaches, such as Sealers Cove.

The west of the state has inland desert regions and, with the exception of the Grampians, is relatively flat. The Grampians consist of sedimentary rock, uplifted by the enormous tectonic pressure between north–south aligned fault lines. The resultant escarpment and generally rugged terrain provides for excellent walking opportunities, notably at Briggs Bluff and Mount Stapylton.

The south-west of the state has in excess of 100 volcanic peaks, some of which ceased activity as little as 4800 years ago. This was due to the north-easterly movement of the continent over a magma 'hot spot' beneath the crust. Many exhibit the 'classic volcanic cone' shape. The south-west coast is home to rock formations known as the Twelve Apostles and the Great Ocean Road. Point Addis Marine National Park offers dramatic coastal cliff scenery, one of Victoria's best beaches, and is a suggested walk in this book.

The central districts contain large expanses of ancient, gold-bearing rocks. As such, the area was greatly affected by the discovery of gold in the mid-1800s, with the landscape being largely remodelled by prospectors. Care must be exercised by walkers, as the area is riddled with unmarked, often deep shafts. The long distance Great Dividing Trail is centred upon the town of Daylesford and extends throughout the goldfields. Close to Melbourne there are innumerable walking opportunities in fine forests at Mount Dandenong, Mount Macedon, nearby Hanging Rock and along the southern slopes of the Great Dividing Range.

Victoria's floral emblem: Pink Heath (Epacris impressa)

Victoria's fauna emblem: Leadbeater's Possum (Gymnobelideus leadbeateri)

8 MOUNT FEATHERTOP

Alps, Victoria

Walk:	29 km retrace (Day one 14.5 km; Day Two 14.5 km assuming two summit ascents)
Time required:	Including minimal breaks, two days (Day one 6 hours; Day Two 6 hours)
Grade:	Two days, medium, backpack
Environment:	Alpine meadow and mountain ascent
Last review date:	March 2006
Map reference:	*Vicmap*, 1:25 000 Harrietville and Feathertop and Map 8
Best time to visit:	November to April, snowbound in winter from June to September

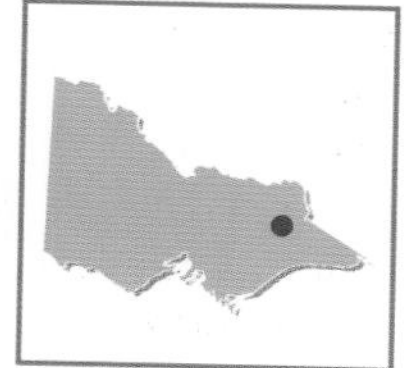

VIC

Bright	J	F	M	A	M	J	J	A	S	O	N	D	Year
Rain av. mm	71	53	57	72	105	116	136	138	124	104	83	75	1136
Temp av. max. °C	29	29	26	21	16	12	12	13	16	20	23	26	20
Temp av. min. °C	10	11	8	5	3	1	1	2	3	5	7	9	6

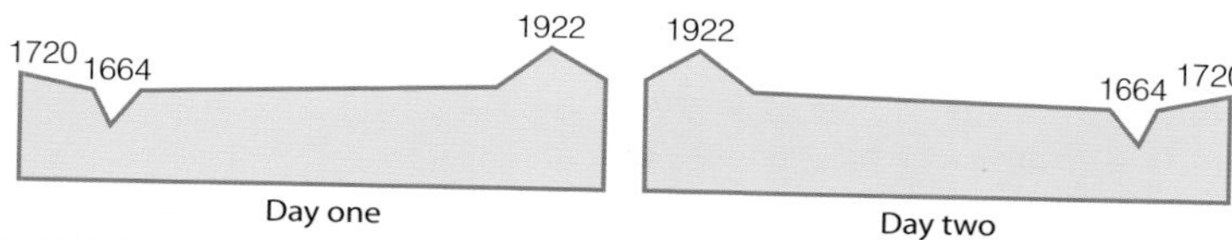

The Razorback Ridge, Mount Feathertop

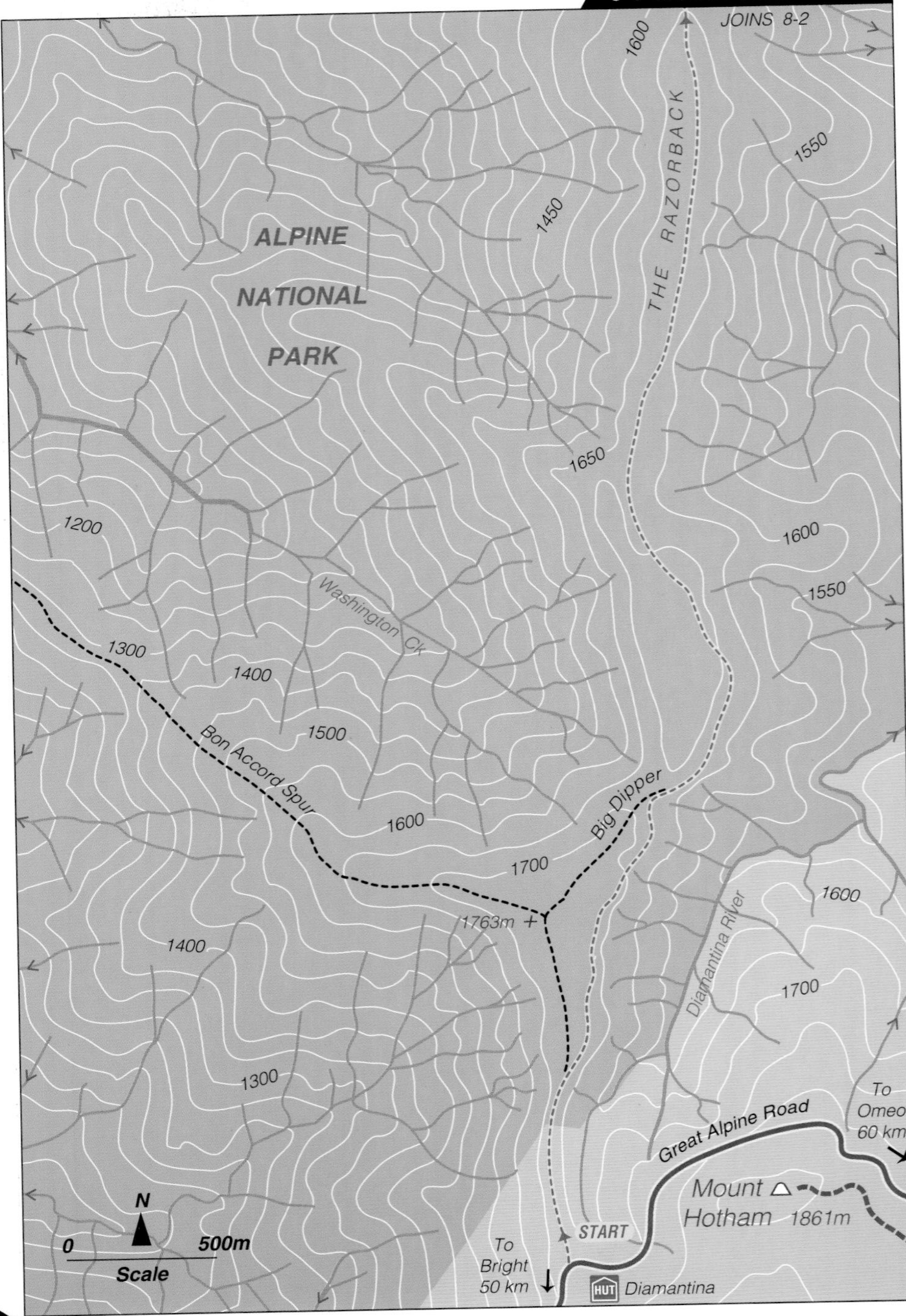

JOINS 8-2

THE RAZORBACK

ALPINE NATIONAL PARK

1600
1550
1450
1650
1200
1600
1550
Washington Ck
1300
1400
1500
Bon Accord Spur
Big Dipper
1600
1700
1763m +
1600
Diamantina River
1400
1700
1300

To Omeo 60 km

Great Alpine Road

Mount Hotham 1861m

N

0 500m
Scale

START

To Bright 50 km

HUT Diamantina

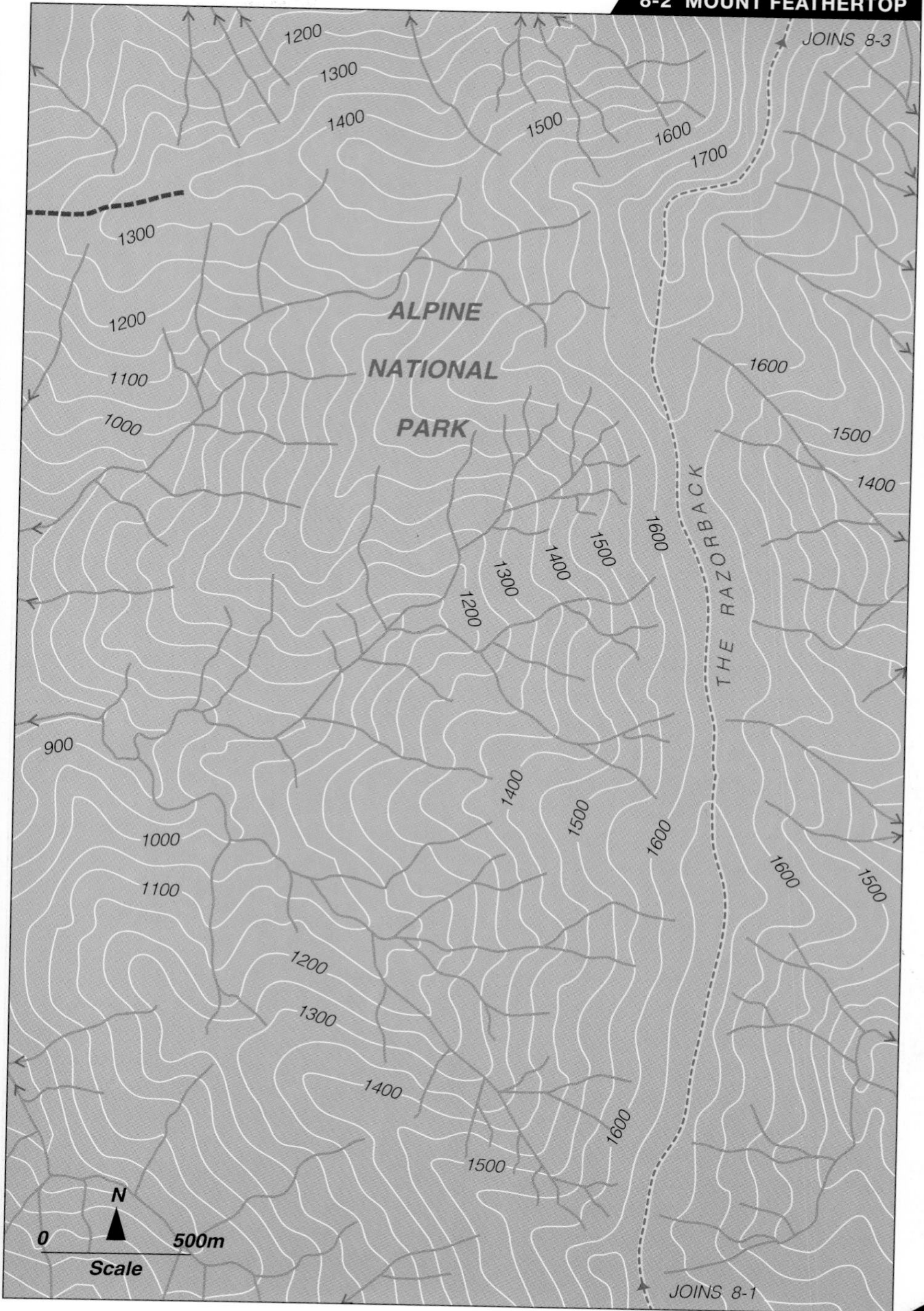

JOINS 8-3
1200
1300
1400
1500
1600
1700
1300
1200
1100
1000
ALPINE
NATIONAL
PARK
1600
1500
1400
1600
1500
1400
1300
1200
THE RAZORBACK
900
1400
1500
1600
1000
1100
1600
1500
1200
1300
1400
1600
1500
N
0
500m
Scale
JOINS 8-1

Snow gums (Eucalyptus pauciflora)

Mount Feathertop is Victoria's second highest peak at 1922 m and is perhaps the only one that looks like a true alpine peak. From most directions, any climb is difficult. Razorback Ridge, however, offers high level walking with views nearly all the way to Mount Feathertop. The route starts from Diamantina Hut on the Great Alpine Road about 1 km west of Mount Hotham. The ridge provides a relatively easy walk and is the most popular of access routes. It is noted that the route attracts inexperienced walkers, some of whom set out from the walk start far too late. Make sure you are walking by 9 am if you are inexperienced.

The district is heavily covered with snow in winter and often in spring, but in summer provides some of Victoria's best walking. During any walk, great care must be exercised in foggy conditions. Remember that in this area, violent and sudden weather changes are frequent. Carry a stove if you wish to cook. Open fires are not permitted on Mount Feathertop or its approaches.

Federation Hut, near Mount Feathertop, is an emergency refuge only and you need to carry a tent. In 2003, wildfire raged throughout the district and millions of snowgums along the Razorback Ridge died. Regeneration is slow because of harsh climate but this classic Victorian walk again holds great interest.

DAY ONE

From Diamantina, head off north on the ridge crest track over exposed grassy tops with broad views. There are stunted snow gums (*Eucalyptus pauciflora*) on the slopes to either side. Snow poles mark the route. Within about 800 m of the start of the walk, the foot track divides. You should veer right rather than continue following the snow pole line over a hill to Bon Accord Spur. You should sidle down eastern slopes into the Big Dipper, a deep saddle 2 km from the

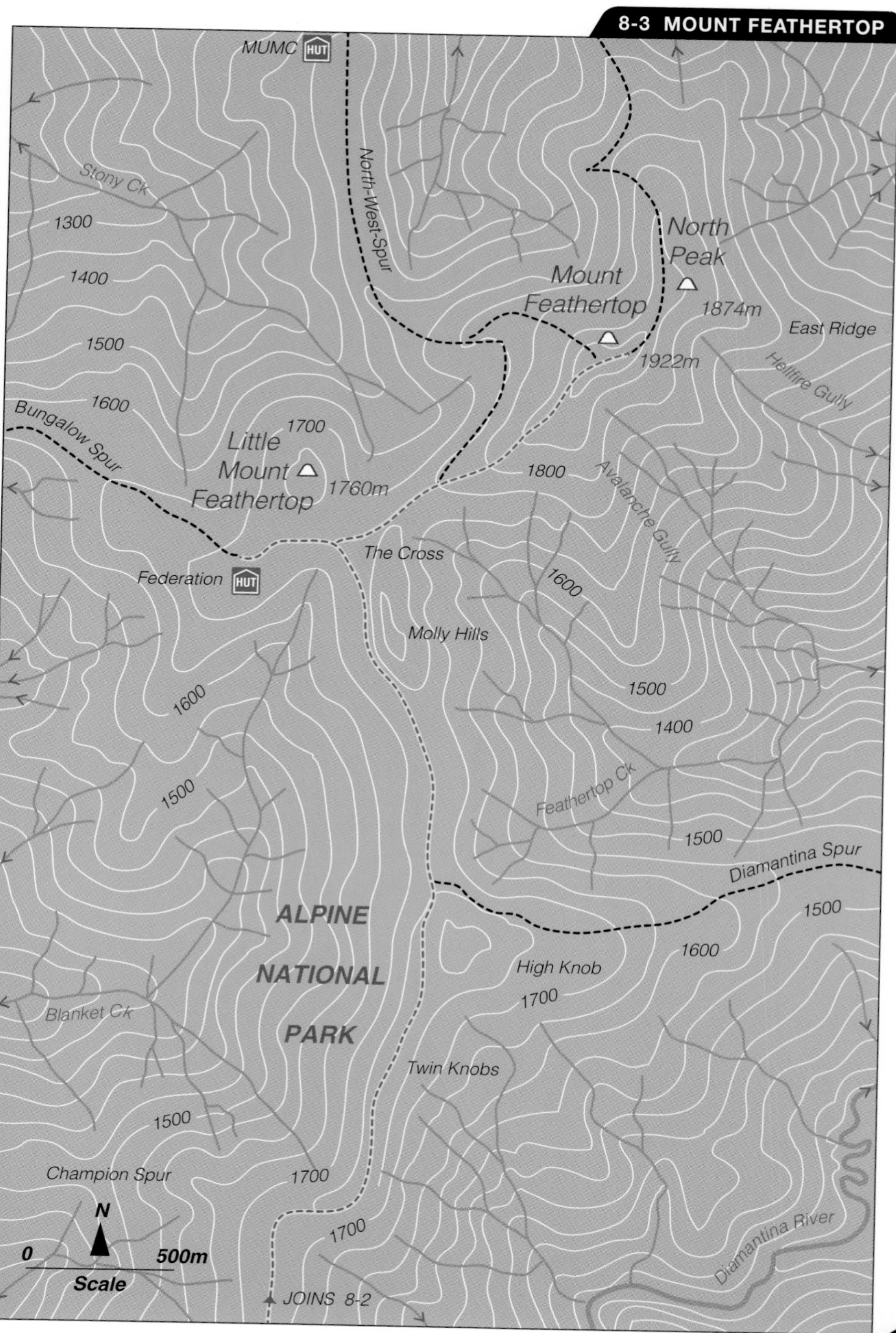
MUMC HUT
North-West-Spur
Stony Ck
1300
1400
1500
1600
Bungalow Spur
1700
Little Mount Feathertop
1760m
Mount Feathertop
1922m
North Peak
1874m
East Ridge
Hellfire Gully
1800
Avalanche Gully
The Cross
Federation HUT
1600
Molly Hills
1600
1500
1400
1500
Feathertop Ck
1500
Diamantina Spur
ALPINE NATIONAL PARK
1500
1600
High Knob
1700
Blanket Ck
Twin Knobs
1500
Champion Spur
1700
1700
Diamantina River
N
0
500m
Scale
JOINS 8-2

walk start. The track then sidles further on eastern slopes to regain the tops gradually.

When 7 km from the walk start and on the crest, the top of Champion Spur is rounded with a short eastwards section of walking. From this point onwards, the scenery becomes quite magnificent. Soon, you pass Twin Knobs where rocky bluffs and summertime wildflowers entice some walkers to camp on tiny grassy clearings. High Knob, which is the top of the Diamantina Spur, lies just north, and the track to follow veers left along its western side. At the north end of the High Knob bypass, 1.8 km from the top of the Champion Spur, Diamantina Spur track links from the east.

Continue ahead northwards on the crest for 700 m, then sidle left another 800 m on the western slopes of Molly Hill down to a saddle known as the Cross. This spot is 10.3 km from Diamantina Hut and there is a track junction in the saddle. Turn left and descend 400 m distance to Federation Hut and camp site on a particularly lovely grassy section of ridge just at the tree line. Snow gums provide shelter and a few escaped the fire. The hut is beside the Bungalow Spur track from Harrietville.

Once at camp and if the weather is good, it is strongly recommended that a side trip be taken to Mount Feathertop summit, 3.8 km return and 200 m higher. If you leave the climb until next morning, bad weather may spoil visibility. As well, if you need water for camp then excellent spring water can be obtained on the return from the summit. The spring is 600 m along the North-west Spur track on the western slopes of the peak. To reach the top, return to the Cross, then head north-east 500 m sidling the slopes of Molly Hill to another saddle. Here, the North-west Spur track veers off left. Continue another 1 km up the main spur crest track to the top and enjoy the great panorama.

Back at camp, ensure that at sunset you walk up the tiny hill behind the hut and toilet to see the sun sink low over Mount Buffalo.

DAY TWO

The recommendation is that you first make a return trip to Mount Feathertop's summit to really get the feel of this wild and beautiful area. The early morning sunlight somehow makes the whole scene entirely different from what it is in the late afternoon. The rest of the day's activities involve retracing the Razorback Ridge route back to Diamantina Hut.

Razorback Ridge and Mount Feathertop

POINT ADDIS
Surf Coast, Victoria

Walk:	11.5 km circuit
Time required:	Including minimal breaks, 4 hours
Grade:	One day, medium
Environment:	Coastal scrub, cliffs and surf beach
Last review date:	April 2006
Map reference:	*Vicmap*, 1:25 000 Torquay and Anglesea and Map 9
Best time to visit:	Suited to any season; carry sunscreen and water

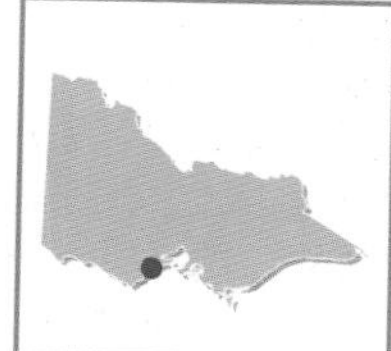

Point Addis and Bells Beach are situated at perhaps the most attractive part of the Surf Coast. Bells Beach is world-renowned in surfing circles and Point Addis, with its towering cliffs, is most scenic. This is also an official clothing optional beach.

Behind the dramatic, high sea cliffs is Ironbark Basin, home to thousands of red ironbark trees (*Eucalyptus tricarpa*). The long-distance Surf Coast Walking Track

Point Addis cliffs

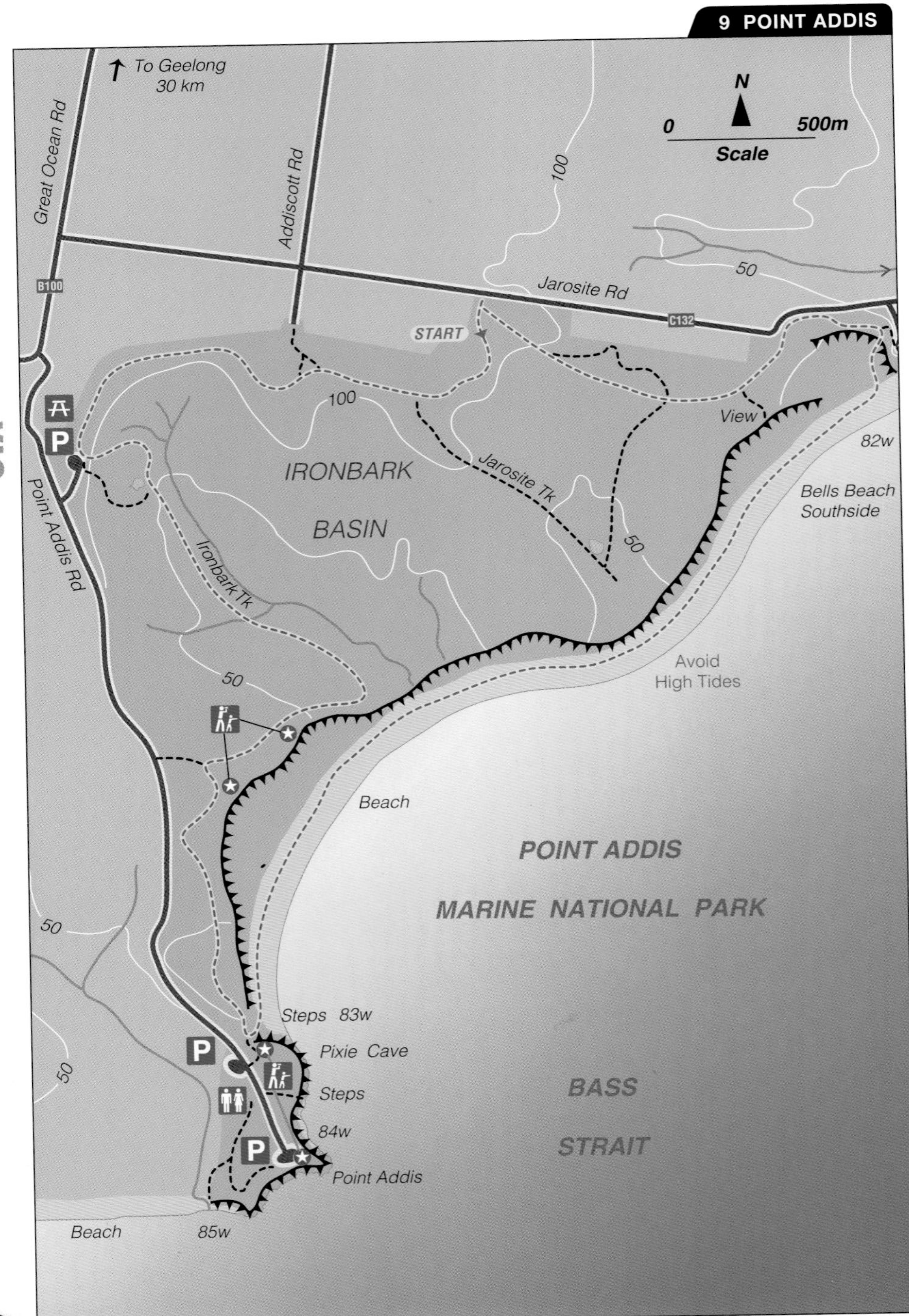
To Geelong 30 km
N
0 500m
Scale
Great Ocean Rd
Addiscott Rd
B100
100
50
Jarosite Rd
C132
START
100
View
82w
Bells Beach Southside
IRONBARK
BASIN
Jarosite Tk
50
Point Addis Rd
Ironbark Tk
50
Avoid High Tides
Beach
POINT ADDIS
MARINE NATIONAL PARK
50
50
Steps 83w
Pixie Cave
Steps
84w
BASS
STRAIT
Point Addis
Beach
85w

Geelong	J	F	M	A	M	J	J	A	S	O	N	D	Year
Rain av. mm	36	31	30	48	49	45	50	49	50	57	49	38	533
Temp av. max. °C	24	24	22	20	16	14	13	15	16	18	20	22	19
Temp av. min. °C	12	13	12	9	7	6	5	5	6	7	9	10	9

passes through the basin and several other walking tracks are present. A great circuit walk can thus be enjoyed. You do need to first check for the time of high tide as a short rocky headland beach near South Bells Beach can be flooded at high tide. Also no drinking water is available at any point. These notes describe the circuit as an anticlockwise route for easiest progress within Ironbark Basin. The description starts at Jarosite Road with the area subject to tides thus being toward the walk end. You may wish to start the circuit at say Point Addis to better suit tidal changes.

Jarosite Road connects the Great Ocean Road with Bells Beach and leads off the Great Ocean Road just north of Point Addis Road. The walk starts at a park gateway along the south side of Jarosite Road about 700 m east of Addiscott Road intersection. Just inside the gate two tracks

Red ironbark (Eucalyptus tricarpa)

veer off into the bushland and you should take the right fork southwards.

The forest here is of somewhat stunted ironbarks with some heathland and grass trees present. The track swings west and after 500 m you pass Jarosite Track off left. That track leads to a former Jarosite mine that existed near the top of the sea cliffs. Jarosite is a sulphate of potassium and iron. Red ochre from the mine was used in paint for former Victorian trains such as Melbourne's 'Red Rattlers'. The track to follow continues west near the southern edge of private properties then turns south-west. It remains at about 100 m above sea level within the stunted dry forest. When 2.1 km from the walk start, you reach a nature trail circuit off left and this spot is just north of a carpark serviced from Point Addis Road. The two ends of the nature trail are about 20 m apart and the loop descends into Ironbark Basin where the forest becomes more dense and includes messmate trees plus many acacias.

Take the left arm of the nature trail for the more interesting walk. You descend over 50 m within 400 m to a small dam and track fork just past it. Instead of following the nature trail up to the right, go south-east down Ironbark Track towards the coastal cliff tops. The track flattens out within the basin and leads into coastal heath land. After 1.3 km, you reach the cliff rim vicinity and get impressive views of the coast and the cliffs.

The track turns right and climbs sharply past a lookout platform to lead south-west above the cliff rim. After 900 m you pass a four-wheel-drive track off right then arrive at another viewing deck. On

Golden wattle (Acacia pycnantha)

again southwards you bypass another pad off right and within 800 m descend to meet the main beach access track for the Point Addis east-side beach (Emergency beach access 83W). You do best to climb 100 m further to the roadway via the beach access track so as to view the tremendous panorama from a deck at the roadside. Toilets are nearby across the road too.

Retrace the 100 m then continue on down many steps on to the beach then consider lunch on the sand, perhaps in the usually sheltered corner of the beach just to your right. This spot is often more suited for swimming than any nearby big surf.

A 4 km beach walk north-eastwards to Bells Beach Southside comes next. Except at very high tide times, most of the distance is broad sandy beach backed by high cliffs. About 1 km along the beach you enter the clothing optional area and here some tea tree and low dunes below the cliffs provide some shade in hot weather. Further along the way you reach some rocks and the beach is narrower. It is here that you need to take care and avoid high tides. At the end of the 4 km, a concrete path leads off the beach as a headland begins (82W) and this takes you up to the carpark at Bells Beach Southside. More coastal views are present in the carpark area.

Where you reach the carpark, the Surf Coast Walking Track leads off westwards above the cliffs. At first it is near the south side of Jarosite Road and soon temporarily uses the actual road. After 1 km among coastal heath land and with some gradual climbing needed you reach a fork of three tracks. The left fork leads to the former Jarosite mine site and the other two tracks parallel each other then rejoin after about 500 m. The left of these two routes is the more narrow but pleasant option as the right fork is adjacent to private properties. Once the tracks rejoin you walk 300 m further west and thereby complete the walk at the Jarosite Road gate.

10 BRIGGS BLUFF

Grampians, Victoria

Walk:	10.8 km retrace
Time required:	Including minimal breaks, 4 hours 30 minutes
Grade:	One day, medium
Environment:	Sandstone formations and cliffs, sparse vegetation
Last review date:	June 2007
Map reference:	*Vicmap*, 1:25 000 Mount Stapylton and Map 10
Best time to visit:	Suited to any season; carry water

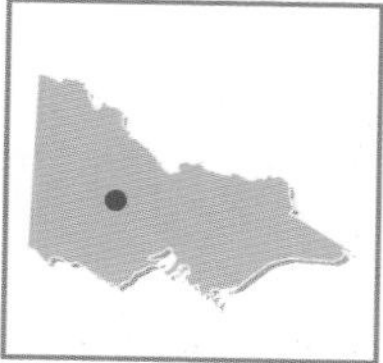

VIC

190 619 190

The Grampians have long been one of Victoria's foremost tourist attractions. These rugged, sandstone mountains are situated between Melbourne and Adelaide and not far from the highway linking these two cities. A climb to Briggs Bluff provides an unforgettable experience, one likely to be remembered for life. It goes through the pick of Grampians terrain and amid some of the best walking country in Victoria. Private transport is needed for access. Horsham and Stawell are the two closest towns and both have a full range of accommodation options, public transport access and hire car availability. To reach the walk start at Roses Gap you need to travel sealed Roses Gap Road from the Western Highway between the two towns.

Beehive Falls, enroute to Briggs Bluff

The foot track is rough in places and sturdy footwear is essential. The walk is not suitable for children under about 10 years of age. The track commences about 800 m west of the intersection of the Halls Gap to Mount Zero Road and Roses Gap Road. There is a small carpark at the start, on the side of sealed Roses Gap Road.

A broad, fairly level track leads for 1.4 km south and south-east up the west bank of Mud Hut Creek to a bridge amid ferns and 200 m short of the lovely, 25 metre-high Beehive Falls. The cliffs in this area get very colourful at times when the sun is low. Cross the bridge below the falls. The track thereafter gets much rougher underfoot. Climb the east bank pad to take a short break and enjoy the

Horsham	J	F	M	A	M	J	J	A	S	O	N	D	Year
Rain av. mm	23	25	23	32	46	50	47	49	46	44	33	27	445
Temp av. max. °C	30	30	26	21	17	14	13	15	17	21	24	27	20
Temp av. min. °C	13	13	11	8	6	4	3	4	5	7	9	11	7

cascading water, swallows and butterflies. Take care not to slip but use stream bed rocks to cross below the falls and then scramble up a steep, rocky track until the top of the cliff is reached. A second, usually dry, small falls should be passed during this short ascent.

The pad then swings south-west then south-east to cross a gully and ascend into wild, rocky, sandstone terrain with the impressive cliffs of Briggs Bluff as a backdrop. Continue up past many rocky turrets, ravines, and escarpments, then swing south-west on to a ridge. Cliff lines abound in this locality. There is a very pretty rocky stream gully just to the east of the pad. About 2 km from Beehive Falls, the track crosses a broad saddle after swinging east, and rises up towards most impressive cliffs containing many high, wind-scoured caverns. Boulders form an arch across the track, which then swings north-east to reach the cliff tops. Proceed from here, 2.6 km from Beehive Falls, and 4.2 km from the walk start, down the left-fork pad. It soon swings north to lead along bare rock near a cliff top, then across a couple of minor streams that form the headwaters of Mud Hut Creek and up the rocky slopes of Briggs Bluff. It is 1.2 km from the track junction to the bluff crest.

In the interests of your safety, and especially if you dislike heights, keep well away from the northern face of the bluff; there is a 400 m drop over the rim. Views here are spectacular. The spot would be good for a lunch break (no water available). Return to the walk start by retracing the same pads.

Briggs Bluff, Grampians

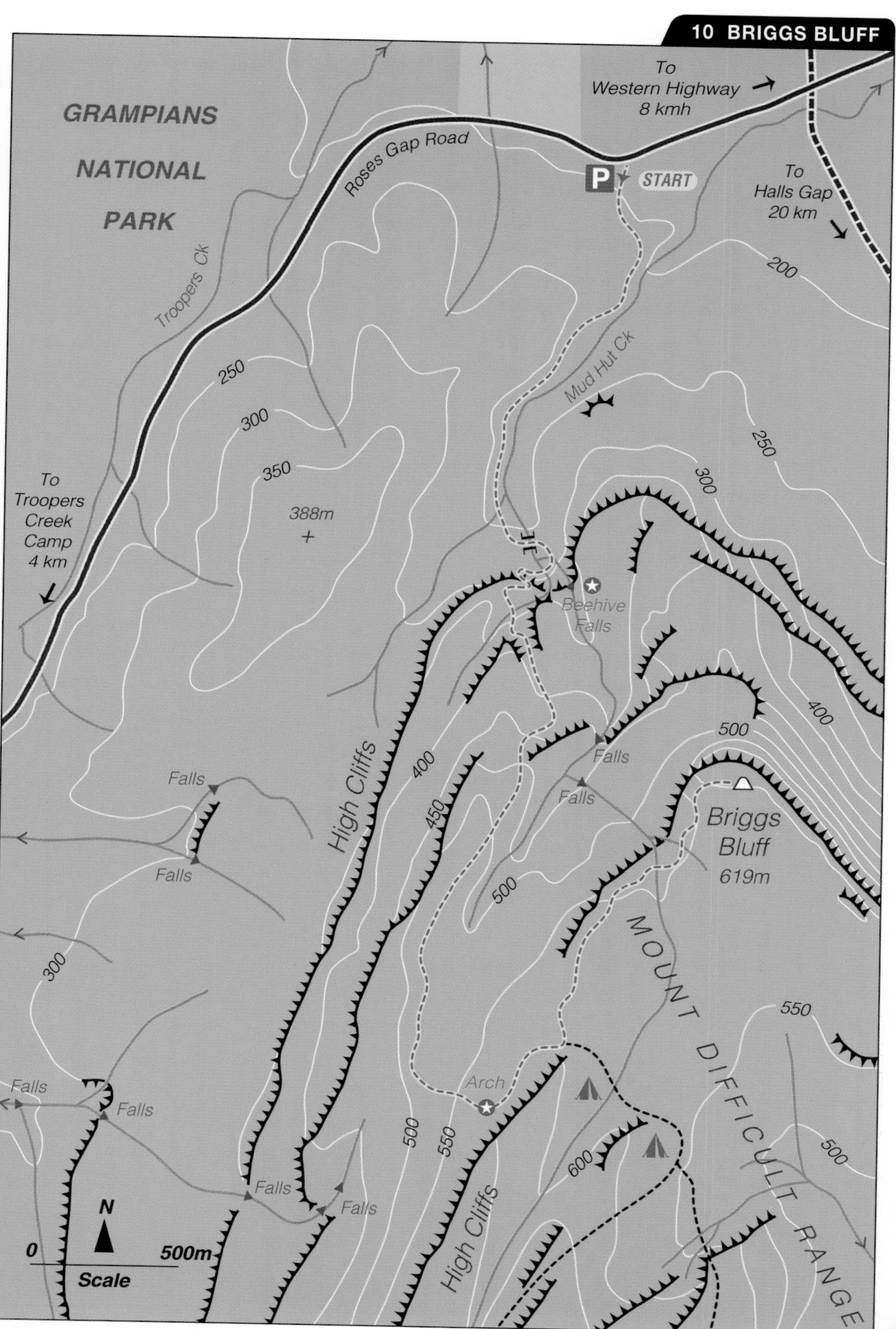
GRAMPIANS
NATIONAL
PARK
To
Western Highway
8 kmh
Roses Gap Road
START
To
Halls Gap
20 km
200
Troopers Ck
Mud Hut Ck
250
300
350
388m
250
300
To
Troopers
Creek
Camp
4 km
Beehive
Falls
400
500
Falls
Falls
High Cliffs
400
450
500
Briggs
Bluff
619m
Falls
Falls
MOUNT DIFFICULT RANGE
300
550
Arch
500
550
600
500
Falls
Falls
Falls
Falls
High Cliffs
N
0
500m
Scale

MOUNT STAPYLTON

Grampians, Victoria

Walk:	5.6 km retrace
Time required:	Including minimal breaks, 3 hours
Grade:	One day, medium with considerable height exposure
Environment:	Sandstone formations and cliffs, sparse vegetation
Last review date:	June 2007
Map reference:	*Vicmap*, 1:25 000 Mount Stapylton and Map 11
Best time to visit:	Suited to any season; carry water

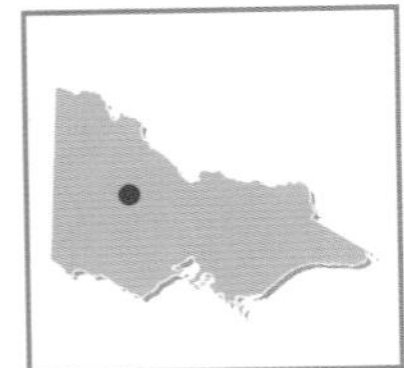

At the extreme north end of the Grampians is the Mount Zero picnic ground just adjacent to Flat Rock. This locality, including nearby Mount Stapylton, is about the most rugged in Victoria's Grampians, and generally has extremely pleasant walking. Reaching the very top of Mount Stapylton is awkward and time-consuming but a great experience. At busy times such as Easter and Christmas, hundreds of people attempt to climb Mount Stapylton every day. Many do not reach the summit.

Taipan Walls, Mount Stapylton

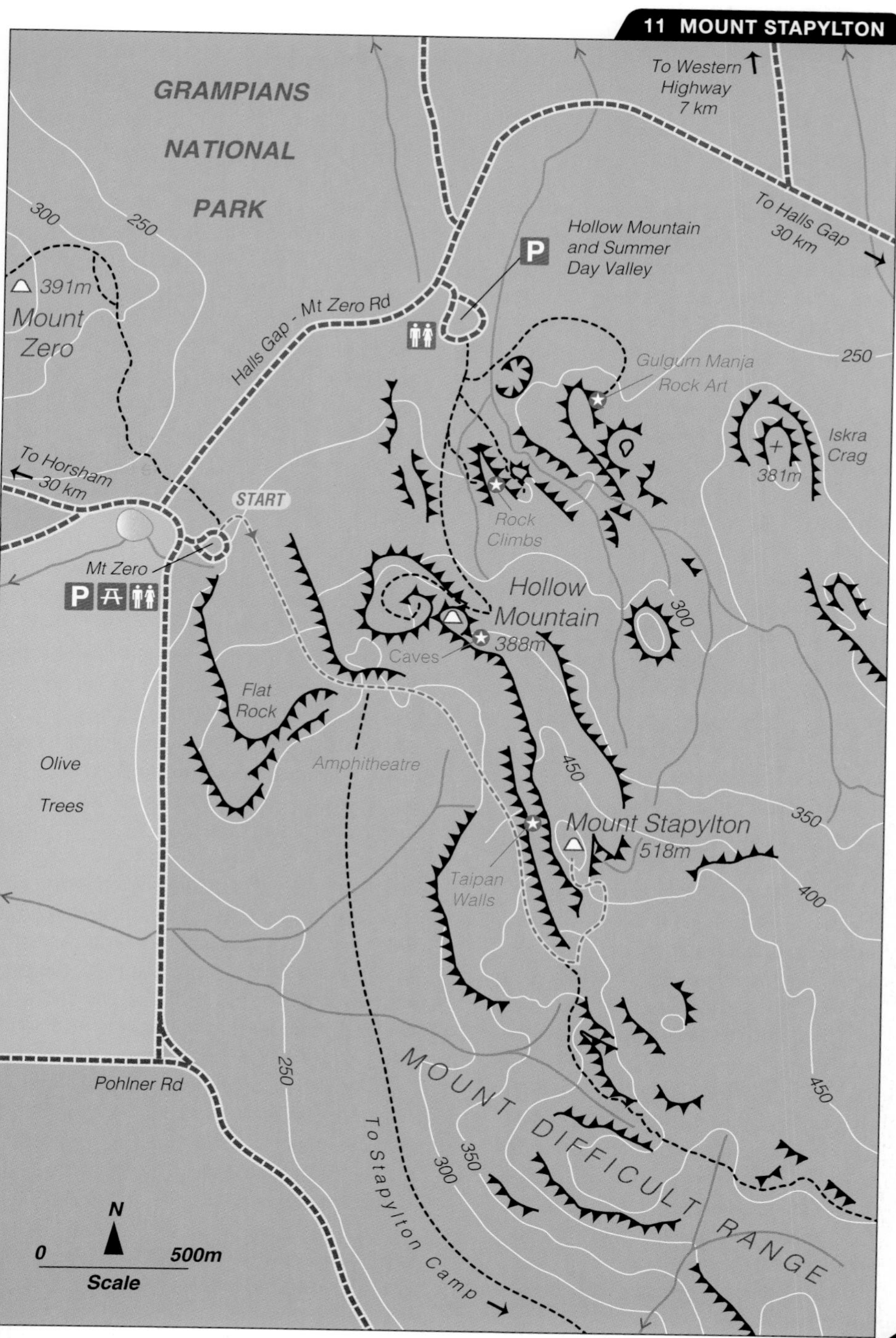
GRAMPIANS
NATIONAL
PARK
To Western Highway 7 km
To Halls Gap 30 km
Hollow Mountain and Summer Day Valley
391m
Mount Zero
Halls Gap - Mt Zero Rd
Gulgurn Manja Rock Art
250
300
Iskra Crag
381m
To Horsham 30 km
START
Rock Climbs
Mt Zero
Hollow Mountain
Caves
388m
Flat Rock
Amphitheatre
Olive Trees
450
350
Mount Stapylton
518m
Taipan Walls
400
Pohlner Rd
MOUNT DIFFICULT RANGE
To Stapylton Camp
N
0
500m
Scale

Horsham	J	F	M	A	M	J	J	A	S	O	N	D	Year
Rain av. mm	23	25	23	32	46	50	47	49	46	44	33	27	445
Temp av. max. °C	30	30	26	21	17	14	13	15	17	21	24	27	20
Temp av. min. °C	13	13	11	8	6	4	3	4	5	7	9	11	7

The Grampians sandstone mountains are situated between Melbourne and Adelaide and not far from the highway linking these two cities. Private transport is needed for access to this walk area. Horsham and Stawell are the two closest towns and both have a full range of accommodation options, public transport access and hire car availability. To reach the walk start at Mount Zero picnic area you need to travel unsealed roads from the Western Highway between the two towns.

A good walking track from the picnic ground to within 500 m of the summit of Mount Stapylton gives access to some of the most scenic spots. The whole route is reasonably easy, with the exception of the final 200 m or so at the very summit. In the interests of your safety you may prefer not to scale this last section because of the exposure on bare rock. The view just below the exposed part is almost as good as the top if the national park-promoted southern approach to the very top is used.

From Mount Zero picnic ground, walk south-east up impressive Flat Rock, a broad sandstone slope with about a 15–20 degree angle. Painted triangles on the rock reveal the route to follow to the higher eastern edge. It tends a little to the left as it rises. At the top of Flat Rock, the pad is just south of a cliff line. It then descends slightly and crosses the floor of a huge amphitheatre on the southern side of Mount Stapylton. Massive colourful cliffs ring much of the amphitheatre and are a rock climbing venue. If you glance up to your left you may see some of those crazy climbers on the enormous rock faces such as Taipan Walls.

Avoid a right-fork pad 900 m from the walk start (Pohlner Road and Stapylton Camp access) and continue on the left-fork track up from the amphitheatre, south-east via a broad ramp formation and past a large bird-shaped rock (Bird Rock), which is seen right on the route of the track markers. No doubt to avoid any falling rock, the section of track up to Bird Rock is realigned away from a former route under the overhanging cliffs. The present alignment uses bare rock surfaces from which you get broad views for much of the climbing section. Almost level ground is attained just south of Mount Stapylton summit and you reach a track junction 2.3 km from the walk start.

Avoid the track off south (Pohlner Road and Staplyton Camp access) and continue on the left fork. The way is then more rocky and leads over a small saddle with the peak of Mount Stapylton just up to your left. You go down and across a small hollow and swing west up a gully into a ravine area just east of the Mount Stapylton summit. As the ravine narrows, the pad divides at abutting rock. Here, many people get confused as to the route, and arrow markers on rocks are less than adequate. From this point there are two routes to the peak summit and a decision must be made. Both routes have advantages and disadvantages.

The left-fork national park-promoted route enables walkers to get very good views without reaching the top if they feel the rock is too exposed. The right fork is equally exposed and far more walkers would be likely to get to the top, but there is no good view via the right fork unless you get to the top. Whichever route you choose, take great care as there are bare rock faces

Mount Stapylton

and cliffs with which to contend. If in doubt or concerned then do not attempt either route to the very top. Be content with the great beauty and rocks all around you. An option for the brave is to ascend one route and descend the other route.

The left fork with painted arrow markers rises up bare sloping rock immediately. It passes a big and lovely wind-scoured cave in the cliffs, right alongside the climbing route. Some 100 m up the slope there is a rocky viewpoint where the climbing route seems to end. Many people make this their turn-around point in rugged wild terrain with great views all around. A few people simply scale the awkward rock face here as this viewpoint is only about 40 m short of the actual summit. However, painted triangles indicate another route down a few metres to a lower broad rock ledge and then off right along ledges to an awkward short ascent. The adventurous can scramble up bare rock, through a squeeze, using many foot and hand-holds to reach the peak. The summit is the highest point in the district and you get a real appreciation of the rugged terrain. A short wander west, down the crest, is most rewarding.

The right-fork access to the summit from the gully below involves walking only a few metres up a rough pad in the ravine to a narrow rock spine protruding east in the middle of the ravine. Scramble on to this rock spine and climb west up its crest. It joins to a cliff-face of Mount Stapylton. This next spot, about 3 m long, is awkward to negotiate and occurs right where the spine joins the face. The difficulty here is noted more on the return. The experience is really just a test of the nerves, rather than any great physical demands. Once past the spot you simply scramble upwards to the top using many hand and foot holds. If using this short approach to the top, the access point from the spine to the cliff needs to be clearly remembered for the return descent. At any time, it is hard to pinpoint.

After climbing Mount Stapylton, simply retrace the route back to the walk start.

SEALERS COVE

Wilsons Promontory, Victoria

Walk:	19 km retrace (Day one 9.5 km, Day two 9.5 km)
Time required:	Including minimal breaks two days (Day one 3 hours 30 minutes, Day two 3 hours 30 minutes)
Grade:	Two day, easy
Environment:	Beach and forest
Last review date:	March 2007
Map reference:	*Vicmap* 1:50 000 Wilsons Promontory National Park Outdoor Leisure and Map 12
Best time to visit:	September to April; other times can be cool and misty

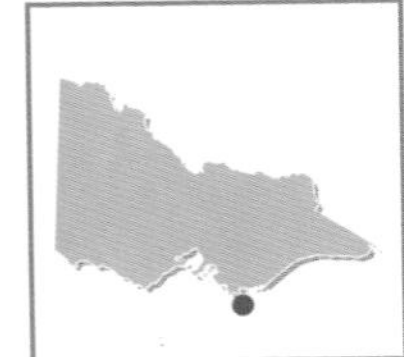

Ferns at Sealers Cove

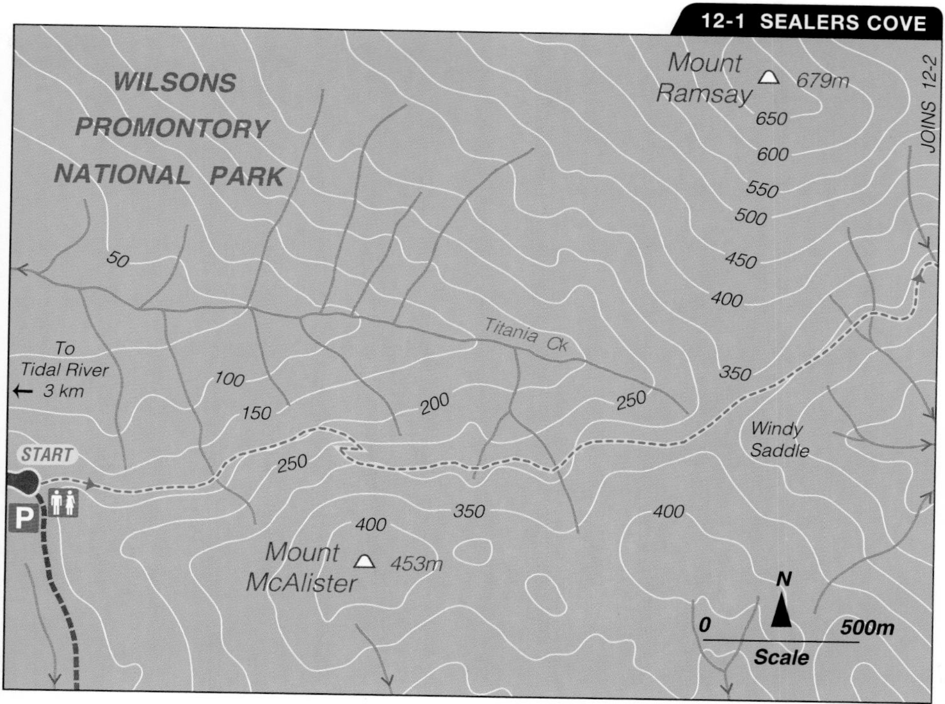

Tidal River	J	F	M	A	M	J	J	A	S	O	N	D	Year
Rain av. mm	50	50	70	90	110	120	120	120	100	90	70	60	1050
Temp av. max. °C	20	20	19	17	14	13	12	12	14	15	17	18	16
Temp av. min. °C	14	14	14	12	11	9	8	8	8	9	11	12	11

On the east coast of Wilsons Promontory is secluded Sealers Cove. It has a crescent-shaped, 1.8 kilometre-long, white sand beach. Each end of the beach is dominated by rugged, forest-clad, high peaks featuring granite boulders. An excellent 9 km walking track leads to Sealers Cove from Mount Oberon carpark at Telegraph Saddle. While the distance and grade is such that you can visit the cove as a day walk, it is far more enjoyable to spend time and camp out overnight. A planned fire burn at nearby Tidal River re-ignited ten days afterwards on 1 April 2005. It burned all the way to Waterloo Bay and the lighthouse area thereby scarring the magnificent landscape along most of the Wilsons Promontory traditional long-distance walking tracks. From Windy Saddle to Sealers Cove and Refuge Cove mostly escaped the fire as did the park north of Tidal River. All tracks in the park have since been reopened.

'The Prom' has national park regulations governing size of camp parties, camp site availability and duration of stay at camps, so first register with the ranger at Tidal River and obtain a camp permit for Sealers Cove. A maximum of twelve persons in a group may camp at Sealers Cove and the overall limit is 60 campers.

You can stay one night only in summer and two nights in winter. Because

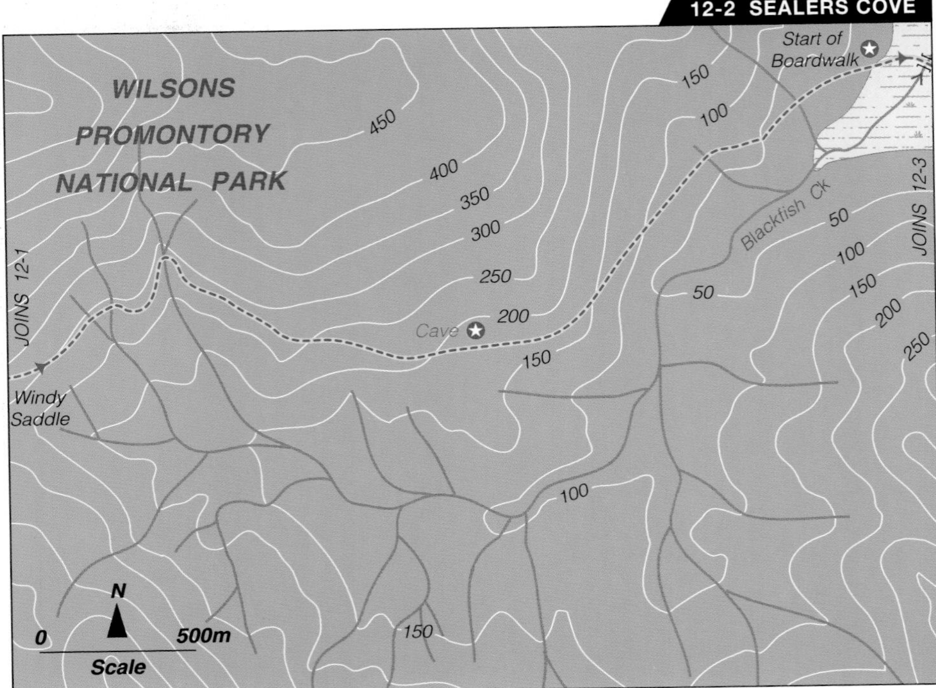

of limited car parking space at Oberon Saddle, a free bus operates continuously from Tidal River for the 3.7 km to the saddle in summer. At the same time the road is closed to all car traffic. Campfires are not permitted so carry a small stove if you wish to cook. Carry insect repellent during summer.

DAY ONE

From the saddle carpark, a foot track leads off east as a broad well-defined route. At first there is a slight downhill section, then a short track switchback. Thereafter, the track ascends gradually to Windy Saddle 3 km from the walk start. The general area is one of low dry eucalyptus forest on northerly aspect slopes. The understorey includes banksia, hakea, grass trees and heaths. Burned areas are left soon after leaving the carpark and have recovered well.

Windy Saddle lives up to its name, but affords good views to both east and west coasts of Wilsons Promontory from its open grassy patch. The saddle is between Mount Ramsay and lofty Mount Wilson. The good track then narrows a little as it continues east down south-easterly facing slopes, around several very ferny gullies. There is a lot of dense, damp, shrubby vegetation including sassafras and beech. Drinking water is usually available in a couple of the gullies, the second of which has a tiny waterfall and is 1 km from Windy Saddle.

About 4 km east of Windy Saddle, the track flattens out to cross swampy areas containing ferns, tea tree, eucalyptus and paperbarks. Long stretches of boardwalk have been erected to facilitate the crossing of the swampy sections. There are a number of ‘Siamese twin’ ferns to be seen, with their trunks joining and dividing.

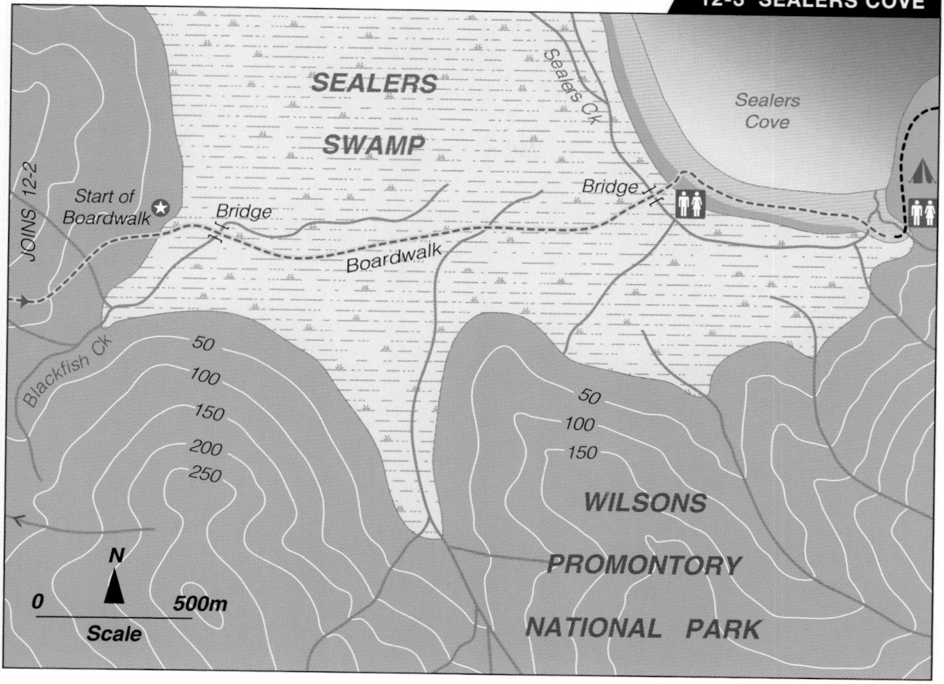

Eventually Sealers Creek should be reached after passing a lot of sword grass (cutting grass) and rushes.

A footbridge spans Sealers Creek. After walking past a toilet, it is just 50 m to the gleaming white sand beach of Sealers Cove. A number of small trees provide shade along the beach and 500 m further south-east is the excellent camp site. It is on the south-east side of the mouth of Sealers Creek within some forest and at the very end of the beach. Sealers Creek may need to be waded knee deep if there is a high tide. Drinking water can be obtained from a small side stream flowing through the camp area into salty Sealers Creek.

It is interesting to know that Sealers Cove once had a jetty and a network of timber-getting tramways spreading inland from the jetty. While in camp you should consider walking a short side trip up the Refuge Cove track. This track rises steeply to some large granite expanses from where there are great views of Sealers Cove and beach. An evening stroll along the beach can be most pleasant, especially on a clear night with a full moon rising in the east.

DAY TWO

On the second day, reverse the journey of day one.

Red parrot

SOUTH AUSTRALIA

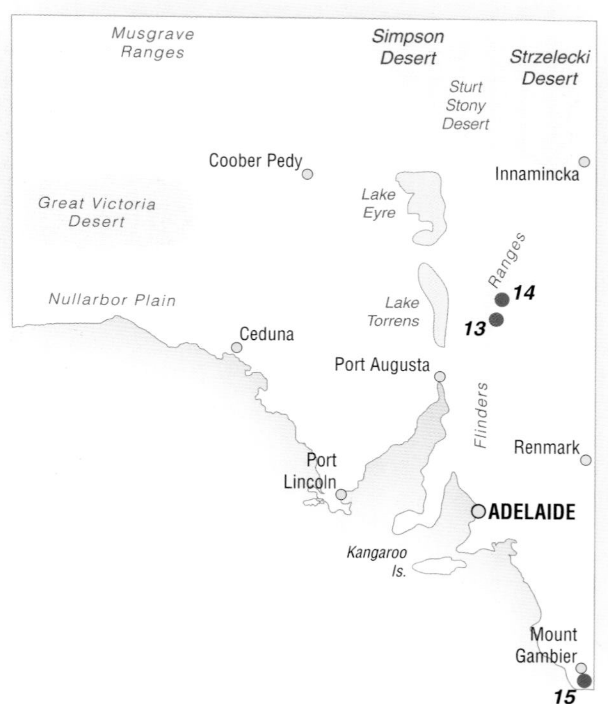

13	St Mary Peak	Flinders Ranges National Park
14	Bunyeroo Gorge	Flinders Ranges National Park
15	Mount Gambier	

SA

Flinders Ranges

South Australia is home to the Flinders Ranges. Hundreds of kilometres long, they reach far inland and also have some of the oldest rock outcrops in Australia. Wilpena Pound is a fine example of a 'geo-syncline' (a bowl-like formation caused by uplift of the Earth's crust) that exposed the oldest rocks at the surface, the highest point of which is known as St Mary Peak, one of the featured walks in this book. The Heysen Trail extends along most of the length of the Flinders Ranges and is a great attraction for walkers. In these areas spring wildflowers are a feature, as are the abundant wildlife, especially following favourable seasonal rains.

Millions of years ago, the Southern Ocean was much further inland than today. The present day Lake Eyre just west of the Flinders Ranges is all that remains of this once vast inland sea, and many marine fossils are to be found in local sedimentary rocks. Also preserved in the stone are the shore-ripples of the ancient waters.

Elsewhere South Australia contains vast areas of desert, semi desert, wheat, and pastoral properties. Substantial prohibited tracts prevent access around Woomera and Aboriginal lands. Coober Pedy is one of the world's few opal mining towns. As it is so far inland and hot in summer, much of the town is underground.

Kangaroo Island lies off the south coast and is a significant draw card for tourism as are the wine growing districts of the Barossa, Coonawarra and Clare valleys. The far western coastal areas adjoin the vast Nullarbor Plain, which extends well into Western Australia. The Eyre Peninsula is well known for its fishing towns and especially for processing tuna and crayfish.

Mount Gambier is the main centre in a large fertile part of the state as a result of past volcanic activity. The centre of town overlies an area of limestone and has a sunken garden within a limestone sinkhole. Adjacent to the town is the major volcanic crater complex, which includes crater lakes. Blue Lake, the largest of these, is the water supply for the entire district. The suggested walk at Mount Gambier takes you around and descends into the presently extinct volcanic craters.

South Australia's floral emblem:
Sturt's Desert Pea (Clianthus formosus)

South Australia's fauna emblem:
Hairy Nosed Wombat (Lasiorhinus latifrons)

13 ST MARY PEAK

Flinders Ranges, South Australia

Walk:	21.2 km circuit
Time required:	Including minimal breaks, 9 hours
Grade:	One day, hard
Environment:	Remote mountain desert, mountain and cliffs
Last review date:	June 2007
Map reference:	South Australian Lands 1:50 000 Wilpena and Map 13
Best time to visit:	May to October; avoid hot summer days from December to March and certainly carry water

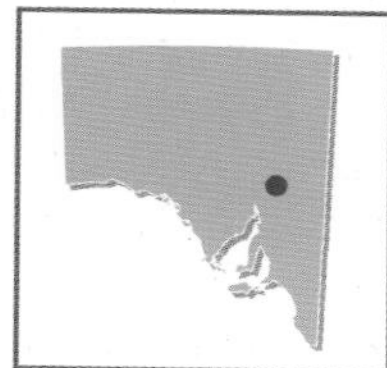

Wilpena	J	F	M	A	M	J	J	A	S	O	N	D	Year
Rain av. mm	20	15	8	7	57	51	62	43	20	17	7	17	324
Temp av. max. °C	31	31	29	23	16	14	12	14	18	24	26	28	22
Temp av. min. °C	16	16	13	8	5	4	2	2	5	9	12	14	9

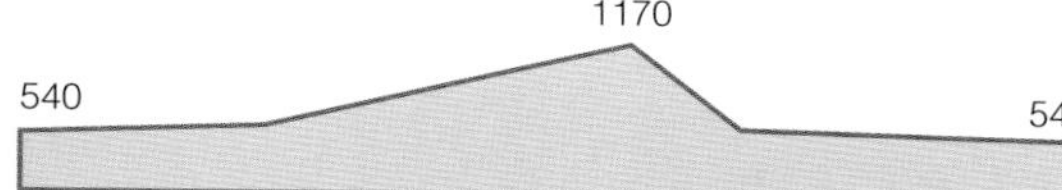

St Mary Peak, Flinders Ranges

SA

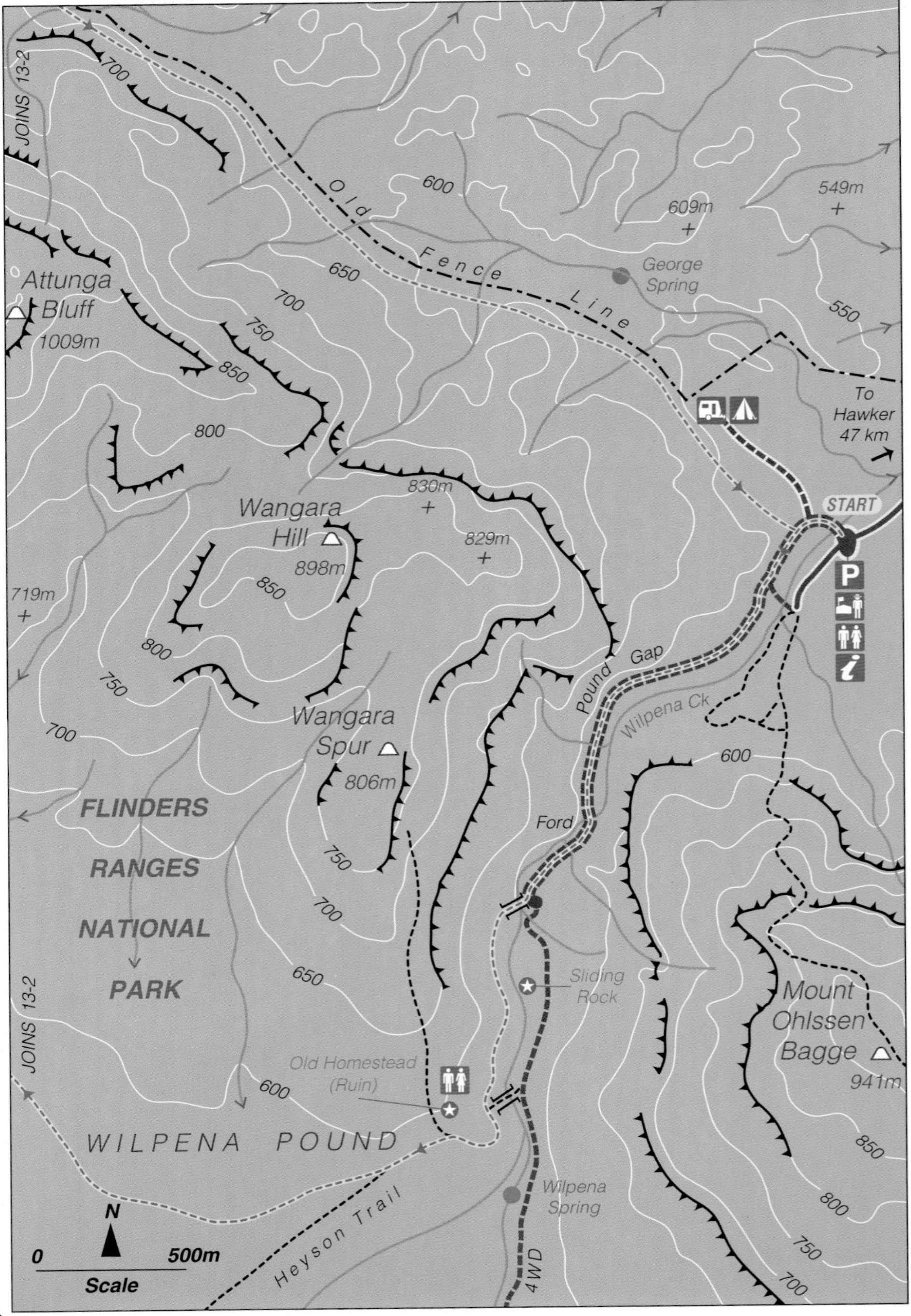
JOINS 13-2
700
Old Fence Line
600
609m
549m
George Spring
650
700
750
850
550
Attunga Bluff
1009m
800
To Hawker 47 km
830m
START
Wangara Hill
898m
829m
719m
850
800
750
Pound Gap
Wilpena Ck
700
Wangara Spur
806m
600
FLINDERS RANGES NATIONAL PARK
Ford
750
700
650
Sliding Rock
Mount Ohlssen Bagge
941m
JOINS 13-2
Old Homestead (Ruin)
600
WILPENA POUND
850
Wilpena Spring
800
N
0
500m
Scale
Heyson Trail
4WD
750
700

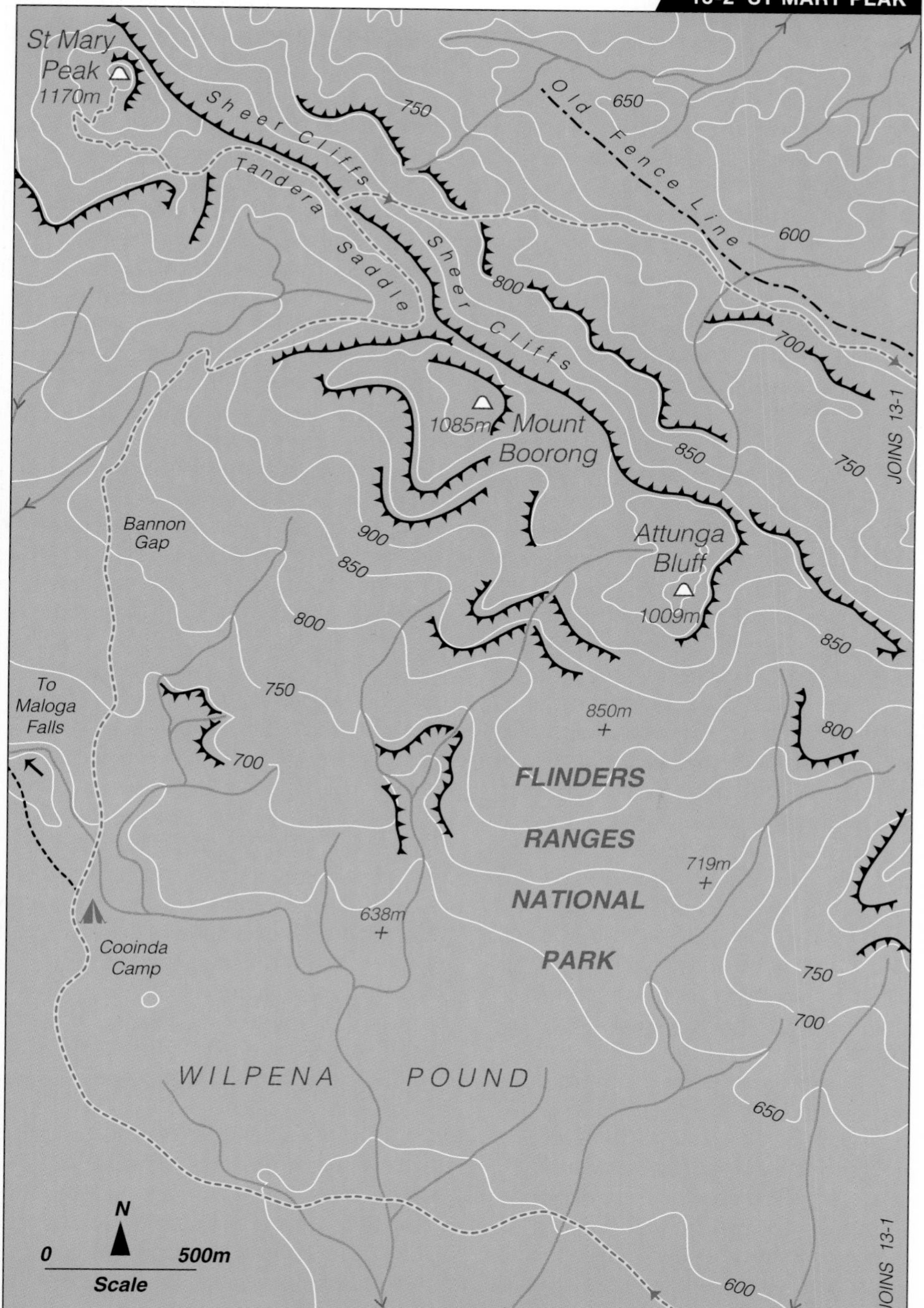

St Mary Peak
1170m
Sheer Cliffs
Tandera Saddle
Sheer Cliffs
Sheer Cliffs
Old Fence Line
750
650
600
800
700
850
750
Mount Boorong
1085m
JOINS 13-1
900
850
800
Bannon Gap
Attunga Bluff
1009m
850
To Maloga Falls
750
850m
800
700
FLINDERS
RANGES
NATIONAL
PARK
719m
638m
Cooinda Camp
750
700
650
WILPENA POUND
600
N
0
500m
Scale
JOINS 13-1

The Flinders Ranges around Wilpena occupy part of one of the oldest landscapes in the world. Geologists claim they are between 600 million and a billion years old. Spectacular, steep, saw-toothed ridges, uplifted, folded, buckled and fractured, are their prominent feature, with many rugged gorges cut through the ridges by streams that rarely flow.

Explorer and navigator Matthew Flinders named the extensive ranges, which now are protected as national parks. The ridges around Wilpena mostly consist of quartzite, which is very resistant to weathering and the rock colours vary from brilliant reds through to dark chocolate-brown. Rock strata below the quartzite in the many cliffs is of sandstone, limestone and shale. The twisting ranges mostly form typical dip slopes and escarpments.

The main tourist focus of the Flinders Ranges is Wilpena Pound, some 450 km north of Adelaide. Here, at the end of the sealed road, is the start of the true outback and dusty dirt roads. Wilpena is an Aboriginal name meaning 'bent fingers' and when viewed from the air, Wilpena Pound is a remarkable, 16 km by 6 km, geological feature. Its huge saucer-shaped synclinal form is easily appreciated from a higher vantage point. Such pounds occur in other parts of the Flinders Ranges but Wilpena is the most noteworthy. Its shape, like two cupped hands, is formed with dramatic cliffs around the exterior of the basin.

St Mary Peak is one of Australia's best arid-country walks. The climb to the summit takes you to the rim of the basin, with seemingly aerial views northwards and southwards over the complex twisting ranges. To the west are seen the vast expanses of the inland plains with Brachina Plains and salt Lake Torrens away to the west. Although only 1184 m high, St Mary Peak is the highest peak for hundreds of kilometres and has a very rugged summit.

The unique vegetation is also of great interest. Many of the usually dry watercourses are lined with beautiful river red gums and each spring, by October, most of the ranges are covered in red hop flowers, mauve salvation jane and other wildflowers. Native pines (*Callitris*) are common and mallee (*Eucalyptus*), grass trees (*Xanthorrhoea*) and wattle (*Acacia*) are prolific on the higher slopes. Overall though, vegetation is sparse and permits good views. Euros, wallabies, kangaroos, including the big red kangaroo, emus, eagles, hawks and birds of the parrot family are very prevalent. The numbers of galahs, budgerigars, and corellas are remarkable. At the time of this review, following prolonged drought, bird and other wildlife numbers were notably less than during past visits.

Wilpena Resort is located at a breach in the wall of the pound where Wilpena Creek drains the internal basin. It is a quiet spot set in an oasis of fine trees and close to interesting cliff lines. In the immediate area, a motel (moderately expensive) with restaurant and swimming pool, is the only real alternative to camping in the 400-site camping ground complete with laundry. A store adjacent to the park visitor centre has a fair range of supplies. Not far south is Rawnsley Park. It has the full range of accommodation from a backpacker hostel to camping, on-site vans, cabins, motel units, and upmarket eco-lodges. There is no public transport available for any access to the Wilpena region.

With an average annual rainfall of just 324 mm, hot north winds and summer temperatures frequently reaching well over 40 degrees from December to March, tourists tend to avoid Wilpena in summer. However, from May to October conditions are very pleasant normally.

Sandstone strata, St Mary Peak

Winter temperatures can drop to freezing overnight due to clear skies, but each day is usually comfortably warm.

The recommended climb to St Mary Peak summit encompasses a 21.2 km clockwise circuit, which at first passes through Wilpena Pound. To reach the top of the peak, climbers need to be agile. There is the option of omitting the time-consuming, somewhat rocky, 3.2 km return side trip along the pound rim to the summit from Tanderra Saddle on the main circuit. Also, you should be aware that Aboriginals consider the summit as sacred and ask you not to climb it. Water must be carried for all of this walk. It is best not to go anticlockwise on the circuit as you would then have an awkward, steep, demanding ascent. Track re-alignments in recent years have added several kilometres to the walk's length. Start the walk early because of the distance.

To start, first follow the minor roadway from the Wilpena Resort and camp, south-west along the western banks of Wilpena Creek towards the pound. Water is nearly always present in this section of the stream and reeds grow in it. After crossing a ford the road meets a barrier 1.8 km from the start. Next, take Sliding Rock foot track back to the west bank and on for another 1 km beside Wilpena Creek to a second footbridge. Here you see a restored cottage to your right and the track swings around to approach the building. It once belonged to an early settler named Hill. A would-be pastoralist, he cleared some of the pound for growing wheat, he tempted fate and lost, failing to take account of harsh climatic extremes and the influence of introduced rabbits and goats, which flourished to plague proportions.

At the cottage, avoid the Wangara Lookout spur trail off to the north (right)

Sturt's desert pea

and continue west-south-west along the well-marked foot trail across the pound. Within another 500 m, veer right to avoid the long-distance Heysen Trail, then go north-west across the pound floor for 5 km to reach Cooinda Camp. There are many native pines along this flat section. You should see both emus and kangaroos. Cooinda Camp, a rather stark, rocky spot, is at the junction of a trail to Edeowie Gorge and Edeowie Creek. If you are considering camping at Cooinda Camp, remember that any available water needs to be boiled as animals frequently drink at the spot. Also, a camping permit is required from the park ranger. No facilities exist at this bush camp. Be careful not to take false leads from the camp. Be sure to locate the next track marker soon after leaving the camp.

A climb north to Tanderra Saddle follows, the saddle marking the rim of the pound. The climb is via a rough but well-defined trail and some 330 m elevation is gained over a 3.5 km distance. Views of the pound walls and an appreciation of the basin structure improve with height. The trail leads through low scrub that includes grevilleas, eucalyptus, and acacias as far as the saddle, so expansive views are a feature. The last section of the climb is re-aligned and doubles back north-west running parallel to the main pound rim. Near the saddle one is suddenly aware of the extreme ruggedness of the rim and exterior cliffs. The circuit crosses the rim and descends steeply. Attractive grass trees grow along the cliff rim. If you have not already eaten at some sheltered spot along the way, a lunch break is a good idea here, while the views are enjoyed.

To continue, turn left (north) and take the 3.2 km return side trip to the summit of St Mary Peak. About an hour and a half to two hours need to be allowed for the rough, re-aligned, return trip along the rocky outcrops. Be careful not to slip if the rocks are wet. You approach the top from the west. The Aroona Valley just northwards is a particular attraction. Far out west is Lake Torrens and vast plains. As you leave from the summit, be careful to locate the track markers. Some are not as apparent as when climbing and it is easy to lose the way.

On returning to Tanderra Saddle, turn sharp left at a break in the cliffs and descend steeply on the clearly marked, but scree-covered, trail. You may need to use your hands to lower yourself in the steepest spots. Only thin vegetation grows in this rocky locality. Within 1.5 km the track flattens out near another saddle, some 300 m below Tanderra Saddle. An old fence line can be seen to the left and from this point onwards the trail remains near the fence. It leads south-east for 4.8 km basically descending amid many native pines, back into Wilpena campground. As you near the camp, the track is well marked and leads across the bottom of a number of spurs of the pound.

14 BUNYEROO GORGE

Flinders Ranges, South Australia

Walk:	8 km retrace
Time required:	Including minimal breaks, 2 hours 30 minutes
Grade:	One day, easy
Environment:	Remote mountain desert, rugged gorge and creek
Last review date:	June 2007
Map reference:	South Australian Lands Department 1:50 000 Oraparinna and Map 14
Best time to visit:	May to October; avoid hot summer days from December to March and carry water

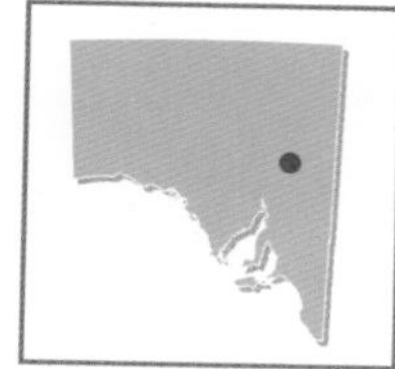

In the Flinders Ranges National Park, Bunyeroo Creek is one of the most beautiful spots for an easy walk. It is a great alternative to the nearby, hard grade St Mary Peak ascent walk in this book. The creek's banks are often green and therefore perhaps more inviting than other gorges and watercourses on warmer days. The often-dry watercourse, remarkably,

290 250 290

passes right through the rugged Heysen Range forming Bunyeroo Gorge. The Flinders Ranges are among the oldest of landscapes in the world. Geologists claim they are between 600 million and a billion years old. There are numerous steep saw-toothed ridges, uplifted, folded, buckled

Bunyeroo Gorge, Flinders Ranges

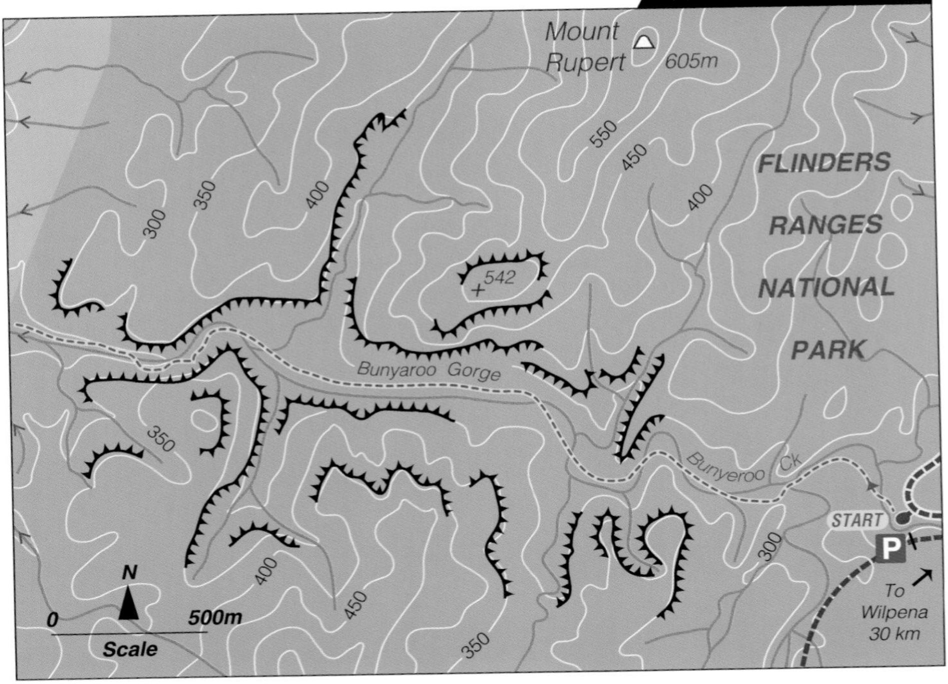

Wilpena	J	F	M	A	M	J	J	A	S	O	N	D	Year
Rain av. mm	20	15	8	7	57	51	62	43	20	17	7	17	324
Temp av. max. °C	31	31	29	23	16	14	12	14	18	24	26	28	22
Temp av. min. °C	16	16	13	8	5	4	2	2	5	9	12	14	9

and fractured, and many rugged gorges cut through the ridges.

Access is via scenic Bunyeroo Road. It starts 4.8 km north of the Wilpena turnoff along the Wilpena to Blinman Road. You need to go 20 km along Bunyeroo Road to a carpark at the head of the gorge. This carpark also services a 9 km circuit walk through the ABC Range. Private transport is needed as there is no public transport to Wilpena and beyond. You should avoid periods of rain as unsealed roads north of Wilpena may be closed to prevent damage to the road and for your safety. The general scenery and views from outlook parking bays along the Bunyeroo Road are outstanding.

The closest accommodation options are at Wilpena and Rawnsley Park. Wilpena has a moderately expensive motel and large camping area. A store for supplies is adjacent to the park visitor centre. Rawnsley Park has the full range of accommodation from backpacker to camping, on-site vans, cabins, motel and upmarket eco-lodges. More distant, Blinman has hotel accommodation. Several Blinman cottages have bed and breakfast accommodation as do some outlying pastoral properties.

Riverbank rock, Bunyeroo Gorge, Flinders Ranges

From the carpark it is only 4 km westwards, right through the gorge and the suggestion is that you go the full distance to a windmill at the western boundary of the national park, then retrace. There is a rough track to follow but it is not fully continuous. Some pegs help you follow the track sections. Walking is normally easy amid sparse vegetation or on sandy creek bed. There are plenty of stepping stones to cross the creek if water is in the bed. River red gums and massive, colourful cliffs make it a very memorable place. A common tree in the ranges, also seen here, is the native pine (*Callitris*). Various wattles, hop bush, daisy bush, and salvation jane are common plants. The presence of any water, attracts huge numbers of birds and other wildlife. Birds of the parrot family seem especially prevalent. On your return upstream, watch the marker pegs. Be careful to maintain the main watercourse and not veer into any side valley, especially those leading south. Basically you retrace in an easterly direction.

Eastern end of Bunyeroo Gorge, Flinders Ranges

MOUNT GAMBIER

South-East, South Australia

Walk:	5 km circuit
Time required:	Including minimal breaks, 2 hours
Grade:	One day, easy with two short, steep ascents
Environment:	Volcanic craters (extinct about 4300 years)
Last review date:	June 2007
Map reference:	South Australian Lands Department 1:50 000 Gambier and Map 15
Best time to visit:	Suited to any time of the year

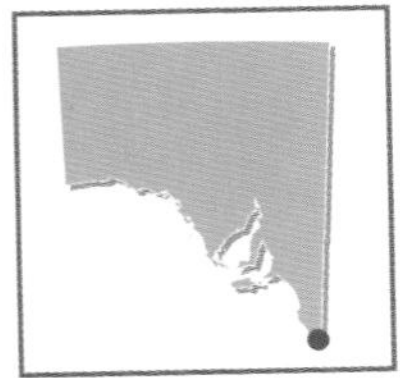

Mount Gambier is one of the most recently active of Australia's many geologically recent, extinct volcanoes and is said to have last erupted some 4300 years ago. It contains nine craters. The whole district has limestone rock under it and contains a number of interesting caves and sinkholes. The volcano has erupted up through the limestone. The most famous

100 187 100

part of the volcano is the Blue Lake crater where the limestone strata is clearly seen in the crater walls. Blue Lake is one of the major tourist attractions of South Australia. Blue Lake owes its name to its colour, which changes strikingly over a few days in November from grey in winter to bright blue

SA

Browne Lake, Mount Gambier

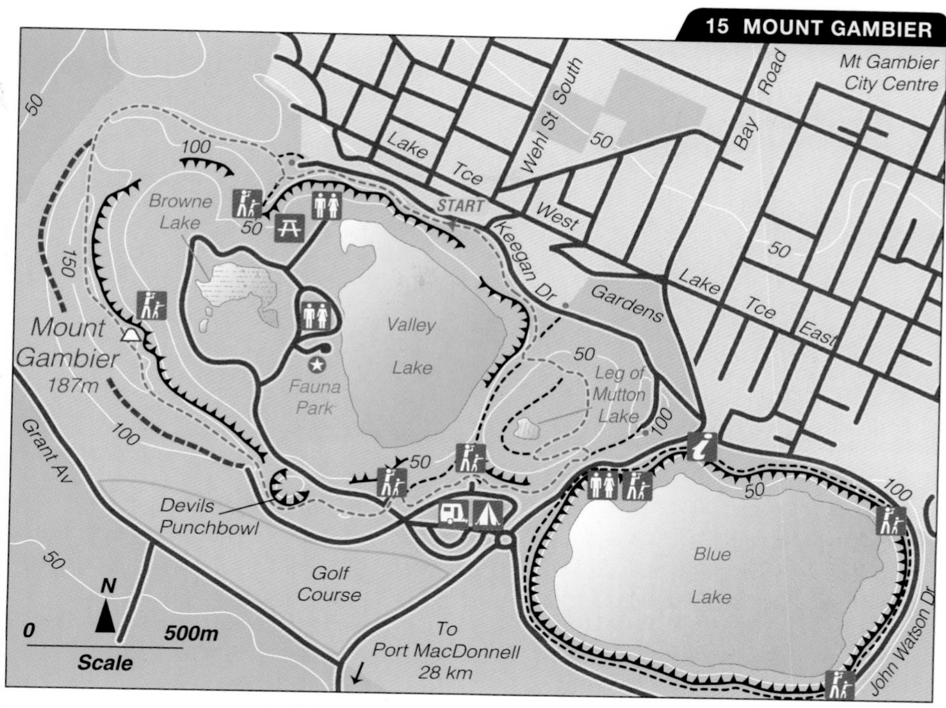

Mount Gambier	J	F	M	A	M	J	J	A	S	O	N	D	Year
Rain av. mm	26	26	34	54	72	84	98	93	72	62	46	37	708
Temp av. max. °C	25	25	23	19	16	13	13	14	15	17	20	22	18
Temp av. min. °C	11	11	10	8	7	5	5	5	6	7	8	9	8

in summer. It reverts to grey each March. The crater lake, known technically as a maar, is over 3 km in circumference and averages some 60 m in depth. The deepest part extends well below sea level. The water surface, as with other crater lakes at Mount Gambier, is at the level of the ground water table in the limestone bedding. Blue Lake's water supplies the whole district with its domestic supply, but the level hardly changes.

In a nearby crater, Valley Lake retains a good water supply, but other craters with higher crater floor levels, dry out in times of drought as the water table sinks. Three craters, all west of Blue Lake, contain water normally but they are not blue. The biggest of these three is Valley Lake while Browne Lake and Leg of Mutton Lake are quite small. Five more craters are dry, although reeds grow in one near the western end of Browne Lake. The highest crater has a floor 91 m above sea level, which is 70 m above the level of the lakes in other craters. A college sporting oval occupies the floor of the westernmost crater. The smallest crater, about 20 m in diameter, is near a fauna park entrance.

The city of Mount Gambier flanks the northern slopes of the volcano so that for decades the mountain has been used as a pleasure and recreation area. Boating

Blue Lake Crater, Mount Gambier

is popular on Valley Lake, a golf club is on the southern slopes of the mountain complex and there are three main walking track circuits. One circuits Blue Lake as a roadside pathway.

Mountain Trail, 4.2 km long, rings both Valley Lake and Browne Lake while Pepperpot Trail, 1.7 km long, circuits Leg of Mutton Lake and passes Blue Lake. A combination of parts of these two walks is recommended. Be aware that some short, steep sections are encountered as the volcanic terrain is typically rugged. Since erupted ash is the principal component of the mountain, erosion occurs easily. The whole system of craters and lakes is packed with interest and contains numerous picnic spots and lookouts. There is a small beach at Valley Lake, a fauna park with an interesting boardwalk and both native plants garden and exotic plantings.

From Mount Gambier business areas, take Bay Road to the edge of the mountain parklands then go west on Lake Terrace West to pass multi-level apartments. At the western end of this former hospital, turn left across a narrow bridge at a motel up Hay Drive and the rim of Valley Lake crater. Parking is available here ready to start walking. The sudden appearance beyond the rim of such a magnificent aspect is certain to enthuse all starters. It is preferable to walk the circuit anticlockwise.

Head off west for 750 m on a foot track close to the crater rim and the south side of the road. The crater system is to your left. You soon reach a picnic area and outlook at the road end. A water reservoir tank is here and foot tracks lead past each side of the tank. Ignore a track off left to a lookout and head past the tank on to the main track system. Go along a crest, pass two craters and climb over a rise called Sugarloaf, which allows more views of Browne Lake and Valley Lake. Steps then take you south up a steep incline on the crest and on to a tower on Mount Gambier summit. Blue Gum Trail veers off to the right at the base of the steps and bypasses the summit. It leads through pines and weed-infested areas so it is best to make the effort to climb over the top. Some pine trees have been felled on the crater slopes. These are quite unsightly but you do get a better view. When a flag is flying on the summit tower, the tower is open to the public for an even better panorama. After this highlight, you descend by pathway to Lions Lookout and a carpark. Blue Gum Trail rejoins here.

Next, go east along Mountain Trail close to Elliott Drive. You soon pass Devils Punchbowl's southern rim and head down to Marks Lookout. From here, you leave Mountain Trail. You follow Pepperpot Trail, which officially has red track markers that are few in number and sometimes indistinct. The trail first continues east, right beside Elliott Drive, past another lookout above the Valley Lake–Leg of Mutton Lake divide and to Mel Hirth Lookout. A native garden is at this lookout. Blue Lake comes into view here and the track leads down to a saddle between Leg of Mutton Lake and Blue Lake. You will see a monument to famous poet Adam Lindsay Gordon and there are three lookouts at the saddle, which is crossed by a main road. A road underpass gives access to the best view of Blue Lake.

At this point an option is to extend the walk length to walk the full crater rim loop around Blue Lake. The extra distance is 3.7 km and a concrete footpath can be used for the full circuit. The path is right beside the tourist ring road. There are great views of Crater Lake, water pumping installations and a different aspect of the mountain summit. It matters little whether you walk clockwise or anticlockwise. A tourist visitor centre is passed during the circuit.

Next, a sealed, former road, leads west from the saddle down to Leg of Mutton Lake crater. Head down around a hairpin bend to be among magnificent deciduous trees to where the road diminishes to a foot track that forms a loop in the crater floor. Soon after the sealed road ends and as you follow the loop track anticlockwise, watch carefully for a rough foot pad up to a saddle between Leg of Mutton Lake and Valley Lake. Take this short climb on to the ridge crest, turn right and ascend further north up the ridge to reach Keegan Drive on the tops. As you climb, take the track that veers left rather than heading up the spur crest. At the roadway, turn left and walk the 300 m to the walk's end by way of a foot track adjacent to the south side of the road.

Leg of Mutton Crater, Mount Gambier

TASMANIA

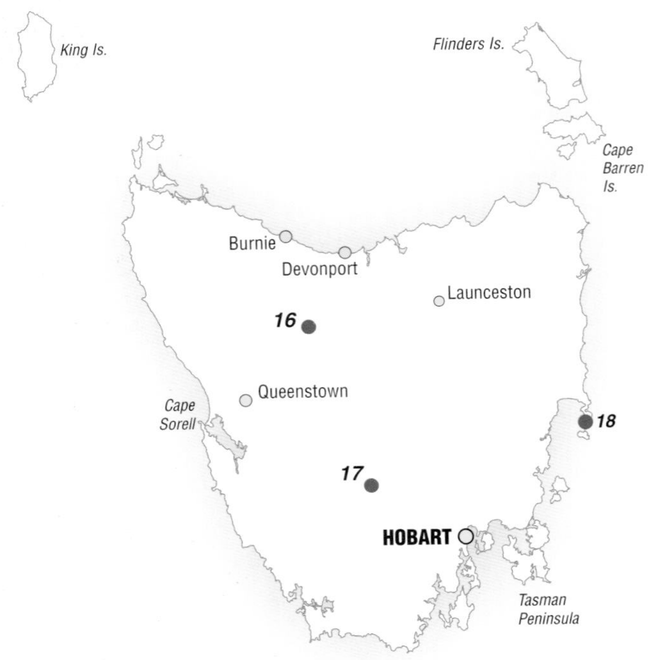

TAS

16	Dove Lake	Cradle Mountain–Lake St Clair National Park
17	Tarn Shelf	Mount Field National Park
18	Freycinet Peninsula	Freycinet National Park

Dove Lake, boat shed, Cradle Mountain–Lake St Clair National Park

Tasmania provides walkers some of the most remote, rugged and challenging terrain in Australia, with many parts of the state only recently mapped to any real certainty. The western half has some of the highest rainfall in the country, which in turn gives rise to spectacular waterfalls, lakes and rivers in a pristine condition. It is also subject to some of the most ferocious weather from the west; the so-called 'roaring forties'. Those venturing into the wilderness here need to take careful note of expected weather conditions and prepare accordingly. At the same time Mount Wellington towers dramatically close to the capital city of Hobart. The residents of the city have wonderful walks nearby.

Some of the most celebrated walks in Tasmania are to be found in the vicinity of Cradle Mountain. The Overland Track as the name suggests, traverses alpine wilderness and is the most popular long distance walk in Australia. Immense peaks, carved by former glaciers, tower over crystal-clear lakes and a sense of being in ancient Gondwana land surrounds you. Trees such as the King Billy Pine (*Antrotaxis selaginoides*) and the deciduous beech (*Nothofagus gunnii*) have remained practically unchanged from their ancient ancestors.

The south-west, with its extremely rugged country, includes Mount Anne, Frenchman's Cap, the Western Arthur Range and Federation Peak areas. These walks are suited primarily to experienced walkers only. Nearer to Hobart (and more accessible) is Mount Field, where Tarn Shelf is situated. A maze of tarns surrounded by button grass moors and other alpine plants are a highlight walk in this book.

Tasmania's floral emblem:
Tasmanian Blue Gum (Eucalyptus globules)

The Great Western Tiers mark the northern rim of the large Central Plateau that includes such scenic places as the Walls of Jerusalem. Some 4000 lakes resulting from past glaciation are on the plateau, and primitive plants such as pencil pines (*Athrotaxus cupressoides*) reflect in the water.

Tasmania's fauna emblem:
Tasmanian Devil (Sarcophilus harrisii)

The east coast, especially at Freycinet Peninsula and Maria Island, has superb white sand beaches backed by rugged granite mountains. The Tasman Peninsula features very high dolerite rock cliffs and pinnacles. A milder climate makes these areas more suitable for walks all year round.

DOVE LAKE
Cradle Mountain, Tasmania

Walk:	5.6 km circuit
Time required:	Including minimal breaks, 2 hours
Grade:	One day, easy
Environment:	Alpine forest, heath land and lake
Last review date:	May 2007
Map reference:	*Tasmap*, 1:25 000 Cradle and Map 16
Best time to visit:	Often snowbound during winter from June to August and snow possible at any time of year, suited best to summer months November to March

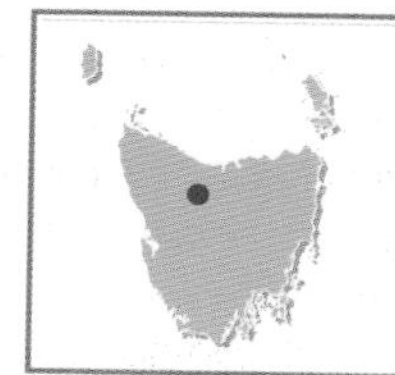

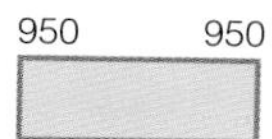

Latitude and altitude bring snow at any time of the year but especially during the long, cold, wet winter. Best walking weather occurs in January, February and March.

Tasmania's biggest focus for walkers is the Overland Track in the vast Cradle Mountain–Lake St Clair National Park. The track appears to be almost as famous as New Zealand's Milford Track. Rugged, glaciated mountains and lakes, tarns, fine forests and snow-capped peaks with jagged, dolerite-capped summits make the

Lakeside vegetation, Dove Lake

Cradle Mt	J	F	M	A	M	J	J	A	S	O	N	D	Year
Rain av. mm	80	75	82	128	162	160	212	201	148	130	113	103	1594
Temp av. max. °C	18	18	16	13	10	8	7	8	10	12	14	16	13
Temp av. min. °C	7	8	7	5	4	2	1	1	2	3	5	6	4

Nothofagus

region quite unique compared to most of the rest of Australia.

Cradle Mountain, at 1545 m, is renowned as one of Australia's most photographed, visited and internationally famous mountains. For a sunburnt country, it is a remarkable alpine-looking peak. In winter it is mostly snow covered. The famous long-distance Overland Track to distant Lake St Clair leads right past the peak. The peak features jagged dolerite rock like many higher Tasmanian peaks.

This day walk area, based from Dove Lake, in the northern part of the park, is higher and more exposed than further south. It is spectacularly beautiful. It contains fine myrtle trees (*Nothofagus cunninghamii*), King Billy pines, pencil pines and many of the smaller nothofagus (fagus or deciduous beech) trees (*Nothofagus gunnii*). This species is extremely colourful in late April and early May.

Access to Cradle Mountain from outside Tasmania is usually by air from Melbourne or Sydney into Devonport or Launceston or by ferry from Melbourne to Devonport. Coaches and private transport operators will take you from Devonport to Cradle Mountain. The tourist office in Devonport is the best venue to arrange such transport.

Accommodation at Cradle Mountain is located just outside the national park. It varies from camping and self-catering cabins to somewhat more luxurious lodge-type hotels and at Pencil Pine. Devonport is a small city with full services.

The Cradle Mountain alpine tops (1200–1545 m elevation) frequently suffer bad weather. Such weather of course limits enjoyable walking possibilities, especially on any exposed, fog-shrouded tops. Dove Lake though is at a lower elevation (940 m) and exposure is not such a major problem. Evidently, in order to reduce costly searches and increase safety, the park authorities have constructed the lower lake circuit and promoted it so as to minimise visitors to the higher circuit. The now far more popular lower circuit walk of the lake has arrows subtly aiming to get everyone walking clockwise to ease congestion on busy summer days. In fine weather there is a stunning mountain backdrop to the lake. Cradle Mountain itself dominates and Weindorfers Tower is just to the east of the summit. Most of the circuit is on boardwalk or on good quality gravel path. There is just one significant climb, but it is of only some 50 m elevation.

This walk begins at a large carpark at the northern end of Dove Lake, on rock debris moraine left by the former, retreating Dove Lake glacier. This spot is some 7 km

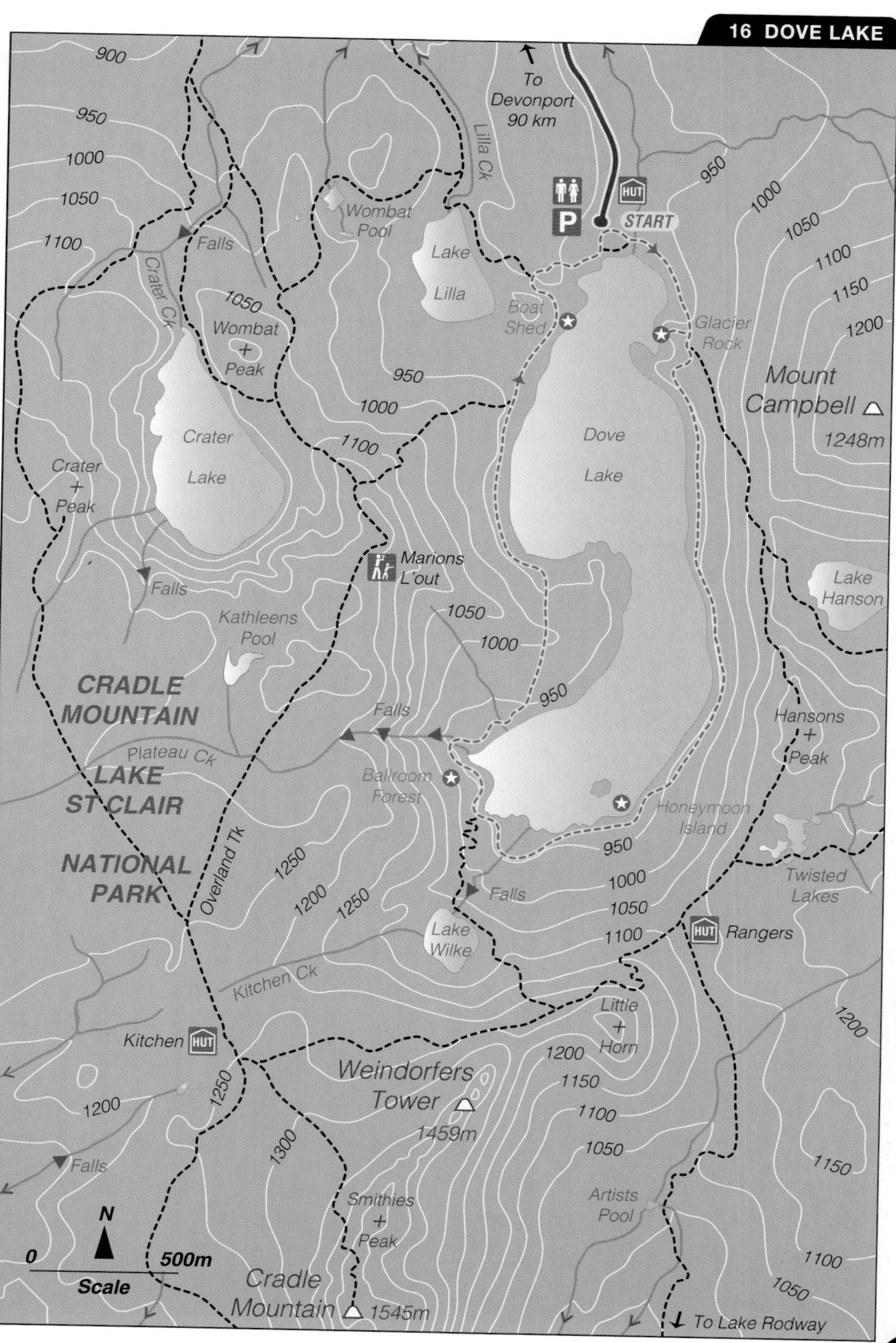

To Devonport 90 km
START
Lilla Ck
Wombat Pool
Lake Lilla
Falls
Crater Ck
Wombat Peak
Boat Shed
Glacier Rock
Mount Campbell
1248m
Crater Lake
Dove Lake
Crater Peak
Marions L'out
Lake Hanson
Falls
Kathleens Pool
CRADLE MOUNTAIN
LAKE ST CLAIR
NATIONAL PARK
Plateau Ck
Falls
Hansons Peak
Ballroom Forest
Honeymoon Island
Overland Tk
Twisted Lakes
Falls
Lake Wilke
Rangers
Kitchen Ck
Little Horn
Kitchen
Weindorfers Tower
1459m
Falls
Smithies Peak
Artists Pool
N
0
500m
Scale
Cradle Mountain
1545m
To Lake Rodway

south of the park's northern entrance and at the end of the road. The view south from here reveals the typical U-shaped valley with steep sides scoured by ice in past ice ages. A shelter hut and toilets are at the carpark. A shuttle bus service operates continuously to the carpark from the park visitor centre for all of the warmer months. This is because the access road is very narrow and winding and the volume of traffic would be too great.

Head off to circuit the lake clockwise. At first you cross a bridge spanning the Dove River as it leaves the lake. You then cross some button grass-covered slopes to the area of prominent Glacier Rock (formerly Suicide Rock). This rock has a gateway for access as great care needs to be taken if you walk on to it. When 500 m from the walk start, you veer right, rather than climb towards Hansons Peak. For the next 2.4 km you basically contour on slopes near the eastern and southern shores. The vegetation is quite attractive and some rocks have glacial striations on them. The view to Cradle Mountain and to nearby waterfalls improves. After rounding the southern end of the lake past Honeymoon Island you reach and pass steps at the Lake Wilks track junction. The vegetation thickens and is very damp.

You go on north 1.8 km into the superb myrtle-dominated Ballroom Forest where Plateau Creek enters the lake. Much lichen and moss covers rocks and more glacial striations are seen. You climb over a spur in an area where the track is at its roughest. Views are great from this spur. You then reach and pass a left-side, lesser track from Marions Lookout. Go 400 m north and reach a shingled boatshed by the water. This spot is particularly photogenic. Many photographs of Cradle Mountain from Dove Lake seem to include the boatshed.

To end the walk, climb 200 m to a track junction. From here you can see Lake Lilla off left. Turn right and descend 300 m to the carpark.

Dove Lake and Cradle Mountain

TARN SHELF

Lake Webster, Tasmania

Walk:	13 km circuit
Time required:	Including minimal breaks, 6 hours
Grade:	One day, medium but can be very wet underfoot
Environment:	Alpine meadow and glacially formed tarns
Last review date:	May 2007
Map reference:	*Tasmap*, 1:50 000 Mount Field National Park and Map 17
Best time to visit:	Suited best to summer from December to March, often snowbound in winter especially July and August

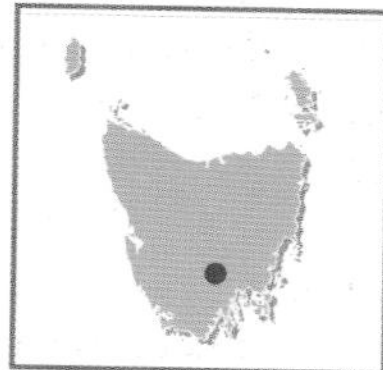

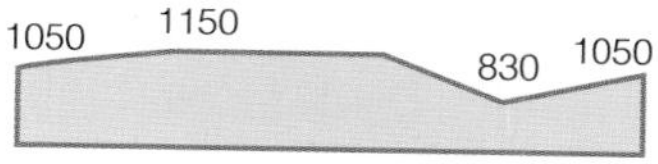

Ice has shaped many of Tasmania's mountains in the past and Mount Field north-west of Hobart is a typical example of the tremendous changes that have occurred. Mount Field West and Mount

Alpine plants, Tarn Shelf

TAS

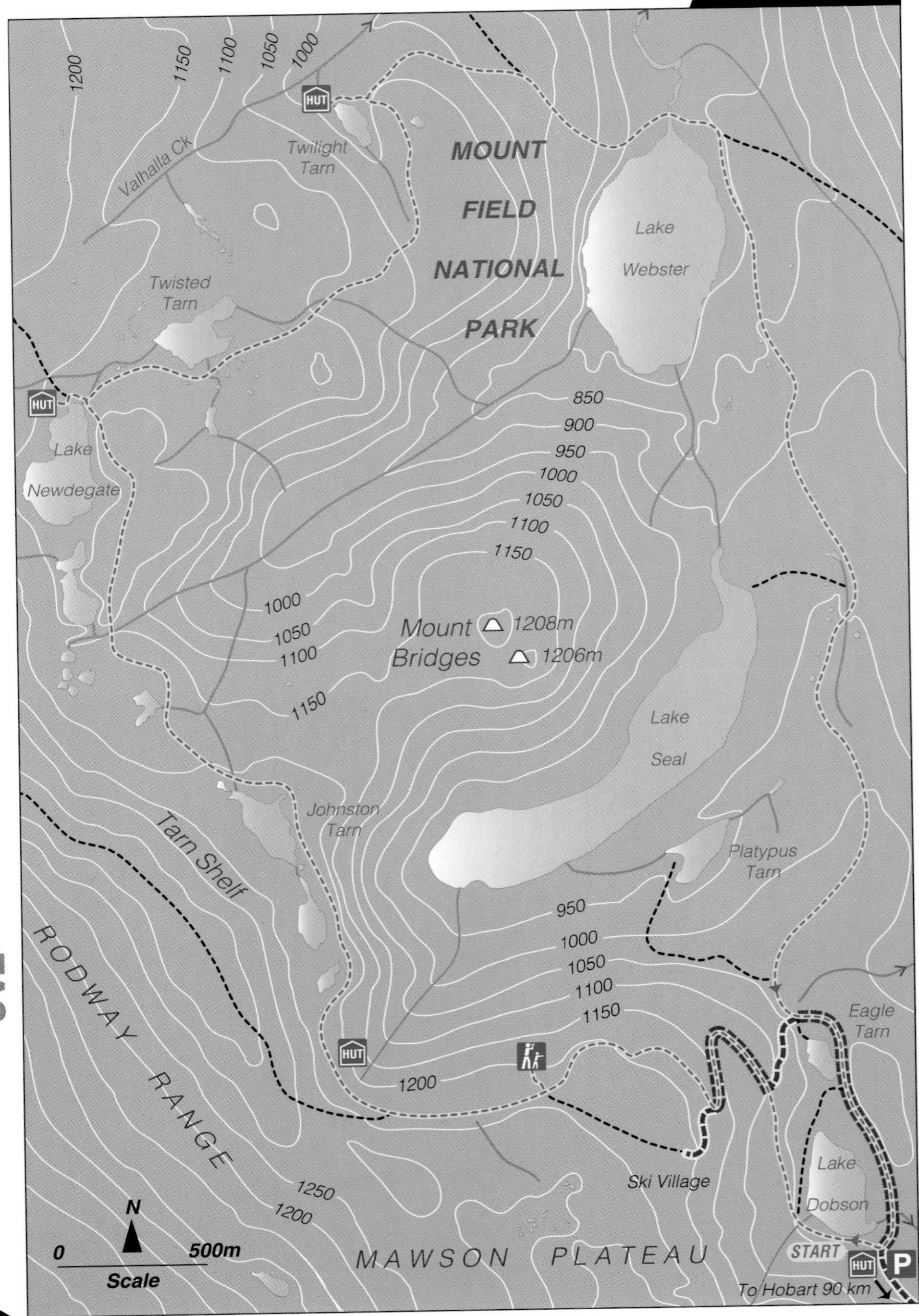
MOUNT
FIELD
NATIONAL
PARK
Twilight Tarn
Valhalla Ck
Twisted Tarn
Lake Newdegate
Lake Webster
Mount Bridges
1208m
1206m
Lake Seal
Johnston Tarn
Tarn Shelf
Platypus Tarn
Eagle Tarn
Lake Dobson
Ski Village
RODWAY RANGE
MAWSON PLATEAU
START
P
To Hobart 90 km
N
0
500m
Scale
HUT
1200
1150
1100
1050
1000
850
900
950
1250

New Norfolk	J	F	M	A	M	J	J	A	S	O	N	D	Year
Rain av. mm	39	34	38	47	44	49	48	46	49	55	47	49	550
Temp av. max. °C	23	24	21	17	14	10	10	12	14	17	19	21	17
Temp av. min. °C	10	11	9	7	4	2	1	2	4	6	8	9	6

Field East form the extremities of what once was a plateau. With the passing of time, ice has scoured out much of the plateau, leaving a series of ridges. Much of the area is of dolerite rock, typical of many higher peaks in Tasmania. If you study a map, K Col is clearly a central point in ridges from Mount Field West to Mount Mawson and between Florentine Peak and the Newdegate Pass area. Glacial action has gouged huge valleys and left typical flat valley floors, steep walls, truncated spurs and an abnormal set of watercourses all radiating out from K Col.

Retreating glaciers left behind an accumulation of debris rock known as moraines. These have caused natural dams behind which lakes, such as Hayes, Belcher, Belton, Seal and Webster, have remained in the valleys. On or near the tops, ice has scoured out innumerable hollows that are now filled with water, an example being the remarkable Tarn Shelf.

A very educational round walk can be taken to see the effects of glacial action. As with most similar areas, the scenery is excellent. The suggested starting point is at the Lake Dobson carpark 15 km up the narrow winding road from the Mount Field National Park entrance. This carpark services a small ski settlement.

Pandani palm (Richea pandanifolia)

Be sure to pick a fine day, so that the glacial valleys can be seen from the tops. Forget the walk if the weather is poor. A shelter hut is at the walk start and three other shelter huts exist along the walk route. This is perhaps indicative of the need to be careful in such exposed alpine country where snow can occur at any time of the year. Late April and early May is a great time to see the resplendent autumn tints on the Tarn Shelf.

Deciduous fagus (*Nothofagus gunnii*), a small endemic tree, grows in the area and is stunningly beautiful as it sheds its leaves. For some, an annual pilgrimage walk to Tarn Shelf on Anzac Day (25 April) to see the fagus at its best has become a tradition. The trees are reflected in the many alpine tarns.

Access to the park is from Hobart and private transport is needed. Accommodation is limited to camping at the park entrance, some cabins and a small hotel at the national park. It is better to use the town of New Norfolk where many options exist.

Take the western shore walking track around Lake Dobson shore for 250 m, passing the Wellington Ski Club building and innumerable varieties of plants along the way. The upper plant storey is of pandani palm (*Richea pandanifolia*), banksia, snow gum, pencil pine, waratah and tea tree. The lower plant storey includes prickly scoparia, bauera and a host of mosses, notably sphagnum moss, lichens, and small alpines including cushion plants. Boardwalk covers wet patches of the track. Veer left next, to climb Urquhart Track for 500 m through forest to a roadway at a hairpin bend. Turn up the road past an outlook point towards ski slopes and lodges. After 500 m take the right fork of the road. Pass three ski lodges and at the nearby road end, head on to Snow Gums walking track. Small animals such as Tasmanian devils and tiger quolls may be seen in this area.

Climb the track west-north-west 500 m via herb and rock-covered scree slopes, to a track intersection, on some open tops. Here, go a few metres north to Lake Seal Lookout. The lake is almost vertically 300 m below the lookout, and you can see clearly how ice has carved the landscape to form the lake and cliffs. Boardwalk is provided on the tracks in this area.

Next, go west from the intersecting tracks for 600 m, then fork right towards Tarn Shelf and Lake Newdegate. Rodway ski tow and a shelter hut are just ahead. It is then 3 km to Lake Newdegate. Much of the way is along the Tarn Shelf. Descend from the shelter hut then continue on to the broad ice-scoured ledge of Tarn Shelf, which is on the slopes of the Rodway Range. Panoramic views are a feature of the whole area. Ice scour marks can clearly be seen on the rocks and scoured hollows contain many delightful tarns. Pencil pines, lichens, wildflowers and other alpine plants including endemic fagus (*Nothofagus gunnii*) make this a plant enthusiasts' and walkers' paradise.

The track is very rocky with many small rises and falls, so progress will be slow. At the northern end of the shelf formation is the larger tarn, Lake Newdegate. The track leads to the lake's north end where there is a nine-bunk hut and minor track junction. Lunch could be considered at the hut.

Turn right (east) to cross 1 km of alpine plateau with more track boardwalk and tarns including lovely Twisted Tarn. The way is then down through stunted eucalyptus north for 800 m to Twilight Tarn where there is another small hut near its north end. This hut is rather rustic and just 200 m west, off the main track.

Descend again east for 1.4 km through more dense eucalyptus forest to the outlet to Lake Webster. The overgrowing Mount Lord track links in on your left during this descent. At the lake outlet, there is a footbridge, across the Broad River.

To the east of the lake there is a small button grass plain, typical of many glaciated valley floors. The soil is too sour to grow trees except on ridges of moraine. The ongoing track forks right, away from a Lake Fenton track. Go south across the button grass plain, then rise on to a rather large moraine ridge. The track then gradually ascends for 3.2 km back to the ski village access road. Banksias, waratahs and eucalyptus form much of the vegetation at first, then the plant life becomes far more varied.

About midway up the rise, in the area of Fairy Tarn and other tiny ridge-top tarns, bypass a track off west, to the outlet to Lake Seal. This finger lake is a typical glacier-formed lake and can be seen from the main track as you climb. When within 200 m of the road and the end of the climb, bypass a track off right down to Platypus Tarn.

The road is reached at a bend. Go down the road for 800 m past the east side of each of Eagle Tarn and Lake Dobson to return to the Lake Dobson car park. The roadside is well endowed with pandani as well as a very diverse range of other plants.

FREYCINET PENINSULA

East Coast, Tasmania

Walk:	13 km circuit
Time required:	Including minimal breaks, 4 hours 30 minutes
Grade:	One day, medium
Environment:	Beaches, granite outcrops and coastal heathland
Last review date:	May 2007
Map reference:	*Tasmap*, 1:25 000 Coles Bay and Graham sheets and Map 18
Best time to visit:	Suited to any season but winter (June, July and August) can be cool

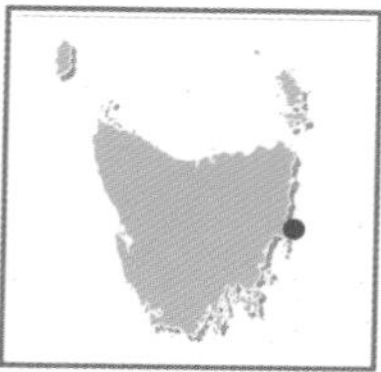

Freycinet Peninsula on the east coast of Tasmania is renowned for its very beautiful beaches backed by massive granite peaks known as the Hazards. The same type of granitic scenery also exists in Tasmania at Maria Island and Flinders Island. About 370 million years ago the volcanic granite welled up amongst rock folds and later was exposed by erosion during sinking and uplifting bouts.

View from Mount Amos of Wineglass Bay, Freycinet Peninsula

Bicheno	J	F	M	A	M	J	J	A	S	O	N	D	Year
Rain av. mm	53	56	56	60	56	60	52	49	43	56	57	69	672
Temp av. max. °C	21	21	20	18	16	14	14	14	16	17	18	19	17
Temp av. min. °C	12	13	11	10	8	6	6	6	7	8	10	11	9

Pink granite at Wineglass Bay

This circuit walk at Freycinet Peninsula, within national park, provides the opportunity for a break at both Wineglass Bay and Hazards Beach with swimming or lazing at either or both beaches. Wineglass Bay is undoubtedly the most beautiful spot so it is suggested that the longer break and perhaps lunch could be taken there. These breaks will naturally extend the estimated 4 hours 30 minutes walk time. Usually the only drinking water is at the south-east end of Wineglass Bay, which also happens to be a bush camp site. This water supply can get brackish at times. Therefore, carry some water and also sunscreen.

Access to the peninsula and its national park is via the Tasman Highway from the small towns of Swansea or Bicheno. Coaches operate along the Tasman Highway. Separate coaches link Bicheno to Coles Bay. However, overall, private transport is best used. Access from outside Tasmania is by air to Hobart or Launceston. Coles Bay is a small settlement with general store, fuel, cafe and boat ramp.

Camping is available at the park with alternative accommodation around Coles Bay being mostly bed and breakfast and cabins. Better accommodation options are available at the more distant towns of Swansea and Bicheno.

Go to the Freycinet Peninsula walking tracks carpark, 3.8 km south of the park ranger's office near Coles Bay. Foot tracks radiate from this now enlarged car park.

From the car park, avoid the Mount Amos track and go south-south-east across a gully on an upgraded foot track. Here you turn left. You then climb steps and a well-defined track. This is in an area of well-drained granitic soils with a westerly aspect, so vegetation is fairly sparse. You may see wallabies in the area. Granite has been used extensively for construction of the many steps and associated track drainage. When 1.5 km from the carpark, you reach a saddle between Mount Amos and Mount Mayson, both rugged pink granite peaks. The saddle is 200 m above sea level and granite boulders surround the locality. The pink tint of the Hazards is caused by iron oxide in feldspar. The granite rock of the peaks consists of feldspar (pink or cream), micas (black) and quartz (white and glassy).

At the saddle, take a side trip (200 m return) to the left on to a viewing deck to get your first view of lovely Wineglass Bay ahead. This lookout is the goal of most walkers at Freycinet Peninsula and once

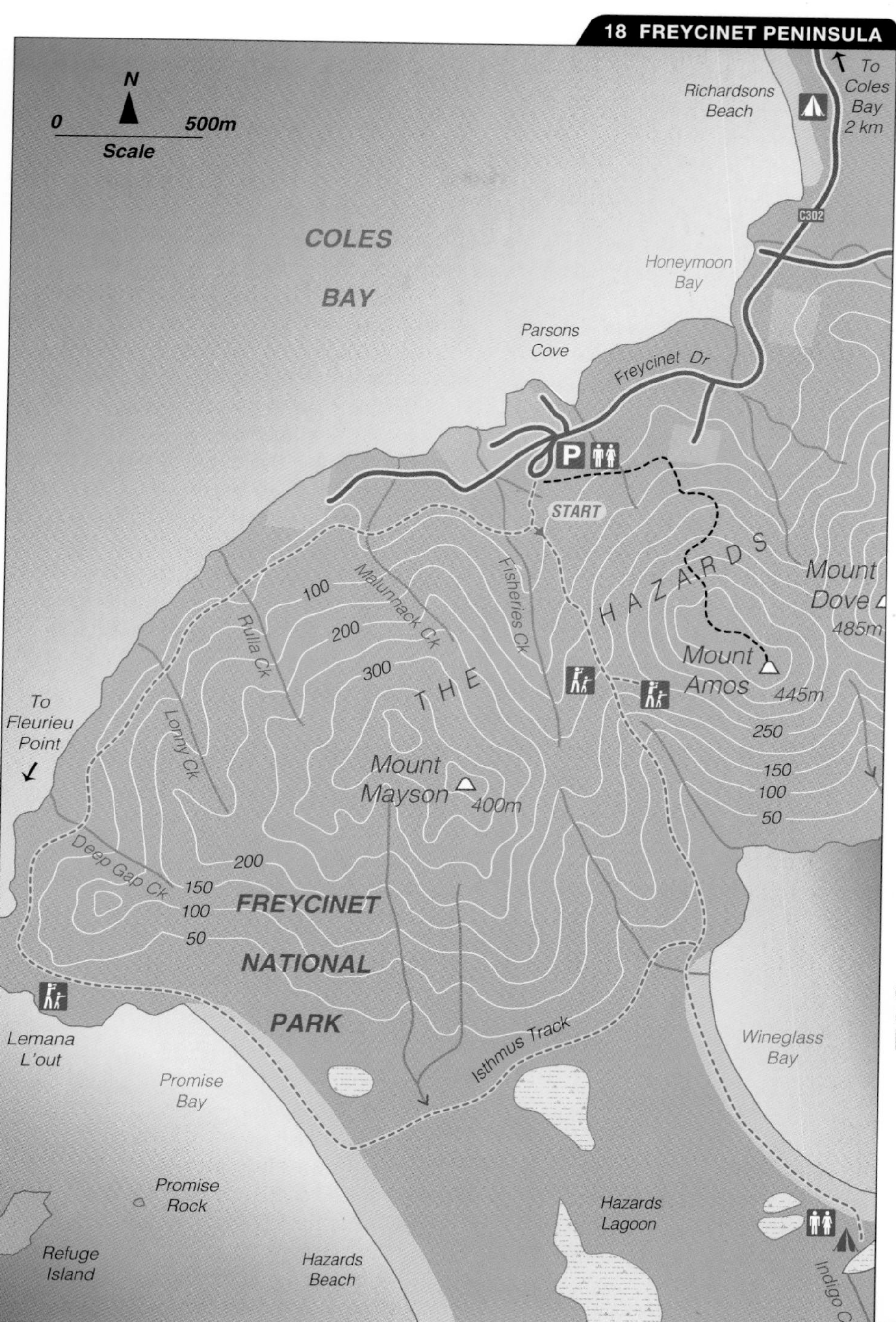

N
0
500m
Scale
COLES
BAY
To
Coles
Bay
2 km
Richardsons
Beach
C302
Honeymoon
Bay
Parsons
Cove
Freycinet Dr
P
START
THE HAZARDS
Mount
Dove
485m
Mount
Amos
445m
Maluunnack Ck
Fisheries Ck
Rulla Ck
Lonny Ck
Deep Gap Ck
To
Fleurieu
Point
Mount
Mayson
400m
FREYCINET
NATIONAL
PARK
Isthmus Track
Lemana
L'out
Promise
Bay
Promise
Rock
Refuge
Island
Hazards
Beach
Hazards
Lagoon
Wineglass
Bay
Indigo Ck

TAS

past it, you tend to have a bit of paradise mostly to yourself.

Leave the saddle and descend the ongoing track for 1.5 km, to the north-west end of the Wineglass Bay beach. The damp forest as you descend contrasts with the dry slopes west of the saddle. Some 30 m before the track links to the beach, another track (Isthmus Track) from Hazards Beach is on your right. This track is your later route. Some of the granite rocks at the beach have colourful orange and silver lichens growing on them.

Walk the full 1.5 km long white-sand Wineglass Bay beach to reach the sheltered far end in about 25 to 30 minutes. There is a bush camp area and a creek mouth at the spot and the usually calm sea here is great for swimming.

Enjoy lunch and preferably take a long break before retracing the beach to turn left on to Isthmus Track. Follow it for a virtually flat 2 km walk to Hazards Beach. The track passes banksia stands with much bird life. In spots near Hazards Lagoon and swamp, there is some boardwalk. The track then crosses dunes to the west side of the peninsula.

Turn north-west (right) at Hazards Beach and go the 1 km to the end of the beach. Another break in this sheltered corner might appeal. There are good views south to the backbone range of the peninsula and across Great Oyster Bay. Refuge Island is seen in the foreground.

Next, follow the Peninsula walking track from the beach end. The track climbs up away from the water's edge, rounds Fleurieu Point, stays roughly parallel to the coast but rises up the slopes and crosses several creeks. It is 4 km from the north end of Hazards Beach back to the car park. The latter part crosses slopes, to avoid private property and an old quarry near the shore. Because the slopes face west, this final leg of the walk can seem hot and tiring on hot summer afternoons.

The Hazards, Wineglass Bay

WESTERN AUSTRALIA

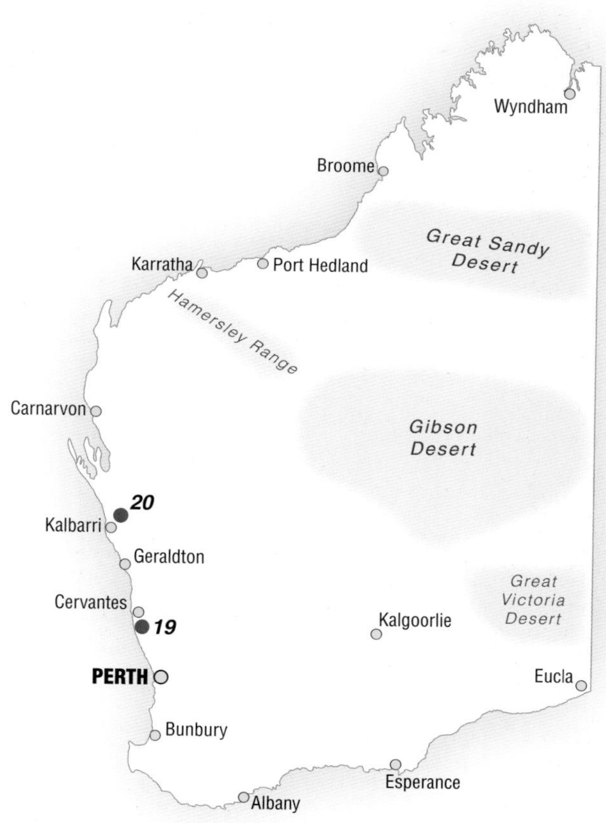

19	Pinnacles Desert	Nambung National Park
20	Murchison Gorge	Kalbarri National Park

Western Australia, the largest of all the states, covering one-third of the country, contains a range of tropical to temperate conditions within its borders. Distances are vast with some roads rendered impassible during the wet season. The Kimberley Ranges in the north have the amazing Bungle Bungles while the Pilbara Ranges of the north-west boast the state's highest mountains and some of the nation's most spectacular gorges and oldest rocks. Mount Augustus is double the size of Uluru and is thought to be the world's largest monocline.

The state is famous for the spring wild flowers, especially in the region of Kalbarri, with many fine varieties of grevillia, banksia and heathland plants. These nectar-rich shrubs support a wide range of birds and mammals. Further south, the Pinnacles are rock formations so ordered in appearance, as to be reminiscent of Stonehenge or the icons of Easter Island. Coral reefs on the tropical coastline include the 260 km

Murchison River Gorge, Kalbarri National Park

Western Australia's floral emblem: Mangles' Kangaroo Paw (Anigozanthus manglesii)

Western Australia's fauna emblem: Numbat (Myrmecobius fasciatus)

long Ningaloo Reef, which is a paradise for snorkellers. It contains 200 species of coral, with turtles, dugongs and some 500 species of fish.

Predominately desert, the state is currently experiencing a mining boom, centred mostly around the Pilbara, Kimberley region and Kalgoorlie. Perth, the state capital, is one of the most remote cities in the world. Some 300 km south can be found the karri forests, among the tallest of trees in the world and with many plant species that exist nowhere else.

The 350 km Bibbulmun long distance walking track from Perth to Albany, traverses mixed, often tall, karri forest in a region of heavy rainfall, and coastal heathland.

The Great Australian Bight marks the edge of the Nullarbor Plain which is mostly a vast limestone plateau indicative of the presence of a former inland sea. This sea effectively isolated Western Australia from the rest of the country allowing flora and fauna to evolve differently.

PINNACLES DESERT
Cervantes, Western Australia

Walk:	5 km circuit
Time required:	Including minimal breaks, 2 hours
Grade:	One day, easy
Environment:	Desert sands with limestone pinnacles
Last review date:	August 2007
Map reference:	Map 19
Best time to visit:	April to November; avoid the very hot summer days from December to April; walk in cooler parts of the day and certainly carry water and sunscreen

The Pinnacles in Nambung National Park are a well-known feature in coastal sandy desert country. They are located 17 km by sealed road south-east of the small town of Cervantes, which is 245 km north of Perth. The town has limited accommodation except for a well-appointed backpacker hostel and a motel. The park has no accommodation. The park's main attraction is the thousands of limestone pinnacles that protrude

The Milk Bottles, the Pinnacles, Nambung National Park

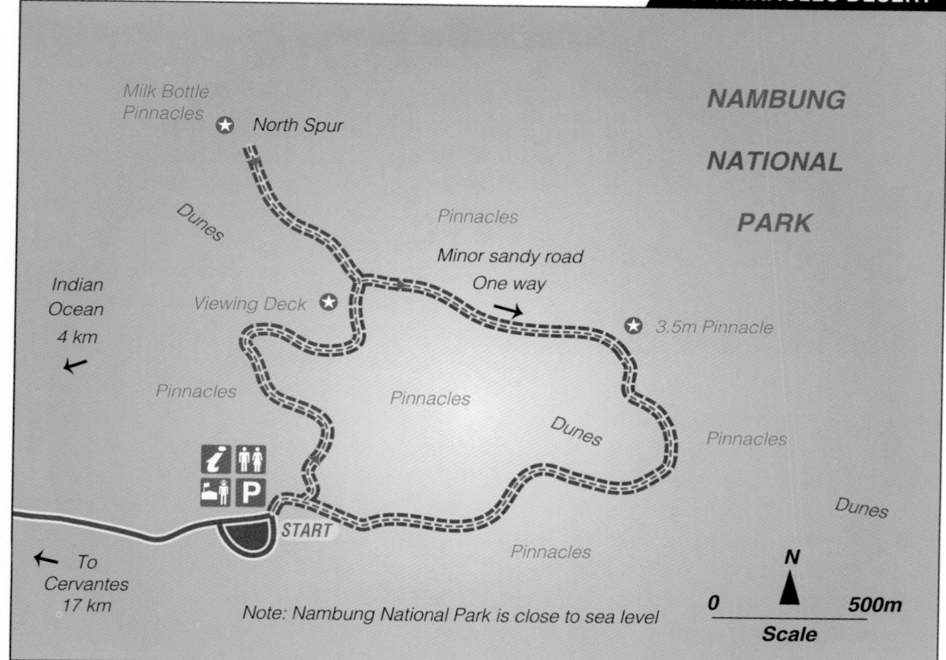

Cervantes	J	F	M	A	M	J	J	A	S	O	N	D	Year
Rain av. mm	9	12	30	40	80	120	110	90	55	35	12	7	600
Temp av. max. °C	37	38	37	32	29	26	25	26	27	29	31	35	31
Temp av. min. °C	23	24	23	19	17	15	14	14	14	16	18	21	18

by as much as 3.5 m from the orange-yellow desert sands. The majority of the formations are needle-like, some having sharp edges, occasionally perforated by holes. They stand like silent sentinels, reminiscent of Stonehenge or Easter Island monuments. However, they are definitely not man-made. There is also fine coastal scenery elsewhere in the park. Most visitors opt to go to the Pinnacles and drive a sandy 3.5 km circuit from the park entrance gate where a fee is charged. Adjacent is a carpark and visitor centre. Visitors stop frequently to admire the formations and take photographs. There is an elevated lookout and a number of dunes from which panoramic views are afforded out to the coast. Seeing the Pinnacles from high points allows you to better appreciate their beauty. The whole of the area lies at close to sea level.

The geology of the Pinnacles is rather interesting. They consist of sand and limestone. The whole district including offshore islands and bluffs has limestone underneath it and forms a major aquifer from which the town of Cervantes draws all its water. Over time, sands made up of sea shell fragments from the nearby coast have washed ashore and blown inland forming dune systems, some of which are the oldest in Western Australia. Sinking

Galah

rainwater during winter, which is slightly acidic, dissolves the calcium carbonate (lime) contained in the alkaline shells that form the dunes. During summers the drying of the material forms calcrete. This hard surface capping has been aided by the presence of plants that accentuate the leaching process. Plants also send down roots, allowing cracking and eroding of underlying softer quartz sand and limestone. Subsequent wind erosion over time has created the columns we see today. The alternate exposure and submerging of pinnacle formation by dune movement continue to slowly change the present balance.

Much of the area is of shifting sands, but numerous plants have adapted to these arid conditions. Acacias prefer the leeward side of dunes while succulents and the more salt-resistant or frontline species grow on the windward side of dunes. The further inland you travel, the larger the plant species tend to become. Banksias, dryandras and casuarinas are common while some small wildflowers are to be seen in season. Animal life includes emus, kangaroos, skinks, pythons, Gould's monitors, emus plus many birds especially birds of prey and birds of the parrot family.

To be fully immersed by the experience, leave your car at the carpark, walk into the desert and complete a 5 km circuit by foot. Make sure you carry water as none is available in the park. Avoid hot days and preferably walk in early morning or late afternoon for best comfort and photographic conditions. The 5 km walk includes a side trip known as North Spur. As this suggested walk is along a sandy route, one must take into account the presence of vehicular traffic, which is usually light, travels a one way route in a clockwise direction and does not mar the experience. A feature of the walk is a viewing deck that is 1.3 km from the walk start. You get views over the Pinnacles and toward the coast. Some 100 m later there is a side track. Follow North Spur 700 m to the road end where you will find a collection of notable pinnacles called the Milk Bottles, nestled at the foot of an imposing dune system. Here one has a chance to truly appreciate this unique desert environment. The hardened calcrete capping on the milk bottle formations is most noteworthy. After you complete the side trip, continue along the sandy road for 700 m to be right alongside the highest recorded pinnacle at 3.5 m. Thereafter, the remaining 1.15 km of sandy road needs to be walked back to the carpark.

The Pinnacles

MURCHISON GORGE

Kalbarri, Western Australia

Walk:	8 km circuit
Time required:	Including minimal breaks, 3.5 hours
Grade:	One day, medium, some rock scrambling involved
Environment:	Cliff rim and river gorge walk
Last review date:	August 2007
Map reference:	1:100 000 Kalbarri and Map 20
Best time to visit:	April to November; avoid hot summer days from December to March; carry water and sunscreen

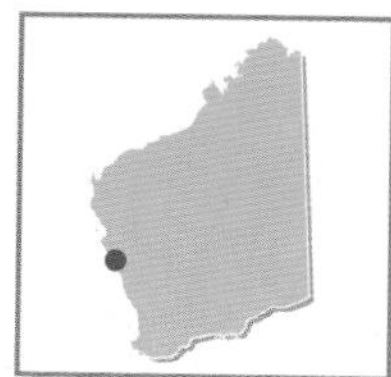

Upstream of the coastal tourist town of Kalbarri, the Murchison River flows through stunningly beautiful scenery of red-brown rock, glistening white-sand beaches and large rock pools. At Murchison Gorge, the river takes an almost complete 7 km loop in one of the most scenic parts of the district. The town itself has a large range of accommodation options from which you can base yourself for this walk. A tourist information office is available in town.

130 40 40 130

Approximately 400 millions years ago, a process of sedimentation began to take

Nature's Window, Murchison Gorge

WA

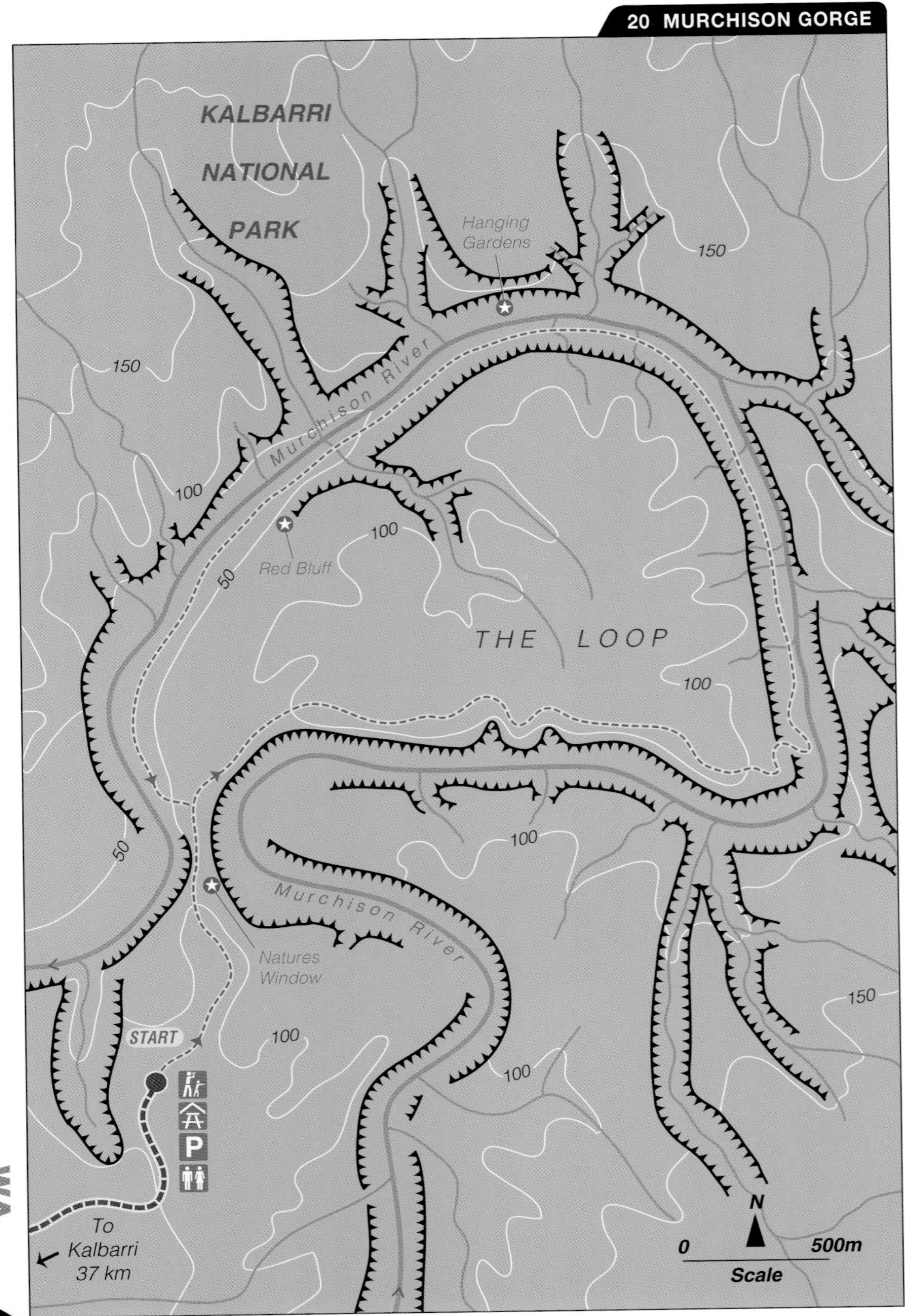

KALBARRI
NATIONAL
PARK
Hanging
Gardens
150
150
Murchison River
100
Red Bluff
100
50
THE LOOP
100
100
50
Murchison River
Natures
Window
START
100
100
150
To
Kalbarri
37 km
N
0
500m
Scale

Kalbarri	J	F	M	A	M	J	J	A	S	O	N	D	Year
Rain av. mm	6	6	21	24	53	90	73	51	26	23	6	1	379
Temp av. max. °C	33	34	33	28	25	22	21	22	23	25	27	31	27
Temp av. min. °C	19	20	19	15	13	11	10	10	10	12	14	17	14

place. This left a relatively flat plateau, which around one million years ago was eroded by the early Murchison River to form the gorge we see before us today. From its beginnings the river flows 700 km west to its mouth at Kalbarri.

This part of Australia could be described as geologically stable from its earliest beginnings to the present day; this is evident by the almost perfectly horizontal layering of the Tumblagooda sandstone. The alternating layers of red and white sediments, whose origin is both wind and water borne over tidal flats, have formed the relatively soft plateau through which the Murchison River has cut its gorge. Many of the iron oxide coloured sands with their characteristically red hue are in stark contrast to the white sands, which can comprise around fifty differing layers within the depth of one metre. It is interesting to note that many of the exposed plates present, exhibit fine wave action on their horizontal surfaces, some of which contain fossilised tracks of ancient marine creatures.

Tumblagooda sandstone at Murchison Gorge

The flora of this region is predominately arid heathland and Kalbarri National Park is centred in one of Western Australia's best wildflower regions. The main species you will encounter on this walk include banksias, acacias and grevilleas. Also present is the characteristic north Australian spinifex grass and grass trees. The river forms a corridor of life in this arid wilderness that supports vast numbers of nectar feeding birds and insects. Nocturnal mammals, notably bats, play their vital role in the pollination of the plants. Rock dwelling kangaroos and wallabies are also prevalent. You will most likely encounter water fowl such as cormorants, black swans and white herons feeding on aquatic life in the deeper pools.

Eleven kilometres from Kalbarri, on the main Ajana–Kalbarri road, turn left on to an unsealed road. Two wheel drive vehicles should only attempt this road in dry weather, which may be closed after heavy rain. Beyond the park entrance (note that an entry fee applies), travel 19 km to a 'T' intersection where you turn left for 'The Loop'. Proceed a further 7 km to a carpark, toilets, picnic shelters and gorge viewing platform.

From here starts one of Australia's most beautiful arid landscape walks via Nature's Window and the Loop, where the river turns back on itself over a distance of some 7 km. It seems many visitors walk the short distance to Nature's Window but few venture further into the equally stunning surrounds. You will see amazing wildlife, have the opportunity to swim the rock

Murchison River

pools and laze on the beaches. You need sturdy footwear because of the presence of so much rock and the track to follow is best walked anticlockwise. The way is well defined with many white track markers (some of which have the loop walk logo) along the way. On rare occasions the river level could make progress slower.

Take the traditional 500 m tourist walk route north from the carpark down to Nature's Window. This feature is on the crest of the narrowest point of the river loop. Barely 300 m separates the river flow; to either side the cliffs drop away some 100 m to the river below. The views improve significantly as you near the well-photographed formation, which is a wind-scoured hole in the spur crest.

Once across the narrow crest northwards, on much bare rock, turn to get great views back towards Nature's Window. Here you will find wind-scoured rock caverns with fine examples of sandstone layering. It is important to stay on the marked route and not venture too near potentially unstable cliffs. Note that the return track also joins at this point.

You next climb a little, following the well-marked track route to the highest point along the rim of the gorge; here the river is 100 m below. Follow the rim track east, past many grass trees until you are about 3.2 km from the walk start. Opposite, impressive ravines join the main gorge. Next, the track leaves the rim and descends steeply to the river at a spot where the flow turns abruptly north. There is a fine beach and pool where you meet the river. This could be a great place for a break. Fine, white-trunked river red gums contrast with the red cliffs and myriad birds surround you.

From here, follow the track markers north on the west bank, mostly on stratified rock ledges, for about 1.5 km. When the river rises you need to climb on to higher ledges in a few spots. Note: at times of flood, debris is carried along the river and may block access to the route. Negotiating such obstacles may require you to deviate slightly from the suggested walk route. After this distance you see a rugged, narrow gorge entering the main gorge from the east. Vertical cliff-faces on the north-east side have remarkable 'hanging gardens'.

Gradually the river swings in an arc to flow west then south-west for another 2.5 km. Along this stretch, beaches and former river bed rock need to be crossed rather than rock ledges. Again, you need to be aware that after floods the track markers on the beaches may be indistinct. There seems to be a profusion of wildflowers here due to large quantities of available underground water and stronger afternoon sunlight, unobscured by cliffs. You pass a prominent rock outcrop (unofficially named Red Bluff) and a deep side canyon. Thereafter, the cliffs on your left give way to a gentle slope. Larger stands of river red gums grow in this area. Eventually you reach broad, sandy river terraces immediately west of Nature's Window and the near completion of the loop.

Track markers show the way up to the terraces via a short rocky slope back to Nature's Window. It is then a 500 m retrace south up to the carpark.

Eucalyptus tree at Murchison River

Overview of Australia

Australia, often referred to as 'The island continent' or 'Great Southern Land', is 4000 km from east to west and 3200 km from north to south. Extending across 30 degrees of latitude, one third of the land mass is within the tropics, however, most of the country is of a desert or arid nature. Australia has the distinction of having the longest, uninterrupted coastline in the world. The majority of Australia's more temperate, habitable regions occupy a relatively narrow band on the eastern and south-eastern slopes of the Great Dividing Range, with an even narrower band in the west and on the extreme west and south-west of the country.

Mount Connor, Northern Territory

Climate of Australia

Temperatures and humidity can vary widely, from many degrees below zero to the high 40s. The presence of winter snow can come as a surprise to overseas visitors. Cyclonic weather every summer across the whole of the northern part of the country releases huge quantities of water on to the landscape. There are definite wet and dry seasons. South of the Tropic of Capricorn, a more temperate, four-seasonal climate exists. The prevailing weather comes from the west. The whole of the east coast is influenced by dominant south-east trade winds. The majority of rain delivered by this weather system falls on the eastern slopes of the Great Dividing Range, leaving inland areas much drier.

Monsoons in the north can affect southern areas, but the south, however, can suffer prolonged periods of drought, especially during times of 'el Niño'. This occurs when large masses of cold water combined with cold air currents impinge on the eastern shoreline, reducing rainfall drastically. The flora and fauna of Australia has had to adapt to changing temperatures and rainfall patterns, as the continent drifted for millennia north-east from the south polar region to its present position.

The large land mass of Australia accentuates wind flows around high and low pressure cells. Much of Australia is desert or semi-desert. This is because the sun warms air at the equator, rises into the troposphere, loses its rainfall and cools. The air then sinks back to Earth as dry air at about 30 degrees south latitude and north latitude creating desert bands around the Earth. At the southern hemisphere solstice, the dry air band lies right across middle Australia. It is for this reason that deserts exist as far south as the Mallee in Victoria.

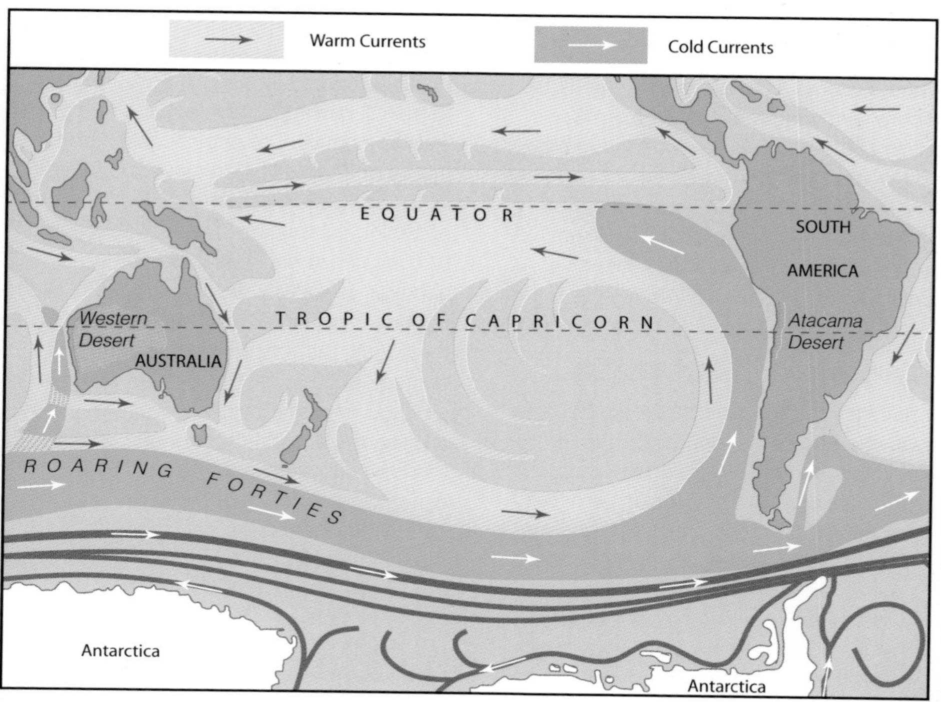

Granite hills with tree

Southern Australia is greatly influenced in winter by the appearance of westerly winds known as the roaring forties. Tasmania bears the brunt of these wind patterns as they encircle the globe. There is no land mass apart from Cape Horn at the tip of South America to slow the winds that hit the west coast causing unpredictable climatic conditions. For this reason it is essential that walkers in the Tasmanian wilderness take this unpredictable influence into account.

Geology of Australia

Australia's geological history shows it was once part of the 'super-continent' known as Pangaea (all-land) surrounded by Thalassa (all-sea). This was deduced from the shape of the coastlines of neighbouring land masses such as Africa, South America, Antarctica and India. Laurasia later separated from Pangaea leaving a southern land mass known as Gondwana. The majority of volcanism was due to the separation of the continental plates. The fact that many fossils and plant species of the same type can be found on these land masses, supports the theory of continental drift: indeed Australia is said to be still moving north-east at a rate of 75mm annually. The original basis for the theory of continental drift was proposed in 1915 by Alfred Wegener. Due to his lack of geological training, it was not accepted by the main stream geological fraternity and was effectively dropped by 1920. With the advent of satellite technology after the 1960s, more accurate positions of the continents could be determined and over a period of time movement was detected proving the original theory was correct. It is now known at plate tectonics. This describes the action of the continents (or plates) floating like rafts on the Earth's molten mantle.

The movement of the continents caused much volcanic activity. This resulted in the formation of metamorphic rock, which is principally either granite

Volcano Formation

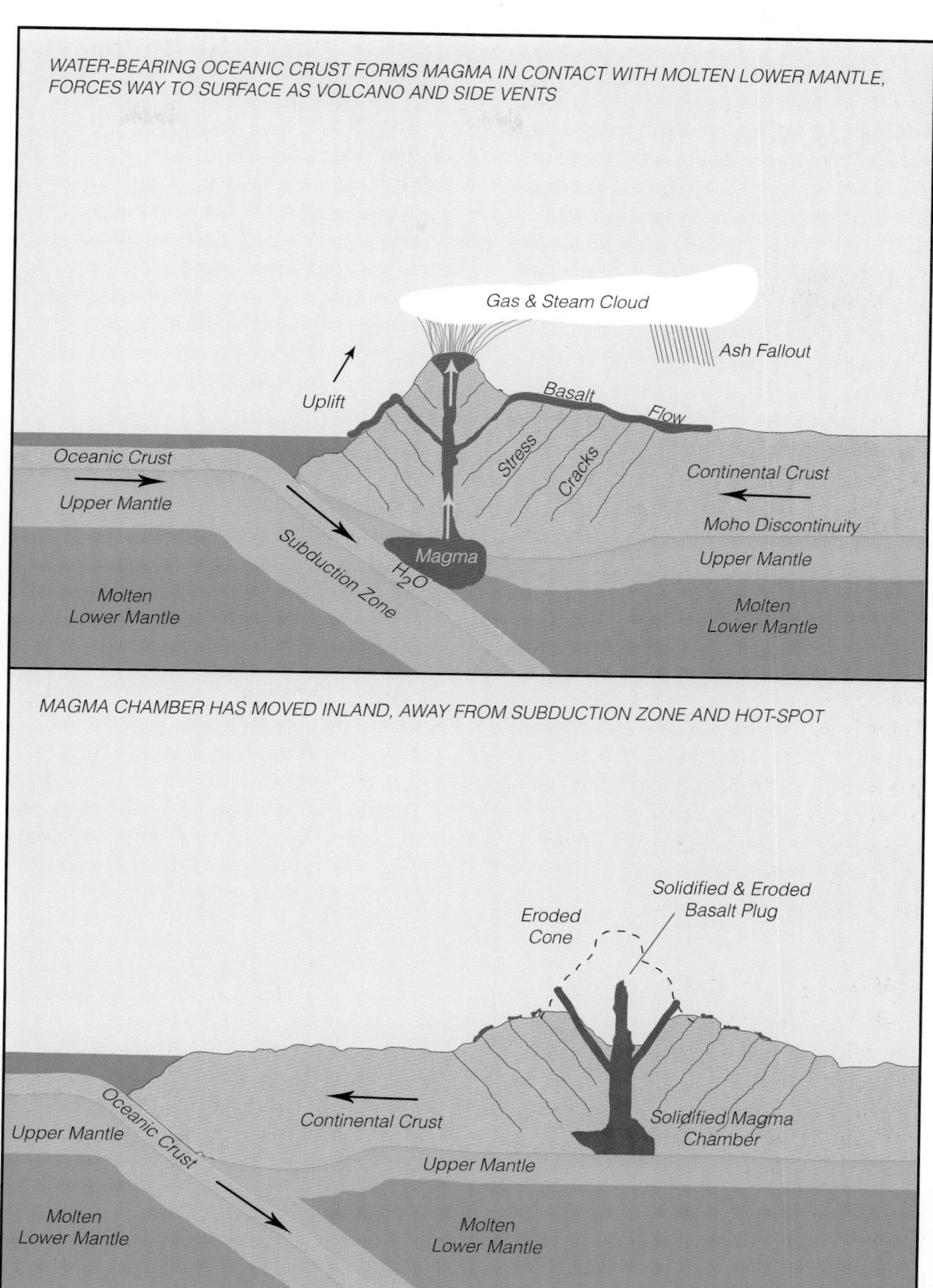

or basalt. Volcanic activity in Australia occurred as recently as 4800 years ago. The activity is concentrated mostly on the eastern side of the country, however, ancient tectonic evidence can be found in practically every region. This geologically 'recent' activity is responsible for most of the Great Dividing Range on the mainland and the peaks of Tasmania (which was part of the original range before sea levels rose). This major mountain building event took place when the Pacific Plate collided with and descended below the Australian-Indian plate. The subduction zone resulted in violent volcanic activity where melting of the Earth's crust occurred deep below the surface. The subduction of the sea floor pushed water-bearing rock deep underground where it encountered the semi molten mantle. This created magma, a mixture of molten rock and water. The steam pressure when brought near the surface through fissures in the Earth's crust allowed the violent release of this pressure.

The formation of granite begins with the upwelling of molten rock that intrudes into the deep overlying crust. It does not break the surface. Over millions of years gradual cooling takes place forming a strong crystalline rock. Subsequent erosion of the softer overlying surface by wind and rain exposes the harder granite, quite often leaving granite boulders resting one on top of another. Large exposures often exhibit rounded forms as a consequence of the original upwelling. Granite occurs at many places along the Great Dividing Range. Excellent examples can be viewed at Wilsons Promontory in Victoria and Freycinet Peninsula in Tasmania.

Crater Bluff, the Breadknife

Pangaea – 50 million years ago

Basalt results from molten rock that is either ejected into the atmosphere or oozed though cracks in the Earth's crust. Thus we have volcanoes such as those in Hawaii that emit basalt (lava) relatively gently. In contrast many other volcanoes exist especially on countries that bound the Pacific Ocean commonly known as the Ring Of Fire. These volcanoes erupt basalt in a violent fashion with little warning, causing great damage and loss of life. Often a super heated cloud of gas and pulverised basalt is released and flows down the volcanic cone at many thousands of degrees Celsius and at great speed.

Notable examples of basaltic volcanic activity featured as walks in this book are the Breadknife, Lord Howe Island and Mount Warning in New South Wales and the Blue Lake at Mount Gambier in South Australia.

The majority of Australia's arable farming land is located in the vicinity of extinct volcanoes where the soils are deep and fertile. On these mineral rich soils derived from basalt, both agriculture and horticulture profit.

With a wealth of mineral deposits, due mainly to the presence of extremely old rock, Australia has some of the world's richest mineral resource areas and could be described as self-sufficient in many minerals. However, one essential ingredient will always be in short supply—water.

Some 500 million years ago, Central Australia was an inland sea. Multiple layers of sand, compressed under a then primeval sea, formed the world's largest sandstone conglomerate: Uluru. Gradual upheaval of the Earth's crust has tilted the rock some 90°. These layers of arkose, a sedimentary sandstone, rich in feldspar, with iron ore give the rock its characteristic red hue. It has defied constant weathering, while all around it a once lush fertile land turned to desert.

Australian soils contain high levels of salt (sodium chloride) left behind from retreating oceans. Evidence of sea life can be found on top of Uluru 360m above the Gibson Desert. Shield shrimps (*Crustacea*) hatch amid puddles each time it rains. Rainfall triggers dormant eggs to hatch in an explosion of life. For the cycle to continue, these tiny short-lived creatures must reproduce before the water dries up, a process their predecessors have performed over the last 150 million years.

Flora of Australia

Australia is predominantly dry or semi-arid with deserts covering over 70 per cent of the land surface. Dry sclerophyll forest, or open forest of eucalyptus and acacia, is the most instantly recognisable 'Australian' forms of vegetation. The interior desert of Australia spans such a huge area that it isolates non-desert flora into the four corners of the continent.

Macroclimates can be divided into specific smaller scale communities or microclimates and likewise the habitats contained within. Each habitat specifically supports the needs of the plants and animals which interact with each other. The forest canopy creates microclimates suited to light sensitive ferns and mosses in habitats below. In some forests, light is reduced almost completely, so only ferns, mosses and a select few other species exist. In rainforest areas, palms tend to occur where light is greater. An example is Mount Warning's flanks. Nearby, a walk through the more shaded Green Mountains reveals large populations of ferns, some of which grow on the side of trees, while others favour streamside positions.
In more open country, a sparse tree canopy often results in good wildflower habitats where sunlight is strong. One common factor is the availability of water throughout the year.

Leaf litter can get burnt by fire or oxidised by the strong sunlight. Deciduous trees discard their leaves in a short space of time, creating a layer of humus that traps moisture and adds carbon to the soil. Eucalyptus drop leaves continuously throughout the year. These are full of oils and waxes and encourage fire to spread and burn very hot. They do not decompose easily, slowing the process of soil conditioning. Some plants have the ability to produce very effective insecticides which protect them. Most native Australian plants are not deciduous.

Continental drift theory attempts to explain how representations from the same plant families are found on different continents now widely separated by oceans. The last links with Gondwana were severed when Australia moved northward from Antarctica and became an island continent. It drifted in isolation north-east towards the equator containing a cargo of ancient flora such as the myrtle beech, Wollemi pine, cycads, ferns and coniferous plants that at one time dominated the Australian landmass.

Tectonic and volcanic activity created a markedly different growing environment from that of the original landscape. Differing microclimates then appeared with a diverse range of temperature and rainfall zones suitable for colonisation by a wider variety of plants. The changing climate forced existing plants to adapt, or face extinction. Species that were able to adapt lead to the creation of new forms.

Much of Australia's flora and fauna has evolved from Gondwana stock. Gondwana was principally rainforest dominated by extensive subtropical rainforests of nothofagus (antarctic beech), and podocarpus (celery top pine). These rainforests contained ancestral representations of both *Myrtaceae* and *Mimosaceae* families. The *Myrtaceae* family produced genus such as eucalyptus and kunzea (heath), capable of adapting to the increasing dry climate and nutrient deficient soils.

It also produced further genus such as syzigium (lilly pilly) and melaleuca (paperbark) to colonise damp and swampy areas. The *Mimosaceae* family produced genus such as acacia (wattles) which did not rise to prominence until much later as they are not rainforest plants. Pockets of tropical rainforest are now restricted to north-east Australia, mostly Queensland, New Guinea and New Caledonia.

One section of the genus *Acacia*, the *phyllodinae*, very successfully adapted to the changing climate of Australia. These include all species containing leaves which are reduced to phyllodes, or to spines, the ultimate sclerophyll adaptation. Smaller leaves reduce evaporation and conserve what little moisture there is in dry climates.

These highly evolved sclerophylls effectively deal with nutrient-deprived soils by creating their own nitrogen through nodules on their roots, which contain a strain of bacteria. This enables the plant to fix nitrogen from the atmosphere to form a nitrate compound essential for growth. This example of a symbiotic relationship has enabled acacias to colonise many arid inland areas where eucalyptus are less prevalent. Sclerophyll adaptation secured a niche for both *Myrtaceae* and *Mimosaceae* families in the modern Australian flora. Acacias especially have now become very widespread.

Those areas of Australia that were inundated by rising sea levels, and received deposits of calcium carbonate in the form of decaying marine organisms, have a higher pH (alkaline) composition. Regions that were the subject of volcanic activity or were overlain by ash fallout, lava flows or both, have a predominately lower pH (acid) composition. As the majority of Australia has soils of volcanic origin, so it is not surprising to find that the majority of indigenous plant forms prefer a low nutrient, acid and generally free-draining medium in which to grow.

Epicormic shoots and lignotubers have enabled eucalyptus and many other plants to regenerate quickly after fire. Banksias and grevilleas among others require heat for scarification of the seed allowing germination and taking advantage of the freshly cleared land for their growing seedlings. These adaptations are not found in nothofagus, or the Wollemi pines, so their occurrence is restricted to small, damp, unburned pockets of forest.

Wallaces Line

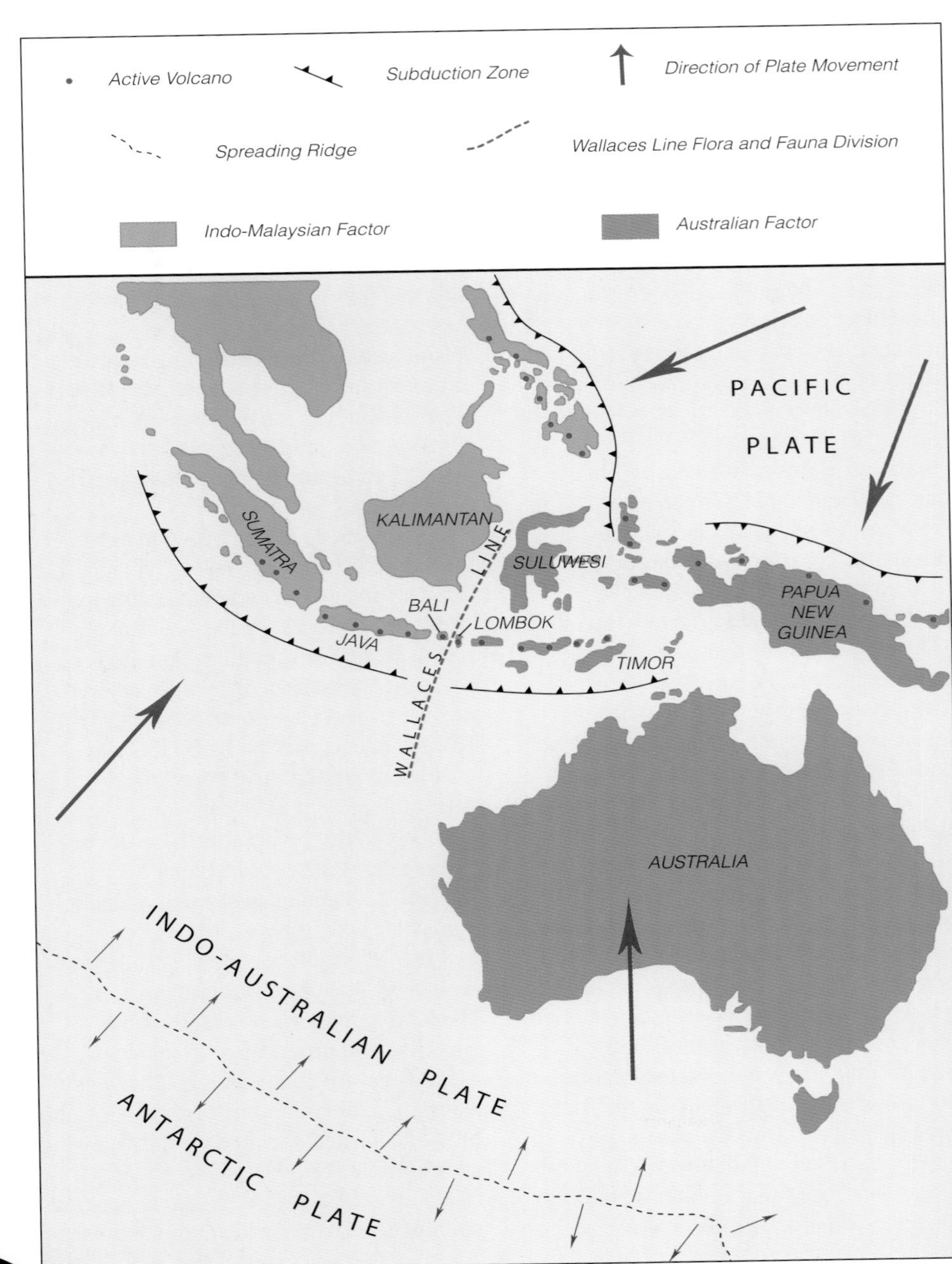

Australian Biomes

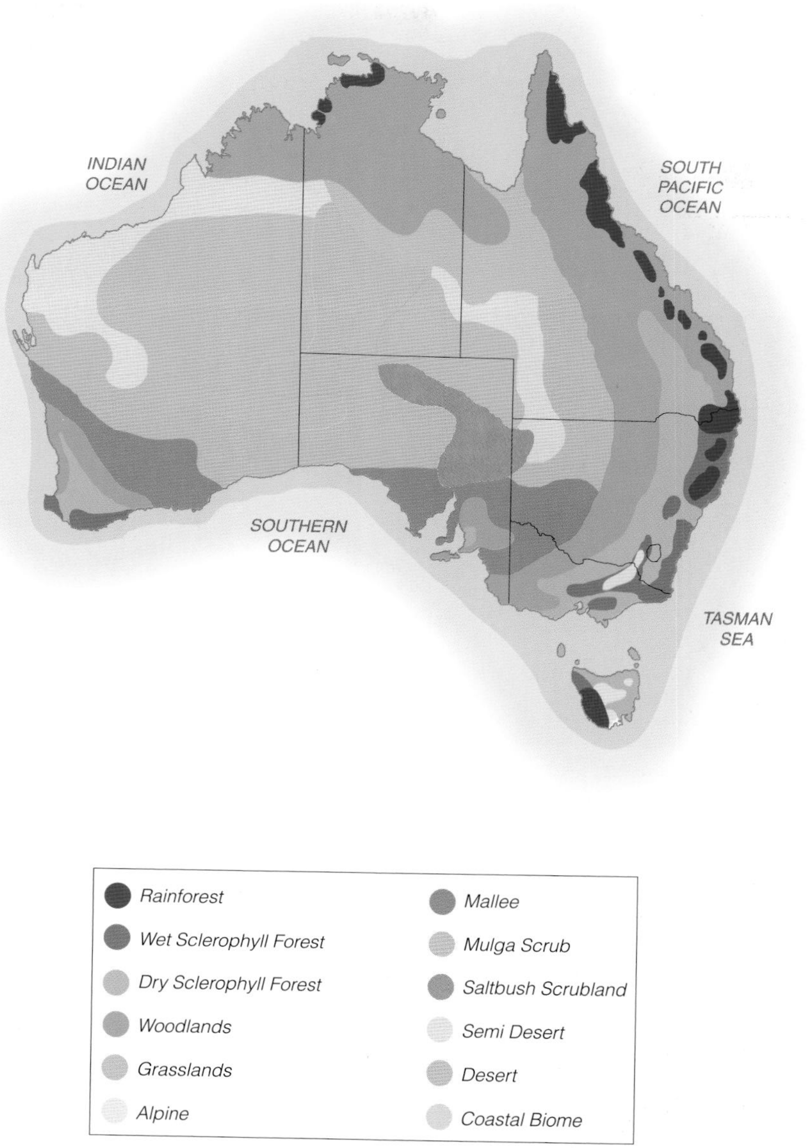

INDIAN OCEAN

SOUTH PACIFIC OCEAN

SOUTHERN OCEAN

TASMAN SEA

Indo-Malaysian Factor plants
Clockwise from top left:
Brachychiton rupistris
Buttressed trees
Bangalow/piccabeen palms (Archontophoenix cunninghamiana)
Epiphytes on Mt Cordeaux
Hoop Pine (Araucaria cunninghamii)

Opposite page
Antarctic Factor plants
Clockwise from top left:
Cycad
Nothofagus gunnii
Wollemi pine
Phyllocladus aspleniifolius

The Australian Biomes

Australia has many different environments or biomes, which vary in temperature, moisture, light, and many other factors. Contained within each biome is a distinctive mix of flora and fauna. Complex interactions take place between a community of plants and animals well adapted to the physical environment, and the governing climatic conditions. Biomes are typically named after the dominant plants and are largely determined by environmental factors impacting on them. As a general rule, we find biomes of like character at similar latitudes around the world. At the equator, there are tropical rainforests. Near the Tropic of Cancer and Tropic of Capricorn, on the western side of continents, there are deserts. Tropical savannah grasslands exist between these two regions. Further away from the tropics, Mediterranean type climates occur on the west side of each continent, while temperate forests exist at the same latitude on the east side of each continent. Further again away from the equator are cool temperate forests which in turn give way to the polar regions. During the history of life on Earth, biomes have been altered and moved many times.

The biomes of Australia have been influenced right back through to the times of Gondwana. In the main, vegetation of Australia today results from three main factors.

The Indo-Malaysian Factor: Rainforests found in New Guinea, Queensland and New South Wales generally show similarities with those found in south-east Asia including trees with buttressed trunks, lianas, (vines), epiphytes (plants which grow on other plants without need for soil) and conifers such as araucaria. Other northern Australian plants also in many cases show similarities to those of Asia.

The demarcation between southern Asia and Australian plants and animals is today known as Wallaces Line (see page 112). In 1876, Alfred Russell Wallace divided the world into zoological and geographical regions. Even though the land to either side of the line is only 24 km apart, a clear distinction can be observed between Lombok and Bali. These islands are volcanic and thought to have repeatedly erupted and slowed the intermingling of species.

Human habitation was affected by these enormous changes to the world's geography, as land bridges formed and retreated during variations in sea levels.

The Antarctic Factor: Ferns, the myrtle beech *(Nothofagus cunninghamii)* and celery top pine *(Podocarpus phyllocladus)* were endemic to Antarctica when that continent was much warmer. The Tasmanian part of the then unified Australian landmass remained joined to Antarctica longer than Africa or South America, so it has the largest representations of Gondwana flora. It is interesting to note that the myrtle beech is Australia's only deciduous tree prior to European settlement and is similar to the European beech. It was also the most prevalent species across much of Australia before the climate became drier. The King Billy pine *(Athrotaxis selaginoides)* is a Tasmanian native conifer and also

The Australian Factor plants
This page from left:
Eucalyptus globulus
Eucalyptus tree
Xanthorrhea australis
Opposite page (clockwise from top left):
Acacia longifolia
Eucalyptus
Kunzea baxteri
Banksia attentuata
Grevillea
Acacia
Acacia pycnantha
Eucalyptus (Mt William)

interestingly it has pollen similar to the North American redwood. Due to its alpine habitat, it does not attain the great height of its American relative.

The Australian Factor: This is represented by widespread eucalyptus woodlands, diverse types of eucalyptus forest and acacia scrublands, which extend to New Guinea and New Caledonia. Banksia, grevillea, hakea and numerous, often prickly and woody species fall into this category.

Australia has been the ongoing recipient of foreign animal and plant species since its separation from Gondwana and before European settlement. This occurred via land bridges with southern Asia and Antarctica, the transportation of seeds in the gut or feathers of migratory birds, seed borne on wind currents and those that arrive by sea and possibly some brought by early Pacific sea-faring peoples.

Availability of water transforms this bleak landscape into something quite different, indeed from the air, green ribbons follow any watercourse, and pools can sustain a huge range of wildlife, a fact not lost on Australia's Indigenous peoples of long ago, who would hunt and alter the landscape around these areas.

Human impact on the natural world

For thousands of years, the nomadic Aboriginal population of Australia influenced the plant and animal life through a process called 'firestick farming'. This involved selectively burning tracts of land to achieve a number of outcomes. Firstly, it cleared thick, impenetrable vegetation to make travel easier; secondly, animals were flushed out of the bush where they could be effectively hunted with spears and other implements for food. Thirdly, it promoted the growth of new, succulent shoots, which attracted animals to these areas to provide extra plant and animal food for the people.

This process, over a considerable period of time, has influenced the type of vegetation that we see today, to the detriment of some plant life that had not adapted to fire, and to the benefit to those that could adapt. Indeed it would be fair to say that many plants and animals have become extinct due to this practice.

The arrival of non-Aborigines in 1788 brought dramatic changes to the landscape and the Aboriginal way of life. The food types familiar to settlers were not naturally available, so there was mass clearing of the land and pasture grasses were introduced, so that food animals such as cattle and sheep could be farmed. These hooved animals, combined with land clearing and ploughing, caused erosion of the thin topsoil.

Whereas the Aboriginals had no concept of land ownership outside of their tribal regions and spiritual beliefs, Europeans drove them off land away from the most productive areas, erected fences and introduced the domestic animals. The most destructive animals included cats, foxes and rabbits. Both cats and foxes caused devastation to those native animals that had no defence against them, now drastic measures are having to be taken to retrieve these populations from extinction, a fact often lost on many pet owners. Rabbits caused severe erosion of the land and provided food for foxes, causing their numbers to increase, putting more pressure on native animal populations. In excess of 60 animal species have become extinct since European settlement.

In some remote areas of Australia, derelict remains of early settlers' homes can be found, giving some impression of the harsh life they must have endured. Many attempts at farming the inland were fruitless. Gradually, the passage of time and the elements are returning these dwellings back to the rubble from which they were constructed.

The introduction of species now considered weeds, such as gorse, holly, boxthorn and blackberry amongst others, have benefited some animals, notably birds. The availability of a rich food source such as blackberry, has enabled many birds to extend their populations into areas not normally available to them, with gorse providing safe nesting sites. At the same time, the plant seeds get dispersed as the bird or animal moves about. Natural selection and evolution of species were greatly accelerated with the introduction of exotic plants. Suddenly, a continent became awash with foreign species including pasture grasses after being effectively isolated for millions of years.

It is interesting to note that because many native animals have adapted to the new plants and habitat, those same animals are now under threat due to the actions of well-meaning environmentalists, who hold the belief that these weed species must be eradicated at any cost. We must question the logic behind removing entire habitats before re-introducing the native vegetation. This would give native animals a chance to re-adapt and to loose their dependence on exotic plants, but even so, is it the correct thing to do?

The introduction of exotic plants may well have saved many animals from extinction, had they not been able to adapt to their new environment with European man. We would do well to remember the processes of natural selection and evolution, which show, sometimes quite remarkably, how well animals adapt to new situations. It is ongoing and will continue to enable most species to co-exist and it must be remembered that species have died out for millions of years, long before man could have any direct effect.

The eradication of riparian trees, such as willows, has allowed erosion to continue along watercourses. The loss of their canopy allows sunlight to heat the water, increasing evaporation and encouraging the growth of algal blooms. Also, many deciduous European trees enhance the soil by adding significant amounts of humus during autumn, as well as providing barriers to bushfire radiant heat, which is often the cause of property loss.

It can be argued that not all introductions of exotic plants are detrimental to the environment, for example, apiarists in South Australia argue that to eradicate Patterson's Curse (salvation Jane in SA) would have a disastrous effect on the bee population. Without bees for pollination, most plants would die out, resulting in starvation of foraging animals and humans. However, an example of an introduced species that has had a negative effect is the cane toad. First released in 1935 from Hawaii to control sugar cane beetle, it has extended its population from Queensland and has been detected in Sydney and the Northern Territory. Highly poisonous to native wildlife, the toad is directly responsible for the demise of the monitor lizard, whose population is becoming critical. This lizard is a traditional food source of the Aboriginal population of the Top End, so the cane toad is having an impact indirectly on humans. Significant and costly control measures are currently being implemented to prevent mass extinction of native wildlife caused by this one species of toad.

Tasmanian Devil
Sarcophilus harrisii

Echidna
Tachyglossus aculeatus

Leadbeater's Possum
Gymnobelideus leadbeateri

Hairy Nosed Wombat
Lasiorhinus latifrons

Fauna of Australia

Prior to the inundation of the land bridges by rising ocean levels, plants and especially animals were able to migrate between the land masses that comprised Gondwana. Following the breaking of the land bridges, animals were effectively isolated on their respective continents. Between Asia and Australia, Wallaces Line marks a boundary of different animal species, just as it does with plant species. The end result is similar animals evolving along different lines. For example, the Australian platypus and the echidna are known as monotremes. These two unusual animals have a reptilian ancestry, in that they both lay eggs, and yet are warm-blooded, aligning them more closely with other mammals.

The platypus has a electrically sensitive, duck-like bill for seeking out aquatic prey in its stream-side habitat. It has webbed feet and nests in burrows and is essentially an aquatic animal.

The echidna closely resembles a porcupine, with many thick, fierce spines along its upper body. A diet of ants has resulted in the development of a long snout and strong front legs with claws, to facilitate digging out the ants nests and termites. A land animal, it has fairly poor eyesight, relying on its sense of smell to find food. Found in mountain and forest country, echidnas can travel quite considerable distances and are surprisingly good climbers. They lay a single egg which develops in a pouch.

Marsupials nurture their young in a pouch on the lower abdomen, examples are kangaroos, possums, wombats, koalas, numbats and bandicoots. They are widespread throughout the country and vary in size from mice-like to the giant red kangaroo. An unusual feature of marsupials is they give birth to highly under-developed young, which then climb through the fur to reach the pouch, which contains the teats for suckling. Kangaroos have the unusual feature of being able to suckle a 'Joey' out of the pouch, a developing embryo suckling in the pouch and a fertilised embryo waiting in the uterus. Throughout the country, the border between pastoral lands and desert landscapes are the best locations to view kangaroos, emus and members of the parrot family.

The Tasmanian devil caused much unrest amongst early settlers with its terrifying nocturnal calls. The largest carnivore still in existence, it raises up to

Numbat
Myrmecobius fasciatus

Red Kangaroo
Macropus rufus

Koala
Phascolarctos cinereus

Platypus
Ornithorhynchus anatinus

four young in its pouch. Unfortunately, a virulent and highly contagious disease is endangering the population of devils. A type of ulcerous infection causes loss of tissue around the mouth, resulting in the animal's starvation. Efforts are underway to secure a disease-free population in isolation from the rest of the state, in case extinction of the wider population occurs.

Two species of crocodile inhabit northern waters. The fresh water crocodile is harmless to humans, however, the salt-water crocodile is dangerous; both are protected.

Approximately 130 species of frog exist in Australia, Two of the more unusual types are the 'gastric-brooding frog', which is unique in that it temporarily transforms its stomach into a uterus to hatch the young, and the 'water-holding frog'. A desert dweller, it conserves moisture during times of drought by forming an underground cocoon and immersing itself until the drought is over.

Among the lizards, perhaps the best known is the frill-necked lizard. When under attack it extends the coloured frill around its neck and makes a hissing sound. Escape is effected by running at high speed on its back legs.

Approximately 100 of the 140 species of snake are venomous. The largest non-venomous snake is the scrub python or amethystine, which can reach 7 m in length. The most venomous land snake is the tiger snake, which reaches up to 2 m in length, followed by the Queensland Taipan. At almost 3.5 m long, it is among the world's most deadly land snakes.

Gippsland in Victoria is home to the world's largest earthworm, growing to over 3.5 m and almost 2 cm in diameter. Related to the earthworm are leeches. They are not considered dangerous, however, the anti-coagulant they inject upon attachment can cause extended bleeding when removed. They are found mostly in damp woodland, especially near water courses.

The funnel-web spider is the most poisonous arachnid in Australia. The male is unusual in being several times more toxic than the female. It is restricted to coastal areas of New South Wales. The famous red-back spider is the opposite, with the female capable of inflicting a painful and highly venomous bite.

Over 700 bird species exist in Australia, at least two of which have an interesting call or song. The bellbirds, as their name suggests, emit a loud call closely resembling a shrill bell. They are most likely to be found in damp bushland. Lyrebirds have the ability of mimicking other birds calls and even extend their range to cover chainsaws and mobile phones! The largest Australian bird is the flightless emu at 1.5 m tall. The male incubates the eggs, which can be almost a kilogram in weight. Related to the European kingfisher, kookaburras are renowned for their laugh. There are two types: the laughing jackass of eastern Australia and the blue-winged variety found in the north to north-west. Galahs and sulphur-crested cockatoos are among more than 50 species of parrot, the smallest of which, the budgerigar, is found in large flocks in more arid regions. The 2.5 m wingspan of the wedge-tail eagle makes it Australia's largest bird of prey. Mostly dark brown in colour, it occurs throughout the country but is more prevalent in arid regions.

By no means is this an exhaustive list. Further information should be sought regarding those areas of interest to the reader which can often be found at local information centres or ranger stations. It is hoped that you will encounter many of these animals and birds as you enjoy your walk.

Safety and commonsense in the bush

Bushwalking is a very enjoyable recreational activity, and common-sense safety precautions will keep it that way. Be prepared for any problem that may arise. In the event of an emergency, free call 000 and ask for connection to fire, police, ambulance or search and rescue.

Planning

Plan your trip and leave details of your route in writing with some responsible person and report back to them on return. Leave details of route, timing, vehicle registration, names, and next of kin and so on. Bushwalkers need to bear in mind that they practise a sport that entails certain elements of risk. You as a bushwalker should be considerate, and remember that the community is not impressed with having to meet expensive search costs because of incompetence. Some park rangers provide walkers' intentions books but you should not rely upon park systems. Pick the right season and hopefully the right weather for the region into which you are headed. Be sensible as to safety and comfort and avoid very cold or hot days. Forget any planned walk on a day of proclaimed total fire ban. On such fire risk days many national parks can be closed.

Always carry maps, compass, mirror, first-aid kit, plenty of paper, warm, bright-coloured, waterproof clothing, whistle, matches in a waterproof container, candle, small sharp knife, torch and emergency rations of food. It is of the utmost importance that you are able to read maps and use a compass.

Accommodation and transport

The large size of the country results in great variations in accommodation availability and means of access to national parks and walking areas. Many parks have campgrounds and some have cabins or huts. A few mountain huts are free of charge. As a general rule, motels are generally a quieter option to hotels, the latter having alcohol licences and public bars. Bed and breakfast should be considered and can be surprisingly affordable. Those on a budget may consider renting an on-site caravan/ trailer at private campgrounds. Also, many backpacker and youth hostels exist around the country. Free camping in remote areas is widely acceptable. Tourist information offices can be helpful in locating suitable accommodation.

There are usually no transport problems between cities and large towns using air, rail, or coach. Rental cars, however, give the most flexibility, especially as travel beyond the large towns is often difficult without a vehicle. Some private operators provide transport to major parks, by coach or four-wheel-drive vehicle. Taxi cabs are in most towns, but can prove expensive if the walk area is distant.

Distance and timing

Never try to rush a trip. Think before you act, watch your route on a map and recognise your limitations, especially with distance. A good walker can cover three to five kilometres each hour but in dense bush perhaps as little as five kilometres in a day. Always keep together when walking in a group and never walk in a party of less than three in remote areas. (If one walker is injured, one can remain to assist while the other seeks help.)

Footwear

Sandshoes (sneakers or runners) are ideal for beach walks or walks in drier regions and on rock surfaces, but certainly not for snow conditions. Boots are needed for alpine country or very wet conditions. Some ankle support is always preferable. Never wear new boots for the first time on any long walk.

Maps

When following suggested walk routes, ensure that you obtain and use the recommended maps so that the maximum amount of information is available to you. Where more than one map of an area is available, you are advised to use both. Maps frequently become obsolete and many government maps have not been updated for years. The detailed maps included in this book should be used in conjunction with other maps wherever possible. Always carry a waterproof map case.

Information

Be aware that spellings of place names on maps, signposts and in books frequently do not match and while many names are official, others are not. Government maps are often outdated as to track and other man-made features. Some names in this book are widely recognised in the bushwalking community but may not appear on official maps. No doubt, in the interest of safety, national park authorities and some other bodies appear to deliberately overstate distances and times in brochures and on signs. This book attempts to state distances precisely.

Conservation

Remember that care of the bushland itself is very important. Many walk routes are in declared national parks and commonsense regulations must be respected. The bush and the life within it are often in a delicate state of ecological balance and, of necessity, there must be no rubbish discarded or damage to wildlife and plants. For the sake of wildlife, pets are banned from all parks. Plants may not be taken from, or brought into national parks, fines often apply. Green timber should not be cut or broken for fires and great care is required with any fire. Before leaving it make sure your campfire is completely extinguished. Remember the adage: the bigger the fire, the bigger the fool. On no account light a fire on a high fire-danger day. Most areas have fire risk indicator boards, and again fines apply. Note that in some parks, fires are totally banned at all times and you may need to carry a small fuel stove for cooking.

Fires, stoves and refuse

Although a stove is always preferable for protection against fire, the campfire is ideal for the majority of waste disposal. However, silver paper, and other foils and cans will not destruct so readily. You need to wash all cans, remove both ends, flatten them, and as with any foil or glass, carry them in a plastic bag to the nearest garbage bin. Burying of rubbish is not permitted. Human waste must be properly buried away from streams and drinking water. Always wash downstream from the camp site and collect drinking water upstream. Remember, other people do not appreciate drinking your bath water.

Off-track walking

This book details walking tracks and with the exception of beaches, are well-defined, park authority endorsed routes. Deviating from tracks and taking 'short cuts' creates erosion problems and may bring you into conflict with the park ranger. Official tracks are usually positioned to provide access to features of interest. We strongly advise against off-track walking.

Water

The purity of drinking water is of course important to walkers and as we all would realise, Australia is basically a very dry country with a shortage of water. Few pleasures can top a cool drink from a high-country lake or mountain stream on a hot day or after a big climb. Fortunately in Australia we do not yet have the major problems of North America where virtually all lakes and streams are contaminated with parasitic *Giardia lamblia*. We can still drink water from most mountain streams relatively safely. Be aware that farmland or town areas upstream can be the main sources of contamination. Use your map if you are unsure of water quality. Avoid water if farms or towns within a few kilometres upstream are shown on the map. At any location, still water is best avoided unless it is in an alpine tarn or remote lake. Inland lakes may be useless because of salt. If in doubt, boil water for about three to four minutes or use water purification tablets. It is best not to use even boiled water if from farmland or near large towns or industry. You are advised to bring water from a treated source.

Snow and exposure

Due to the variability of weather, violent weather changes and snow storms can occur even at the height of summer in the higher parts of southern Australia. In alpine areas of New South Wales, Victoria and Tasmania you should carry protective and warm clothing at all times, and make note of the position of huts or other shelter if needed. Good footwear is therefore also very important. In winter, snow can fall as far north as the Queensland border.

If, in spite of planning, you do find yourself caught in snow when camping, stay in the tent. Do not try to walk out until the weather clears. Learn how to interpret cloud formations and winds in advance so that you do not get caught in exposed positions and so that you can get off high, wild places well before foul weather sets in. It is our view that most situations where walkers have been holed up for days by snow or floods could have been avoided by reading the signs of the cloud formations and acting to avoid the problem. During electrical storms, lightning frequently strikes on mountain tops. At such times keep off lookout towers and away from large or solitary trees, or metal objects.

Flooding of streams

Flooded streams can cause delays and even prevent you from continuing along your intended route. Do not camp on sandy creek beds. A thunderstorm upstream can quickly turn a dry creek bed into a torrent. Some areas mentioned in these track notes are subject to flooding and you should use discretion. In this book, Murchison Gorge and Bunyeroo Gorge are two such examples where care should be excercised. Wet weather gear is essential in Tasmania virtually at all times.

Hot days

Australian conditions mean that for most of the country temperatures can rise to over 40°C. This applies to areas as far south as Melbourne. The northern one-third of the country is tropical and bushwalking is often uncomfortable. On hot days, especially if a northerly wind is predicted in southern Australia, rise very early if you have to walk and start before the main heat of the day. Wet a small towel or similar item in a creek at the bottom of any big climb and cool off as you climb by mopping your brow. The towel should be left draped over your shoulders to dampen and cool you as you climb. Use sunscreen, especially at high altitudes and wear a hat.

Bushfires

If the day is a proclaimed total fire ban day then abandon your walking plans. If you are unlucky enough to be threatened by bushfire while walking—do not panic. Never run uphill or run to try and outstrip a fire without giving some thought to the situation. Consider the area, the approach direction of the fire and the wind direction and velocity.

In taking action remember that northern slopes are usually hot and dry and therefore an area of greater risk. Fire tends to turn uphill and is usually most fierce on ridges and spurs. Choose the nearest clear space, then place some obstruction between you and the fire, quickly clear away all flammable material, leaves and so on. Cover your body completely with clothing, preferably wool and preferably wet. Wear proper footwear, not thongs; wet any towels and lie face down in the clearing. Cover all exposed skin surfaces. Radiant heat from the fire kills, as well as the flames. Do not be tempted to lift your head too much because if you do, you will inhale smoke or get smoke in your eyes. The freshest air is right next to the ground surface. If you are near a deep stream or deep dam get right into it. Concrete and galvanised iron tanks should be avoided as concrete tanks can explode with heat and iron tanks can buckle and burst open. Do not try to run through a fire front unless it is no wider than 3 m and no higher than 1.5 m. If you have a car parked in an open spot, get in and shut all the windows. Lie low on the floor of the car away from the radiant heat. Ensure flammable material is well away from the car. Remember that modern cars include a significant amount of plastics, and while a car may be the safest place, there are no guarantees. Do not chance driving in dense smoke.

Generally, it is safest to lie low in an open space covered with wet clothing unless a deep stream or deep dam water is very close.

First aid at a glance

Dial 000 free call for emergency. It is essential that any emergency can be dealt with adequately.

A first-aid book and kit should be carried by at least one member of every walking party. The kit should include bandages, safety pins, adhesive tape, small adhesive dressing strips, gauze pads, antiseptic, tweezers, small scissors, sunscreen, insect repellent, aspirin, anti-fungal powder/cream, antacid tablets and antihistamine tablets.

The most likely troubles to be encountered are listed opposite for rapid reference, because in many cases there is not time to do research in a more comprehensive first-aid book. In virtually all serious situations, the patient needs to be rested and reassured, often while another person obtains medical assistance. For this reason walk parties in any remote place should never be less than three in number. One walker should stay with the patient while the other goes for aid.

Lost?

If lost, ***stop!*** Only move after you have sat down and logically and carefully thought things through. Generally it is best to stay in the spot until help comes. Remember that any movement is normally best made on ridges and spurs, not in scrub-choked gullies. You should be absolutely sure of directions and should leave a prominent note indicating your intentions and time of leaving. Preferably wear brightly coloured and warm clothing and ration the food you have with you. Parties should not split up and the physically stronger should help others cope.

Once moving, check the compass frequently, remain on as straight a line as possible and leave notes along the route. If you become tired, stop and rest. Do not over-exert yourself. Remember that severe physical and mental strain, plus cold, can bring death by exposure. Over the years, far too many people have died unnecessarily, or suffered serious injuries, mainly because they have not understood the seriousness of being caught unprepared in the bush, and have not been able to cope with the situation. The accepted distress signal is three long whistles, coo-ees, mirror flashes, or any other signal repeated in threes every minute. Do not force yourself physically; rather, do things objectively and calmly, with plenty of rest. If you feel confused, make a campfire in a sheltered spot, but where you can be seen from the air.

Theft

Years ago, theft from a car left at a trackhead was rare. Now, equipment has become increasingly sophisticated, such as GPS, iPods and mobile phones, which are worth stealing. There are more walkers, too. Wilderness trackheads are not safe so never leave valuables unattended.

Be wary of anyone waiting around when you arrive. A ploy used is for thieves to wear a rucksack on the back as if genuine walkers. After you leave, the thieves, having watched you hide your valuables, fill the rucksack with your belongings.

Parks system

It is time to make several critical observations about the state of our ever-changing parks system. Overall, we must appreciate the huge growth in the amount of our country rescued from logging and other threats to be set aside for national and other parks. This means staff and funding are far more widely dispersed. We should be grateful that at least a lot more land is seemingly better protected.

COMPLAINT	TREATMENT
BLISTERS	Apply an adhesive foam patch; wear extra socks; if possible, do not break the blister as this increases the risk of infection.
HEAT EXHAUSTION	Replenish body fluids with plenty of drinks of water or fruit juice and take a little salt if badly dehydrated. Rest in a cool place and fan the patient. Remove excess clothing from the patient.
ABDOMINAL PAIN/FEVERS	Rest is essential. Give plenty of liquid to the patient.
BURNS	Immediately immerse burn area in cold water to chill. Clean thoroughly, despite the pain, and apply a clean bandage. Immobilise the burn area.
EXPOSURE TO COLD	Do not rub the skin or apply direct heat or give alcohol. These cause blood to come to the skin surface, which then returns to the heart, cooler. The body trunk and brain must be warmed. Insulate the entire body; give sugar in easily digested form (for example, sweetened condensed milk). Put the patient in a sleeping bag, preferably with a warm person. Cover the bag with insulation, provide a wind break and pitch a tent over the patient. If breathing stops, apply mouth-to-mouth resuscitation. Only move to a warmer place if in doing so the patient will in no way be physically exerted. Avoid patient standing as fainting will follow. The recognisable signs of the onset of exposure are: pallor and shivering, listlessness, slurred speech, poor vision, irrational and violent behaviour, collapse. It is wet cold particularly that kills.
SPRAINS	Immobilise the area of the sprain and rest it. Promptly immerse in cold water (stream, etc.).
SNAKE BITE	Most bites are of a minor nature but it is wise to treat all bites as if dangerous. Many people have a disproportionate fear of snake bite so need reassurance and rest. The majority of bites are to limbs rather than the body trunk, so first aid is easier. If bitten deeply by a full-grown deadly snake on the neck many kilometres from anywhere, then there is probably little that can be done and in these circumstances, prayer and writing your will seem like worthy options. But the instances of such bites are extremely rare. For first aid for practically all bites, you need to restrict venom movement in the body. Therefore, a broad bandage should be applied to a limb bite area or pressure kept firmly on bites to the body trunk. The bite area should be kept immobilised, with pressure applied to bandage or pad until antivenene is received from a doctor. Immobilisation can best be achieved by binding a splint to any limb bite area. Cutting the bite and washing venom off skin should not be attempted. Cutting upsets the patient, and can cause complications. Venom retained on the skin can be tested later to identify the snake species. To maximise rest, transport should be brought to the patient. Apply mouth-to-mouth resuscitation and artificial respiration, (CPR) until medical aid is given.

Today legal claims for injuries suffered by park visitors have cost the parks system dearly and we now find safety measures, duckboards, railings and safety signs everywhere, effectively removing much former feeling of wilderness. Negative rather than positive attitudes prevail in signage and general communication. Walkers are now often deprived of the spirit of adventure or challenge with map and compass. In many instances you can no longer have that campfire and all sorts of regulations are in place. The cost of all these measures, often to satisfy the liability issue, has meant other aspects of park management suffer.

An amazing number of tracks simply get closed if a storm washes out a bridge, and they then stay closed until assessment and insurance issues are settled.

A heavy emphasis is placed upon economics and protecting assets that are situated too close to forests and parks, and so control burns are now far too frequent. Park authorities have heavily promoted the valid fact that most Australian native plants benefit from burning. However, authorities do not point out that some plants can be wiped out, thus reducing the variety of plants we may find in the natural environment. Eucalyptus has become the dominant species as a result of burning and more fire helps this trend, to the detriment of other plants. The oils contained in eucalyptus are the most combustible element in the bush and the more we burn, the more we increase the problem. Fire management tampers with the balance in flora, which in turn directly affects fauna. Their food sources or nectar-bearing flowers are removed. Authorities seem oblivious to the fact that the huge amount of smoke is worsening global warming. Carbon contained within living or dead plant material is released needlessly into the atmosphere. A number of control burns have escaped, causing horrific damage, while some control burns have proved ineffective when wildfire occurs. At these times there is little access to fight the fire as hundreds of four-wheel-drive tracks have been closed and have become overgrown. The fire therefore becomes huge and only rain helps. Asthmatic sufferers are badly affected by the smoke too, as it blows over cities and towns.

Erosion can be dreadful if heavy rains follow fires. Billions of small animals, including lizards, frogs and small birds, plus especially the all-important small and microscopic fauna of the forest floor and soils perish. 'Research' burns are often carried out to assess the environment's ability to recover after fire. These burns only serve to compound the problem. This 'research' is perhaps akin to those countries that kill whales in the name of scientific research.

In undertaking the walks in this book, you need to be aware that some problems, and especially problems of so-called temporary track closures, will occur. Perhaps you might agree with the works and the emphasis upon safety; or perhaps you won't and you will express your disapproval to rangers. We believe many walkers will simply find places to walk that are not in the park system. Others may consider walking too 'tame' and lacking adventure, and so turn even more to the increasingly popular extreme sports.

A conservation-related plea

In stark contrast to controlled burning policies, regeneration programs are common. They use plastic tree guards extensively. Many of us have been induced as volunteers to help plant and place the tree guards in position. However, usually the plastic does not get removed later. Plasticised milk cartons also get used. Each look unbelievably ugly at any time, but especially when lying about or blowing around as rubbish. Our national pride seems tarnished by this neglect. Their use negates the policy directed at the general public to stop using so many plastic bags. If you inspect any plants in an area of tree guards you usually find at least half of all plants are dead through lack of after-care. Trees that do survive are eventually restricted in their growth to the width of the tree guard. Many trees up to even 10 m tall are virtually strangled with plastic, or are affected by fungi under the plastic, which rots the tree base.

This conservation-related plea is to pass the message around that if plastic guards are used at all, rather than say a perimeter fence, then authorities and volunteers need to tend to that vital after-care of watering and plastic removal. The worst offenders for lack of after-care seem to be the main roads authority and local councils, but park authorities also seem remiss at times. Additionally, there appears to be an emphasis of revegetating treed areas with grasses and shrubs, which do not equate to the same carbon storage. So-called 'plant a tree days' are often for grass planting. This is at a time when we are all warned of global warming and how important it is to increase, not reduce, the number of trees. Another anomaly is that the cost of tree guards often exceeds the cost of the plant, so perhaps we should question the use of guards at any time. For the same cost, we could plant twice as many unguarded plants and not cut down trees for use as stakes. One stated reason for guards is to stop foraging animals. Our busy freeways and main roads, where so many millions of guards exist, certainly have few animals present, as animals would be scared off by traffic. Once the presence of neglected tree guards is pointed out, it is hard to not see the problem which is right before your eyes.

Family walking advice

It is stressed that parents or party leaders attempting walking trips should at no time leave children unattended as becoming lost is a very unhappy experience for a child and parents alike. It must be emphasised that any walking along roads should usually be done facing oncoming traffic. However, The Pinnacles Desert walk suggested in this book recommends walking against this advice, but extremely slow-moving traffic is encountered here. Children should be instructed not to wander away from the party and if they do become separated or lost, to wait where they are until help arrives. It is also important that children be instructed not to drink from streams without supervision and not to eat tempting looking berries in the bush. Many leaves, fruit, berries and fungi, if not poisonous, can cause acute discomfort. It is unwise to take babies on walks that expose them to the hot sun, wind, undue jarring while walking or injuries from stumbling. Do not leave children (or pets) in vehicles while out walking.

By using a little extra care and avoiding placing children in dangerous situations, great family enjoyment can be had. The bush is full of wonders and what better way is there to give children fresh air, exercise and a first hand knowledge of the wonder that is the Australian bush?

Equipment and food suggestions for walks

Safety equipment

(*See also* ***Safety and commonsense in the bush***.) Maps, compass, small mirror, paper, whistle, matches in a waterproof container, sharp knife, small candle, small torch, a waterproof marking pen, first aid kit, safety clothing (consisting of warm sweater or pullover, thick woollen socks, bright coloured shirt and bright coloured waterproof coat) and safety food rations (such as nourishing concentrated foods plus a little bulky food like dried fruit, chocolate, nuts, fruit and seed bars and brown rice).

Sunglasses and sunscreen are needed if snow is a possibility. A balaclava, mittens and wool trousers should be taken on all snow country walks. Waterproof over-trousers also help. Gaiters can be helpful.

Other equipment

Overnight walks: tent, tent poles, tent pegs, tent guys, good quality sleeping bag, inner bag, plastic ground sheet, a newspaper (fire lighting and bed mattress), toilet items, and if you wish to cook: a small stove, a billy (saucepan), billy lifters and pot scourer. In wet weather, plenty of plastic bags should be carried for waterproofing items in your pack. A pack liner also helps. Include a deck of cards or a book of crosswords for the days when you might be tent-bound.

All walks: shirt or blouse (woollen in winter), shorts, jeans, handkerchief, walking boots, runners or gym-boots with good tread and ankle support, mug, bowl, cutlery, small towel, lightweight bathers for summer, sunscreen, hat, waterbag (canvas type with zip top), water bottle (aluminium or plastic), can opener and pack.

Food

In addition to emergency rations, which are to be used only in an emergency, the following foods should be carried in quantities according to the number of days that the walk will occupy: nuts, dried fruit, chocolate, fruit and seed bars, hard-boiled eggs, packet or cube soups, fruit drink powders, rice and packet rice preparations, pasta, fresh fruit, honey, wholemeal bread, Vegemite, salami, fruit cake, coffee, tea or other hot drink, salted bacon, carrot, packet mashed potato and some muesli or porridge. Cans should only be carried by people accustomed to carrying heavy packs. Empty cans should be washed and, along with any foils or glass, carried out of walk areas to garbage bins. Thought should be given to the energy content of foods with respect to their weight.

Weight of backpack

The most important consideration when carrying an overnight pack is the combined weight of the contents. If you carry no more than stated in this list of equipment and food suggestions, you should not encounter trouble. Some extras, such as a camera, might be considered worthwhile. However, far too many people include that little extra item or two, or overestimate the quantity of food that they could possibly eat and so suffer the consequences when they have to climb a hill bearing 'a ton of bricks'. They defeat the purpose of the walk by becoming too tired to enjoy the trip.

Mapping and navigation

Navigation procedures are best learned from experience in the field, using map and compass. This is sometimes difficult to arrange if one does not have a friend who can teach you in the field. Usually, there are excellent opportunities to learn navigation when walking with a bushwalking club.

Clubs help walkers with safety, advice, experience and companionship. Usually their organised walks are led by experienced leaders, often with transport arranged. Inquiries of a general nature and those concerning the various clubs can be made from the local Federation of Walking Clubs.

This book provides a map of the immediate area of every walk suggestion. To some extent the maps will assist with navigation, but to rely entirely on these maps would be unwise. (For example, you might travel off the map coverage while lost.) It is strongly recommended, therefore, that every endeavour be made to purchase government or other maps before setting out on these trips.

Besides maps suggested in this book, other maps are on sale which usefully supplement their information. Such maps are available in the bigger cities at sales outlets of government departments, and at larger book shops and especially shops catering for bushwalkers' needs. Map coverage is also available using the Internet. The best government-produced maps available for the walks in this book tend to be of the 1:25 000 scale sheets; there is broad coverage of walk areas in these series. The 1:100 000 scale sheets covering even greater areas are useful for planning and car touring. Remember that many government maps have been in circulation for a long time, often more than thirty years, and often lack recent changes to roads, tracks and other man-made features.

One important point with which all walkers should be familiar is that magnetic north is at present about eleven degrees east of true north.

Glossary

adit an underground mine entrance

alluvial soil sand, silt and clay, resulting from deposition by streams, glaciers and lakes

amphitheatre semi-circular formation of cliffs resembling ancient man-made gallery for audience

anabranch former watercourse usually crescent shaped and often with billabong

anticlines deeply folded rock strata, the middle of which arches upwards

arable land normally used for growing grains for food

basalt hard, fine-grained, dark-coloured, extruded, volcanic rock

benched track a track that runs across a slope with a high-side embankment excavated to provide a flat walking surface

billabong a usually permanent waterhole found in the bed of a former stream or river, particularly anabranch

bushbash (also scrub-bash) to traverse trackless terrain amid bushland

bracket fungi the visible fruiting body resembling a round plate, often found on decaying trees especially in damp conditions

cairn usually small mound of rocks, erected to mark summits and track alignment, especially for unmaintained, minor tracks in rocky terrain

confluence the meeting of two streams

conglomerate pieces of various rock types naturally cemented together

continental drift movement of the tectonic plates that comprise the crust and surface of the Earth with respect to each other

endemic found only within a particular location

El Niño (as opposed to La Niña) weather system resulting from the combined effects of cold ocean currents and dry onshore winds causing reduced rainfall

epicormic cells specialised, dormant cells triggered into growth following damage such as fire, notably eucalyptus trees

escarpment rock formation, often cliffs, caused by sections of the crust being thrust to the surface during sideways compression along faults

fauna any form of animal life including insects and fungi

flora any form of plant life dependant on photosynthesis for growth

geo-synclines folded rock strata forming a central depression often with escarpments on the outer limits

GPS (Global Positioning System) a device used to define elevation and position by decoding satellite signals

granite course-grained, light-coloured, intrusive, volcanic rock formed deep underground and in places, later exposed by erosion

gulch a ravine or cleft, usually narrow, eroded by a stream or the sea

indigenous native to a particular region or country

isthmus narrow neck of land connecting promontory, point or cape to mainland

latitude divisions used to locate points on the surface of the Earth with respect to the Equator and the poles, 0–90 degrees + north and 0–90 degrees – south where '0' is the equator

lava plug the solidified core of a volcanic vent following eruption, often exposed at the surface by erosion

longitude divisions in hours, minutes and seconds to locate points on the Earth's surface parallel with the Equator at any latitude, up to 24 hours from the Greenwich Meridian near London

maar a volcanic crater that does not lie in a cone and was formed by a single volcanic event. Maars usually contain a lake.

magma molten rock, often containing water and mineral elements. When ejected from a volcano forms lava and ash; when trapped underground forms granite

metamorphic rock chemically or structurally changed by intense heating and pressure

mineral deposits rocks and sediments containing ores including oil, coal and precious metals

monsoon usually torrential rainfall preceded by rising humidity particularly in the tropics, often with cyclones (hurricanes or typhoons)

monolith solid usually large rock formation devoid of variation in density or mineral composition

moraine an accumulation of rock debris by retreating glaciers

mudstone mud cemented by pressure and mineralisation

pad a minor, unmaintained walking track or defined animal track

pastoral land usually grazed by sheep and cattle for food or wool production

peakbag when one reaches the top of a significant peak for the first time

pound common name for the depression within a geo-syncline, for example Wilpena Pound in the Flinders Ranges, South Australia

rain shadow an area rendered dry because mountains regularly block prevailing weather and rainfall

saddle a low point along a ridge crest between two hills

sandstone sand cemented by pressure and mineralisation

sedimentary rock formed through the progressive deposition of particles on the bottom of lakes and seas, for example sandstone and mudstone

sidle to walk, following along a map contour or across the side of a hill

spur a sloping ridge that links lowlands with highlands

symbiosis a mutually beneficial association between two or more organisms, often differing species, for example a bacterium and a plant

synclines deeply folded rock strata, the middle of which arches downwards

tarn a small alpine lake

telegraph (line, station) early system of electronic communication utilising morse code to transmit the alphabet via overland wiring

tops the highest areas of high-country plateau, ridge crest or mountain

trackhead the starting point of a walking track, often at a road or car park

treeline the upper limit at which trees will grow due to severe weather

trig point (trigonometric point) a marker on many significant mountain tops for survey mapping now largely superseded by satellite navigation

tropics the regions of the earth 23 degrees, 28 minutes north and south of the Equator bounded by the Tropic of Capricorn in the south and the Tropic of Cancer in the north

volcano vent in the Earth's crust through which magma escapes from the mantle, usually found close to the collision or separation of continental plates.

Australian road atlas

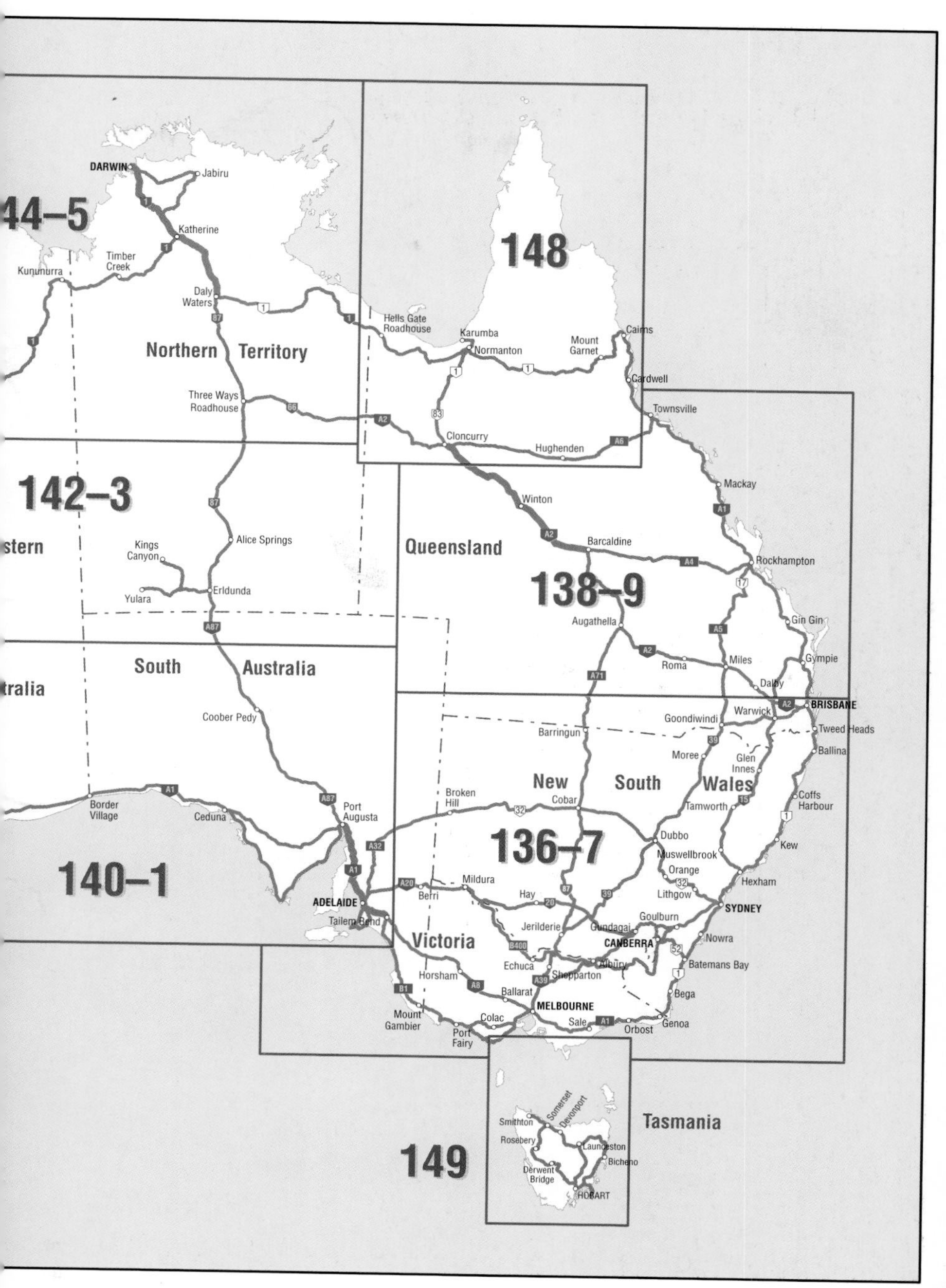

44–5
148
142–3
138–9
136–7
140–1
149
DARWIN
Jabiru
Katherine
Timber Creek
Kununurra
Daly Waters
Northern Territory
Three Ways Roadhouse
Hells Gate Roadhouse
Karumba
Normanton
Mount Garnet
Cairns
Cardwell
Townsville
Cloncurry
Hughenden
Winton
Mackay
Barcaldine
Queensland
Rockhampton
Alice Springs
Kings Canyon
Yulara
Erldunda
stern
tralia
South Australia
Coober Pedy
Augathella
Gin Gin
Roma
Miles
Gympie
Dalby
Warwick
BRISBANE
Goondiwindi
Tweed Heads
Barringun
Moree
Glen Innes
Ballina
New South Wales
Broken Hill
Cobar
Tamworth
Coffs Harbour
Border Village
Ceduna
Port Augusta
Dubbo
Muswellbrook
Kew
Orange
Hexham
Mildura
Berri
Hay
Lithgow
SYDNEY
ADELAIDE
Tailem Bend
Jerilderie
Gundagai
Goulburn
Victoria
CANBERRA
Nowra
Echuca
Albury
Shepparton
Batemans Bay
Horsham
Ballarat
Bega
Mount Gambier
MELBOURNE
Colac
Sale
Orbost
Genoa
Port Fairy
Tasmania
Smithton
Somerset
Devonport
Rosebery
Launceston
Bicheno
Derwent Bridge
HOBART

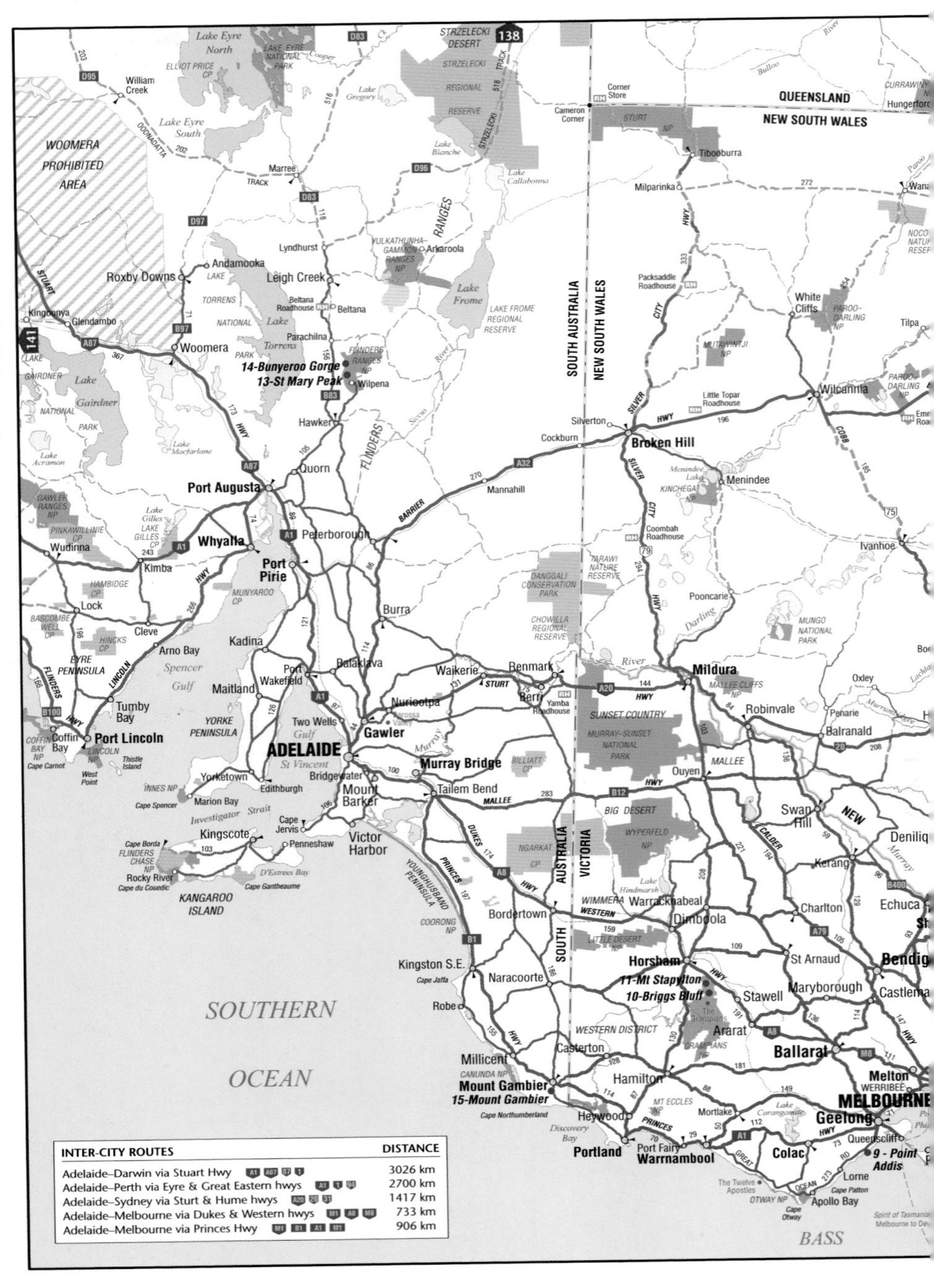

INTER-CITY ROUTES

INTER-CITY ROUTES	DISTANCE
Adelaide–Darwin via Stuart Hwy A1 A87 87 1	3026 km
Adelaide–Perth via Eyre & Great Eastern hwys A1 1 94	2700 km
Adelaide–Sydney via Sturt & Hume hwys A20 20 31	1417 km
Adelaide–Melbourne via Dukes & Western hwys M1 A8 M8	733 km
Adelaide–Melbourne via Princes Hwy M1 B1 A1 M1	906 km

INTER-CITY ROUTES		DISTANCE
Sydney–Melbourne via Hume Hwy/Fwy	31 M31	881 km
Sydney–Melbourne via Princes Hwy/Fwy	1 A1 M1	1037 km
Sydney–Brisbane via New England Hwy	1 15	1001 km
Sydney–Brisbane via Pacific Hwy	1 1 M1	966 km
Melbourne–Adelaide via Western & Dukes hwys	M8 A8 M1	733 km
Melbourne–Adelaide via Princes Hwy	M1 A1 B1 M1	906 km
Melbourne–Brisbane via Newell Hwy	M31 A39 39 A39 A2	1676 km

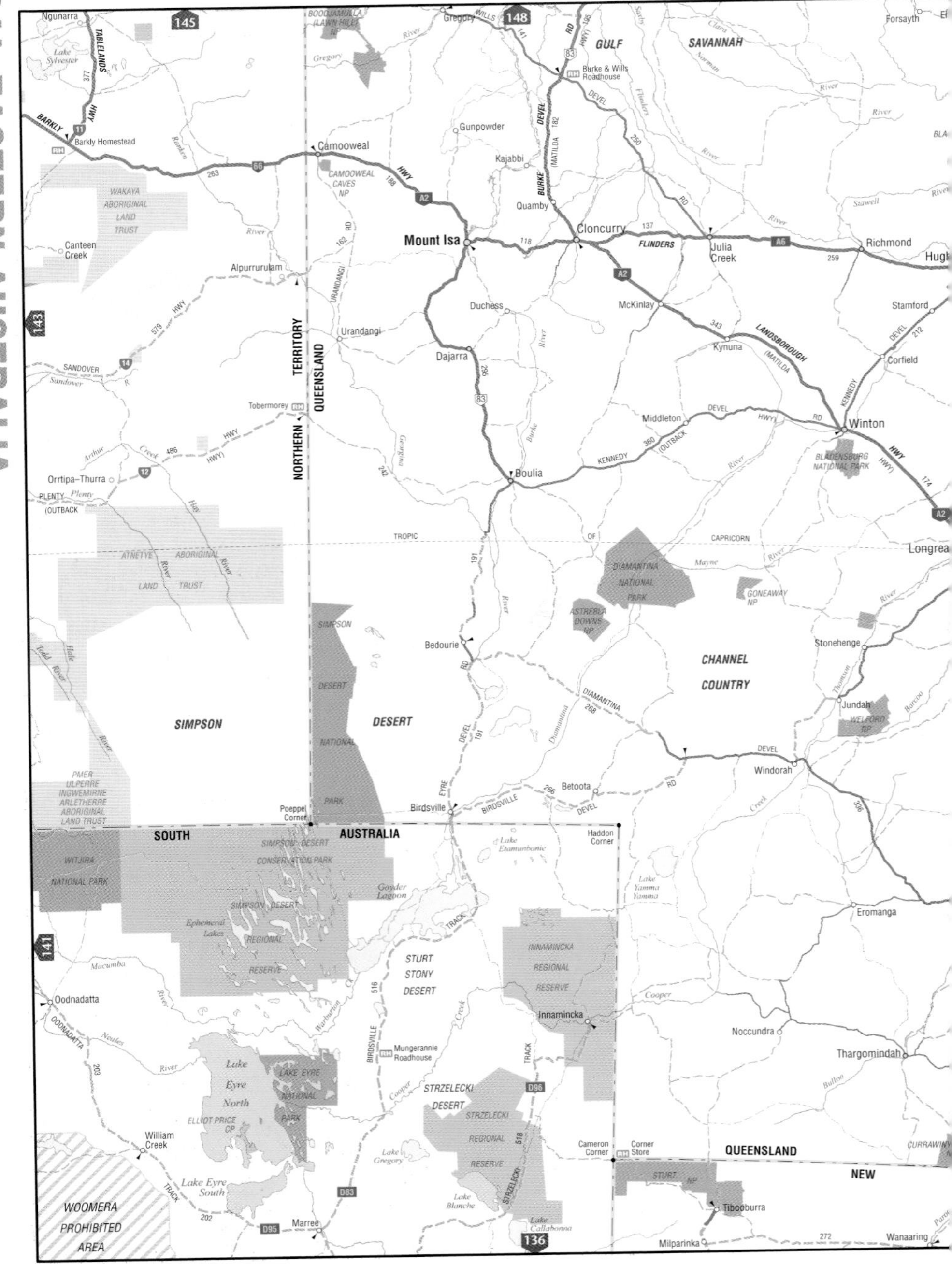

Ngunarra
Gregory
Forsayth
Burke & Wills Roadhouse
GULF
SAVANNAH
Barkly Homestead
Gunpowder
Camooweal
Kajabbi
CAMOOWEAL CAVES NP
Quamby
WAKAYA ABORIGINAL LAND TRUST
Mount Isa
Cloncurry
Julia Creek
Richmond
Canteen Creek
Alpurrurulam
Duchess
McKinlay
Stamford
Urandangi
Dajarra
Kynuna
Corfield
Tobermorey
Middleton
Winton
Orrtipa–Thurra
Boulia
BLADENSBURG NATIONAL PARK
TROPIC OF CAPRICORN
Longreach
NORTHERN TERRITORY
QUEENSLAND
ATNETYE ABORIGINAL LAND TRUST
DIAMANTINA NATIONAL PARK
GONEAWAY NP
ASTREBLA DOWNS NP
Bedourie
Stonehenge
CHANNEL COUNTRY
SIMPSON DESERT NATIONAL PARK
SIMPSON
DESERT
Jundah
WELFORD NP
Windorah
PMER ULPERRE INGWEMIRNE ARLETHERRE ABORIGINAL LAND TRUST
Betoota
Poeppel Corner
Birdsville
SOUTH
AUSTRALIA
Haddon Corner
WITJIRA NATIONAL PARK
SIMPSON DESERT CONSERVATION PARK
SIMPSON DESERT REGIONAL RESERVE
Lake Etamunbanie
Goyder Lagoon
Lake Yamma Yamma
Eromanga
STURT STONY DESERT
INNAMINCKA REGIONAL RESERVE
Oodnadatta
Innamincka
Noccundra
Mungerannie Roadhouse
Thargomindah
Lake Eyre North
LAKE EYRE NATIONAL PARK
ELLIOT PRICE CP
STRZELECKI DESERT
STRZELECKI REGIONAL RESERVE
William Creek
Cameron Corner
Corner Store
QUEENSLAND
NEW
STURT NP
Lake Eyre South
Tibooburra
WOOMERA PROHIBITED AREA
Marree
Lake Blanche
Lake Callabonna
Milparinka
Wanaaring

CENTRAL EASTERN AUSTRALIA

INTER-CITY ROUTES	DISTANCE
Brisbane–Sydney via New England Hwy 15 1	1001 km
Brisbane–Sydney via Pacific Hwy M1 1 1	966 km
Brisbane–Melbourne via Newell Hwy A2 A39 39 A39 M31	1676 km
Brisbane–Darwin via Warrego Hwy A2 66 87 1	3406 km
Brisbane–Cairns via Bruce Hwy M1 A1	1703 km

0 50 100 150 200 km

Scale

LITTLE SANDY DESERT
142
GIBSON DESERT NATURE RESERVE
MUNGILLI ABORIGINAL LAND
HWY
GUNBARREL
STOCK ROUTE
CARNARVON RANGES
CANNING
Lake Naberu
Carnegie Homestead
Lake Carnegie
NGAANYATJARRA ABORIGINAL LAND
Boyd Lagoon
Lake Breaden
Warburton Roadhouse
Warburton
Warakurna
Warakurna Roadhouse
RD
231
HWY
Surveyor Generals Corner
Pipalyatjara
CENTRAL AUSTRALIA ABORIGINAL LAND TRUST
WESTERN AUSTRALIA
250
Tjukayirla Roadhouse
CENTRAL (OUTBACK
Lake Wells
Wiluna
Lake Way
GOLDFIELDS
Mount Keith
WANJARRI NATURE RESERVE
174
DE LA POER RANGE NATURE RESERVE
Lake Throssel
315
GREAT
YEO LAKE NATURE RESERVE
Cosmo Newbery
COSMO NEWBERY ABORIGINAL LAND
CONNIE SUE
4WD only
Neale Junction
NEALE JUNCTION NATURE RESERVE
Leinster
141
131
HWY
Rason Lake
GREAT VICTORIA DESERT
Laverton
124
Leonora
Jubilee Lake
GREAT VICTORIA DESERT NATURE RESERVE
Lake Carey
Lake Minigwal
PLUMRIDGE LAKES NATURE RESERVE
Lake Ballard
Kookynie
Lake Barlee
Lake Raeside
Menzies
Lake Rebecca
275
91
146
MOUNT MANNING NATURE RESERVE
GOONGARRIE NP
QUEEN VICTORIA SPRINGS NATURE RESERVE
NULLARBOR
Broad Arrow
Cundeelee
Loongana
RAILWAY
Reid
AUSTRALIA
TRANS
Kalgoorlie–Boulder
Lake Yindarlgooda
Zanthus
Rawlinna
Coolgardie
38
ALT 94
GOLDFIELDS WOODLAND NP
HWY
Kambalda
Southern Cross
EASTERN
186
94
BURRA ROCK NR
Lake Lefroy
Mundrabilla Roadhouse
BOORABBIN NP
Widgiemooltha
HWY
195
Marvel Loch
166
Lake Cowan
Cocklebiddy
158
Madura
JILBADJI NATURE RESERVE
94
EYRE
191
HWY
Balladonia
Caiguna
EYRE
Red Rocks Point
Norseman
182
1
Point Dover
DUNDAS NATURE RESERVE
Lake Dundas
NUYTSLAND NATURE RESERVE
Point Culver
Lake Johnston
G
Varley
313
FRANK HANN NP
PEAK CHARLES NP
Salmon Gums
Lake Tay
203
Grass Patch
CAPE ARID NP
Israelite Bay
Point Dempster
Lake King
Young R
Condingup
Ravensthorpe
COAST
187
HWY
65
Cape Pasley
LAKE MAGENTA NR
1
SOUTH
Esperance
CAPE LE GRAND NP
113
Hopetoun
N
Jerramungup
FITZGERALD RIVER NP
179
0 50 100 150 200 km
Scale
Bremer Bay
Cheyne Bay
Ledge Point

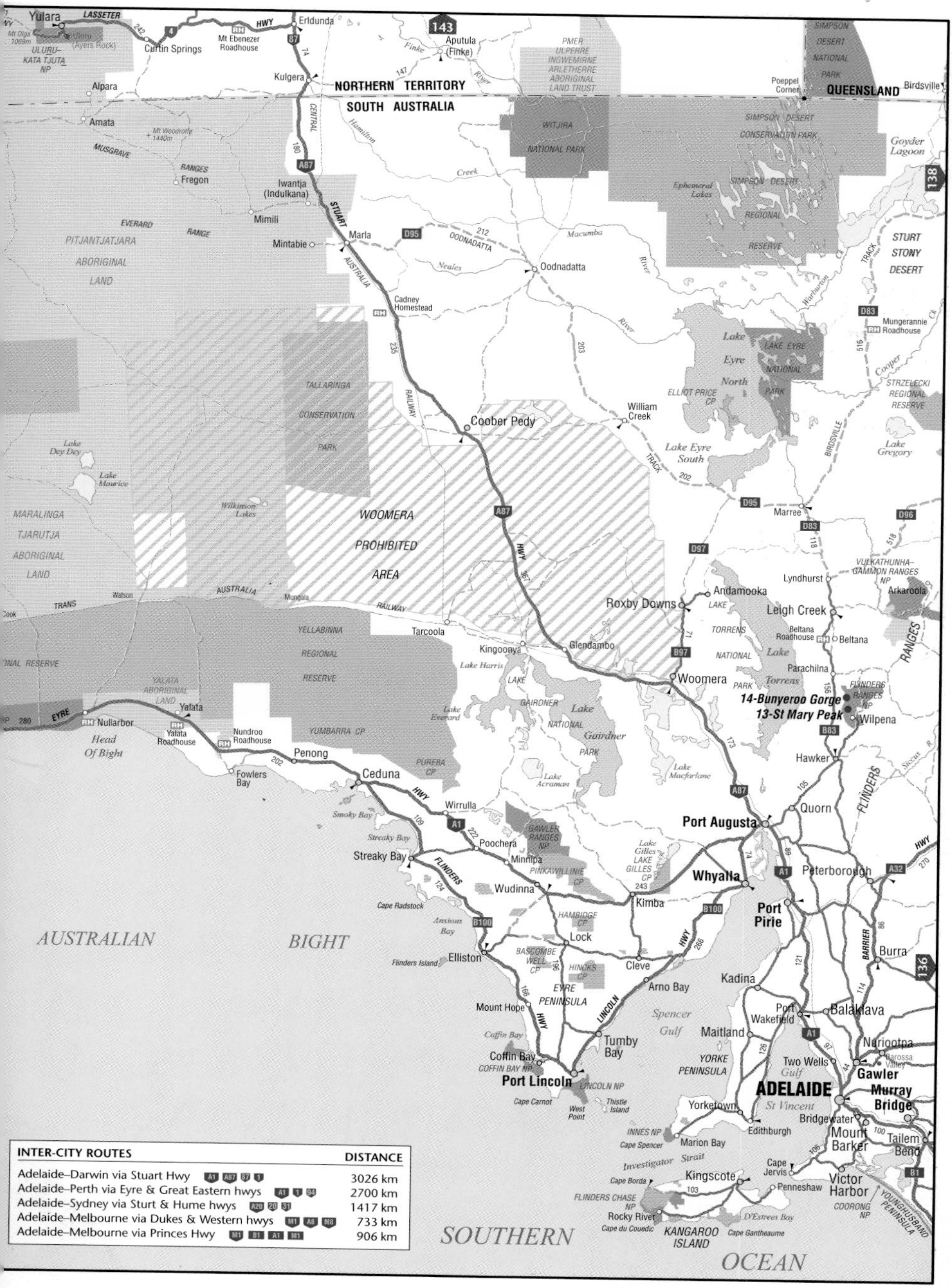

INTER-CITY ROUTES		DISTANCE
Adelaide–Darwin via Stuart Hwy	A1 A87 87 1	3026 km
Adelaide–Perth via Eyre & Great Eastern hwys	A1 1 94	2700 km
Adelaide–Sydney via Sturt & Hume hwys	A20 20 31	1417 km
Adelaide–Melbourne via Dukes & Western hwys	M1 A8 M8	733 km
Adelaide–Melbourne via Princes Hwy	M1 B1 A1 M1	906 km

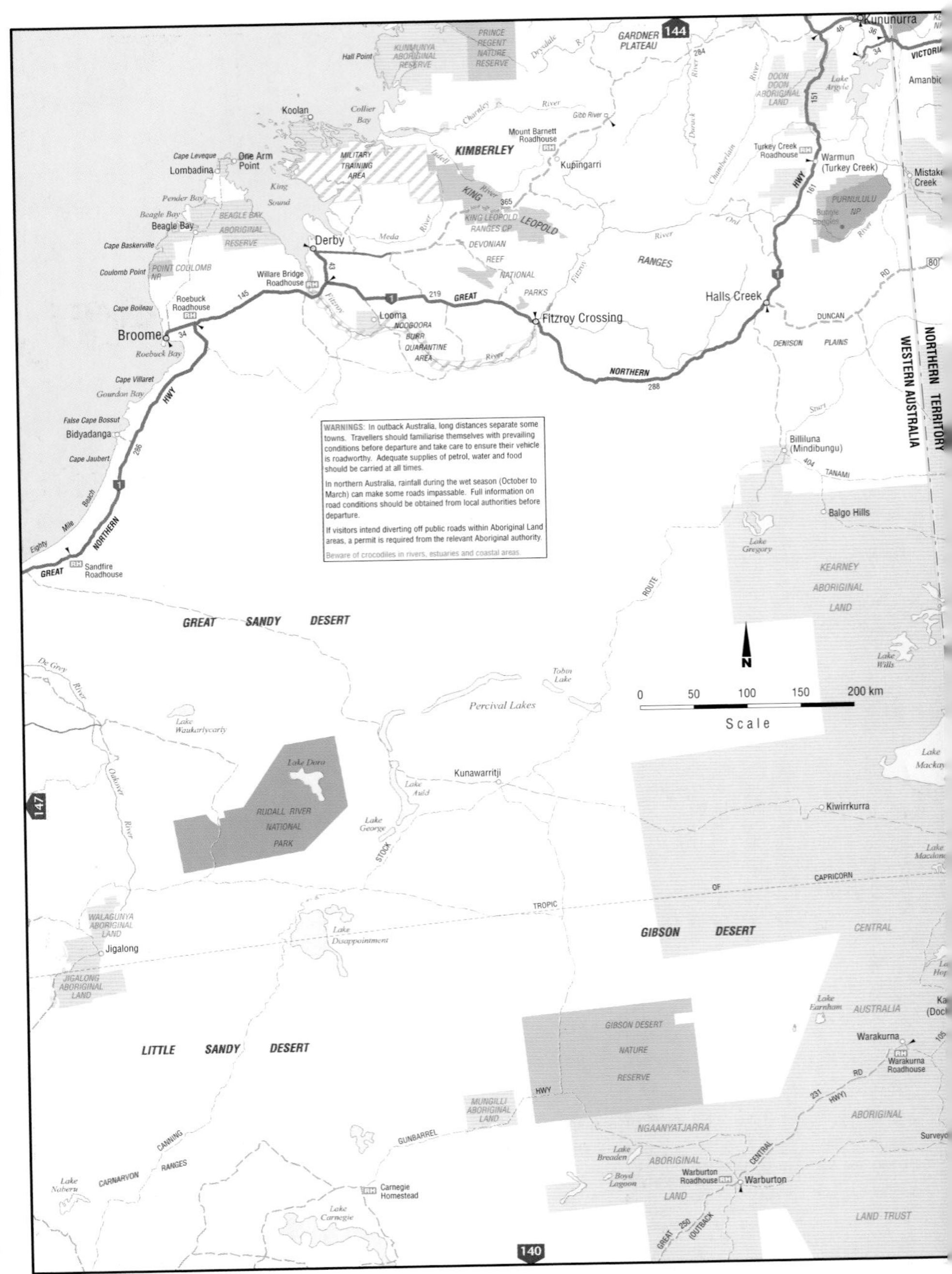
WARNINGS: In outback Australia, long distances separate some towns. Travellers should familiarise themselves with prevailing conditions before departure and take care to ensure their vehicle is roadworthy. Adequate supplies of petrol, water and food should be carried at all times.
In northern Australia, rainfall during the wet season (October to March) can make some roads impassable. Full information on road conditions should be obtained from local authorities before departure.
If visitors intend diverting off public roads within Aboriginal Land areas, a permit is required from the relevant Aboriginal authority.
Beware of crocodiles in rivers, estuaries and coastal areas.
Kununurra
GARDNER PLATEAU
144
Hall Point
KUNMUNYA ABORIGINAL RESERVE
PRINCE REGENT NATURE RESERVE
Koolan
Collier Bay
Cape Leveque
One Arm Point
Lombadina
MILITARY TRAINING AREA
KIMBERLEY
Mount Barnett Roadhouse
Gibb River
Kupingarri
King Sound
Pender Bay
Beagle Bay
BEAGLE BAY ABORIGINAL RESERVE
KING LEOPOLD RANGES CP
Cape Baskerville
Derby
DEVONIAN REEF NATIONAL PARKS
Coulomb Point
POINT COOLOMB NR
Willare Bridge Roadhouse
RANGES
Cape Boileau
Roebuck Roadhouse
Looma
NOOGOORA BURR QUARANTINE AREA
GREAT
NORTHERN
HWY
Fitzroy Crossing
Halls Creek
Broome
Roebuck Bay
Cape Villaret
Gourdon Bay
False Cape Bossut
Bidyadanga
Cape Jaubert
Eighty Mile Beach
Sandfire Roadhouse
DOON DOON ABORIGINAL LAND
Lake Argyle
Turkey Creek Roadhouse
Warmun (Turkey Creek)
PURNULULU NP
Bungle Bungles
VICTORIA
Amanbidji
Mistake Creek
DUNCAN
DENISON PLAINS
NORTHERN TERRITORY
WESTERN AUSTRALIA
Billiluna (Mindibungu)
TANAMI
Balgo Hills
Lake Gregory
KEARNEY ABORIGINAL LAND
ROUTE
Lake Wills
GREAT SANDY DESERT
De Grey River
Tobin Lake
Percival Lakes
Lake Waukarlycarly
Lake Dora
RUDALL RIVER NATIONAL PARK
Oakover River
Kunawarritji
Lake Auld
Lake George
STOCK
Kiwirrkurra
Lake Mackay
Lake Macdonald
CAPRICORN
OF
TROPIC
WALAGUNYA ABORIGINAL LAND
Jigalong
JIGALONG ABORIGINAL LAND
Lake Disappointment
GIBSON DESERT
CENTRAL
AUSTRALIA
Lake Earnham
Warakurna
Warakurna Roadhouse
LITTLE SANDY DESERT
GIBSON DESERT NATURE RESERVE
MUNGILLI ABORIGINAL LAND
NGAANYATJARRA ABORIGINAL LAND
GUNBARREL
CANNING
CARNARVON
RANGES
Lake Nabberu
Carnegie Homestead
Lake Carnegie
Lake Breaden
Boyd Lagoon
Warburton Roadhouse
Warburton
OUTBACK
LAND TRUST
Surveyor
140
147
0 50 100 150 200 km
Scale
N

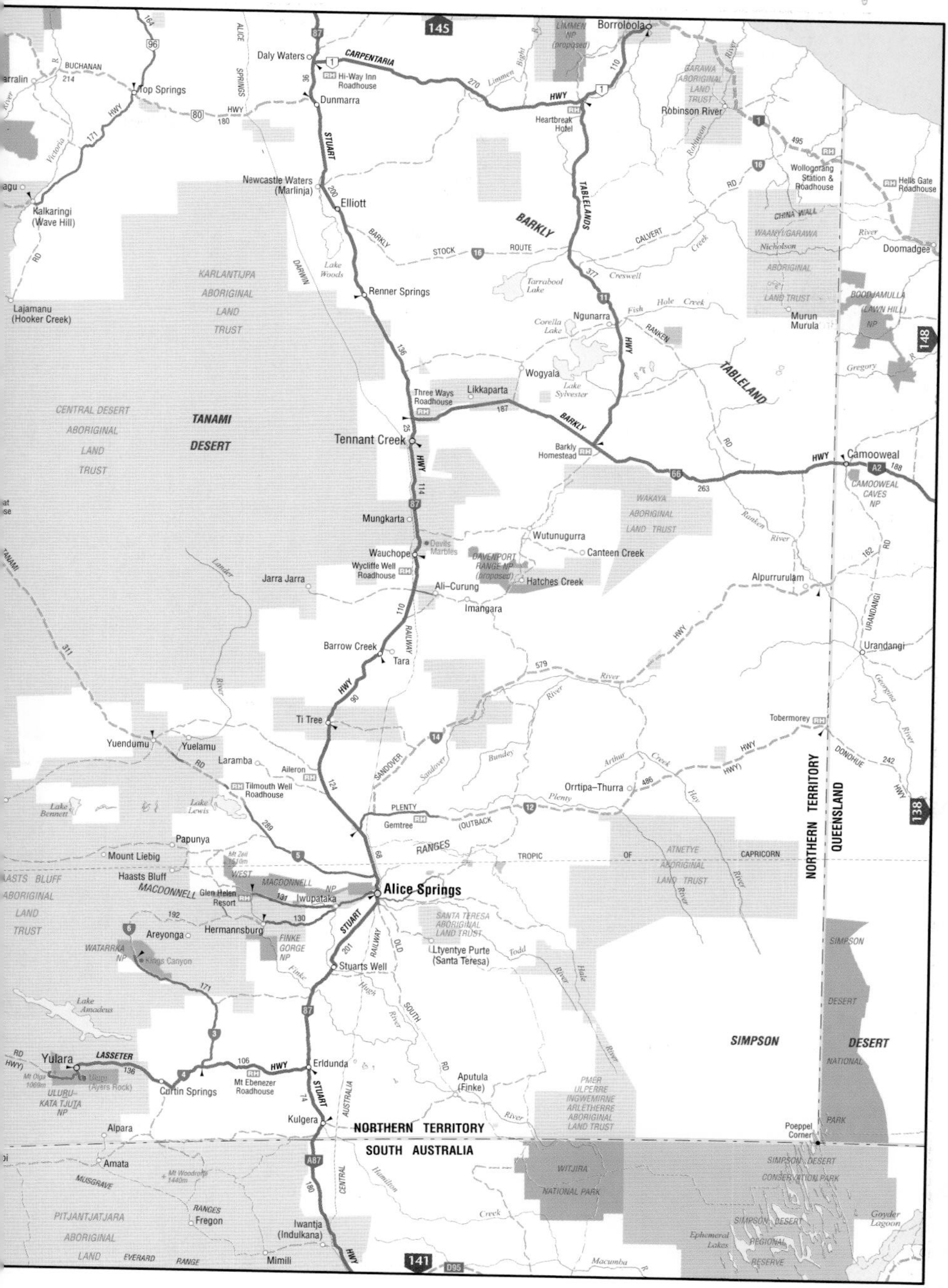

145

Daly Waters
CARPENTARIA
Hi-Way Inn Roadhouse
Dunmarra
BUCHANAN
Top Springs
Kalkaringi (Wave Hill)
Lajamanu (Hooker Creek)
Limmen NP (proposed)
Borroloola
Heartbreak Hotel
Robinson River
Garawa Aboriginal Land Trust
Wollogorang Station & Roadhouse
Hells Gate Roadhouse
China Wall
Waanyi/Garawa Aboriginal Land Trust
Doomadgee
Newcastle Waters (Marlinja)
Elliott
STUART HWY
TABLELANDS HWY
BARKLY
BARKLY STOCK ROUTE
CALVERT RD
Lake Woods
Renner Springs
Tarrabool Lake
Creswell Creek
Ngunarra
Corella Lake
Fish Hole Creek
RANKEN
Murun Murula
Boodjamulla (Lawn Hill) NP
148
Gregory R
Karlantijpa Aboriginal Land Trust
Wogyala
Lake Sylvester
TABLELAND
Three Ways Roadhouse
Likkaparta
BARKLY HWY
Central Desert Aboriginal Land Trust
TANAMI DESERT
Tennant Creek
Barkly Homestead
Camooweal
Camooweal Caves NP
Wakaya Aboriginal Land Trust
Mungkarta
Wutunugurra
Canteen Creek
Wauchope
Devils Marbles
Wycliffe Well Roadhouse
Davenport Range NP (proposed)
Hatches Creek
Jarra Jarra
Ali-Curung
Imangara
Ranken River
Alpurrurulam
Urandangi
TANAMI
Lander River
Barrow Creek
Tara
RAILWAY
Sandover River
Ti Tree
Tobermorey
Yuendumu
Yuelamu
Laramba
Aileron
Tilmouth Well Roadhouse
Bundey
Arthur Creek
Orrtipa–Thurra
Hay River
DONOHUE HWY
138
Lake Bennett
Lake Lewis
PLENTY (OUTBACK) HWY
Plenty River
Gemtree
Papunya
Mount Liebig
RANGES
TROPIC OF CAPRICORN
Atnetye Aboriginal Land Trust
Haasts Bluff
Haasts Bluff Aboriginal Land Trust
MacDonnell
West MacDonnell NP
Mt Zeil 1510m
Glen Helen Resort
Iwupataka
Alice Springs
NORTHERN TERRITORY
QUEENSLAND
Areyonga
Hermannsburg
Finke Gorge NP
Santa Teresa Aboriginal Land Trust
Ltyentye Purte (Santa Teresa)
Todd River
Hale River
Simpson Desert National Park
Watarrka NP
Kings Canyon
Stuarts Well
Finke River
Hugh River
OLD SOUTH RD
Lake Amadeus
SIMPSON DESERT
Yulara
LASSETER HWY
Mt Olga 1069m
Uluru (Ayers Rock)
Uluru-Kata Tjuta NP
Curtin Springs
Mt Ebenezer Roadhouse
Erldunda
Aputula (Finke)
Pmer Ulperre Ingwemirne Arletherre Aboriginal Land Trust
Kulgera
CENTRAL AUSTRALIA RAILWAY
Alpara
NORTHERN TERRITORY
SOUTH AUSTRALIA
Poeppel Corner
Amata
Mt Woodroffe 1440m
MUSGRAVE RANGES
Witjira National Park
Simpson Desert Conservation Park
Hamilton Creek
Pitjantjatjara Aboriginal Land
Fregon
Iwantja (Indulkana)
Simpson Desert Regional Reserve
Ephemeral Lakes
Goyder Lagoon
EVERARD RANGE
Mimili
141
Macumba R

INTER-CITY ROUTES	DISTANCE
Darwin–Adelaide via Stuart Hwy 1 87 A87 A1	3026 km
Darwin–Perth via Great Northern Hwy 1 95	4032 km
Darwin–Brisbane via Warrego Hwy 1 87 66 A2	3406 km

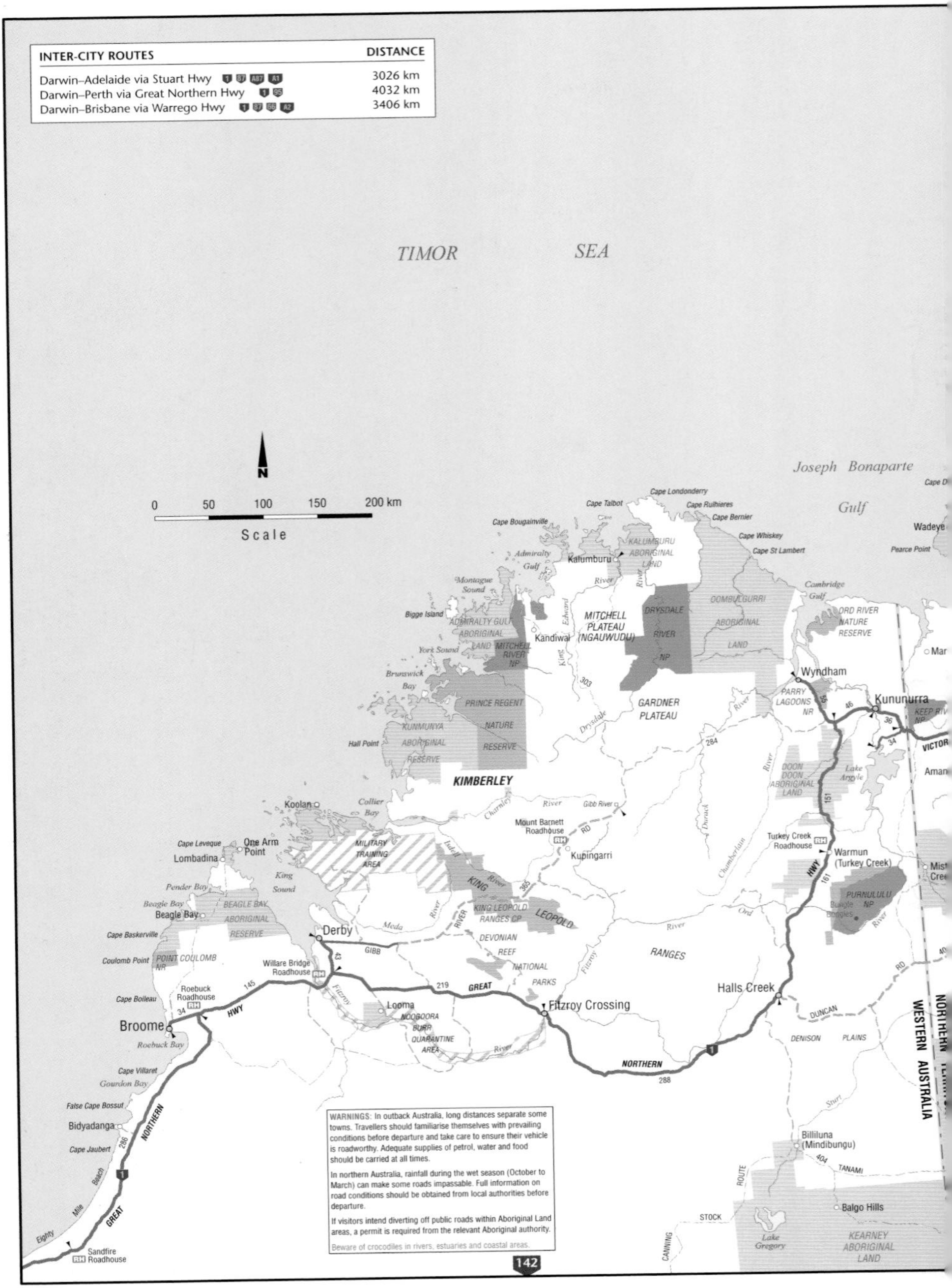

TIMOR SEA

N

0 50 100 150 200 km

Scale

Joseph Bonaparte Gulf

Cape Londonderry
Cape Talbot
Cape Rulhieres
Cape Bernier
Cape Bougainville
Cape Whiskey
Cape St Lambert
Wadeye
Pearce Point
Admiralty Gulf
Kalumburu
KALUMBURU ABORIGINAL LAND
Montague Sound
Cambridge Gulf
Bigge Island
ADMIRALTY GULF ABORIGINAL LAND
MITCHELL PLATEAU (NGAUWUDU)
DRYSDALE RIVER NP
OOMBULGURRI ABORIGINAL LAND
ORD RIVER NATURE RESERVE
Kandiwal
MITCHELL RIVER NP
York Sound
Brunswick Bay
Wyndham
PARRY LAGOONS NR
Kununurra
KEEP RIVER NP
PRINCE REGENT NATURE RESERVE
GARDNER PLATEAU
KUNMUNYA ABORIGINAL RESERVE
Hall Point
VICTORIA
KIMBERLEY
DOON DOON ABORIGINAL LAND
Lake Argyle
Koolan
Collier Bay
Gibb River
Mount Barnett Roadhouse
Kupingarri
Cape Leveque
One Arm Point
Lombadina
MILITARY TRAINING AREA
King Sound
Turkey Creek Roadhouse
Warmun (Turkey Creek)
Pender Bay
Beagle Bay
BEAGLE BAY ABORIGINAL RESERVE
KING LEOPOLD RANGES CP
PURNULULU NP
Bungle Bungles
Cape Baskerville
Derby
DEVONIAN REEF NATIONAL PARKS
RANGES
Coulomb Point
POINT COULOMB NR
Willare Bridge Roadhouse
Cape Boileau
Roebuck Roadhouse
Halls Creek
Broome
Roebuck Bay
Fitzroy Crossing
Looma
NOOGOORA BURR QUARANTINE AREA
DUNCAN
DENISON PLAINS
GREAT NORTHERN HWY
Cape Villaret
Gourdon Bay
False Cape Bossut
Bidyadanga
Cape Jaubert
Eighty Mile Beach
Billiluna (Mindibungu)
TANAMI
Balgo Hills
Lake Gregory
KEARNEY ABORIGINAL LAND
CANNING STOCK ROUTE
Sandfire Roadhouse
NORTHERN TERRITORY
WESTERN AUSTRALIA

WARNINGS: In outback Australia, long distances separate some towns. Travellers should familiarise themselves with prevailing conditions before departure and take care to ensure their vehicle is roadworthy. Adequate supplies of petrol, water and food should be carried at all times.

In northern Australia, rainfall during the wet season (October to March) can make some roads impassable. Full information on road conditions should be obtained from local authorities before departure.

If visitors intend diverting off public roads within Aboriginal Land areas, a permit is required from the relevant Aboriginal authority.

Beware of crocodiles in rivers, estuaries and coastal areas.

142

ARAFURA SEA

COBOURG PENINSULA
Croker Island
Gul Gul
Minjilang
Dundas Strait
GARIG GUNAK BARLU NATIONAL PARK
Cape Cockburn
TIWI ABORIGINAL LAND TRUST
MELVILLE ISLAND
Murgenella
Goulburn Islands
Warruwi
Braithwaite Point
Pickertaramoor
Van Diemen Gulf
Cape Hotham
DJUKBINJ NP
Gunbalanya (Oenpelli)
Border Store
Maningrida
Cape Stewart
Milingimbi
Nangalala
Ramingining
Manmoyi
ARNHEM LAND ABORIGINAL LAND TRUST
Howard Springs
ARNHEM HWY
MARY RIVER NP (proposed)
KAKADU NATIONAL PARK
Jabiru
ARNHEM LAND PLATEAU
KAKADU HWY
Adelaide River
Emerald Springs Wayside Inn
Hayes Creek Wayside Inn
Mary River Roadhouse
Pine Creek
Douglas Daly Tourist Park
NITMILUK NP
Manyallaluk
Jodetluk (George Camp)
Katherine
Maranboy
Barunga
CENTRAL ARNHEM RD
Bulman
Wilton River
Mann River
Rose River
Ngukurr
Roper Bar Store
ROPER HWY
ELSEY NP
Mataranka
MANGGRRAYI ABORIGINAL LAND TRUST
Minyerri
ALAWA 1 ABORIGINAL LAND TRUST
LIMMEN NATIONAL PARK (proposed)
NATHAN RIVER RD
Limmen Bight
Maria Island
MENNGEN ABORIGINAL LAND TRUST
GREGORY NP
Victoria River Roadhouse
BUNTINE HWY
Larrimah
Hodgson River
ALAWA ABORIGINAL LAND TRUST
Minamia
ALICE SPRINGS
Daly Waters
Hi-Way Inn Roadhouse
CARPENTARIA HWY
Borroloola
Dunmarra
STUART HWY
Heartbreak Hotel
BUCHANAN HWY
Top Springs
Newcastle Waters (Marlinja)
Elliott
Lake Woods
BARKLY
BARKLY STOCK ROUTE
CALVERT
TABLELANDS HWY
Kalkaringi (Wave Hill)
Lajamanu (Hooker Creek)
KARLANTIJPA ABORIGINAL LAND TRUST
DARWIN RAILWAY
Renner Springs
Tarrabool Lake
Creswell
Ngunarra
Fish Hole Creek
RANKEN
Corella Lake
Wogyala
Lake Sylvester
Three Ways Roadhouse
Likkaparta
BARKLY HWY
CENTRAL DESERT ABORIGINAL LAND TRUST
TANAMI DESERT
Tennant Creek
Barkly Homestead
TABLELAND
Mungkarta
Wutunugurra
WAKAYA ABORIGINAL LAND TRUST
Wauchope
Devils Marbles
Wycliffe Well Roadhouse
DAVENPORT RANGE NP (proposed)
Hatches Creek
Canteen Creek
Alpurrurulam

Cape Wessel
WESSEL ISLANDS
Marchinbar Island
Guluwuru Island
Drysdale Island
Elcho Island
Point Wilberforce
Galwinku
Gunyangara
Nhulunbuy
Yirrkala
Arnhem Bay
GOVE PENINSULA
Gapuwiyak
Garrthalala
Cape Grey
Baniyala
Cape Shield
Isle Woodah
Milyakburra
Umbakumba
Angurugu
GROOTE EYLANDT
Cape Beatrice
Numbulwar
GULF OF CARPENTARIA
West Island
SIR EDWARD PELLEW GROUP
North Island
Vanderlin Island
GARAWA ABORIGINAL LAND TRUST
Robinson River
Wollogorang Station & Roadhouse
Hells Gate Roadhouse
CHINA WALL
WAANYI/GARAWA ABORIGINAL LAND TRUST
Nicholson River
Doomadgee
BOODJAMULLA (LAWN HILL) NP
Murun Murula
Gregory River
NORTHERN TERRITORY
QUEENSLAND
Camooweal
CAMOOWEAL CAVES NP
URANDANGI

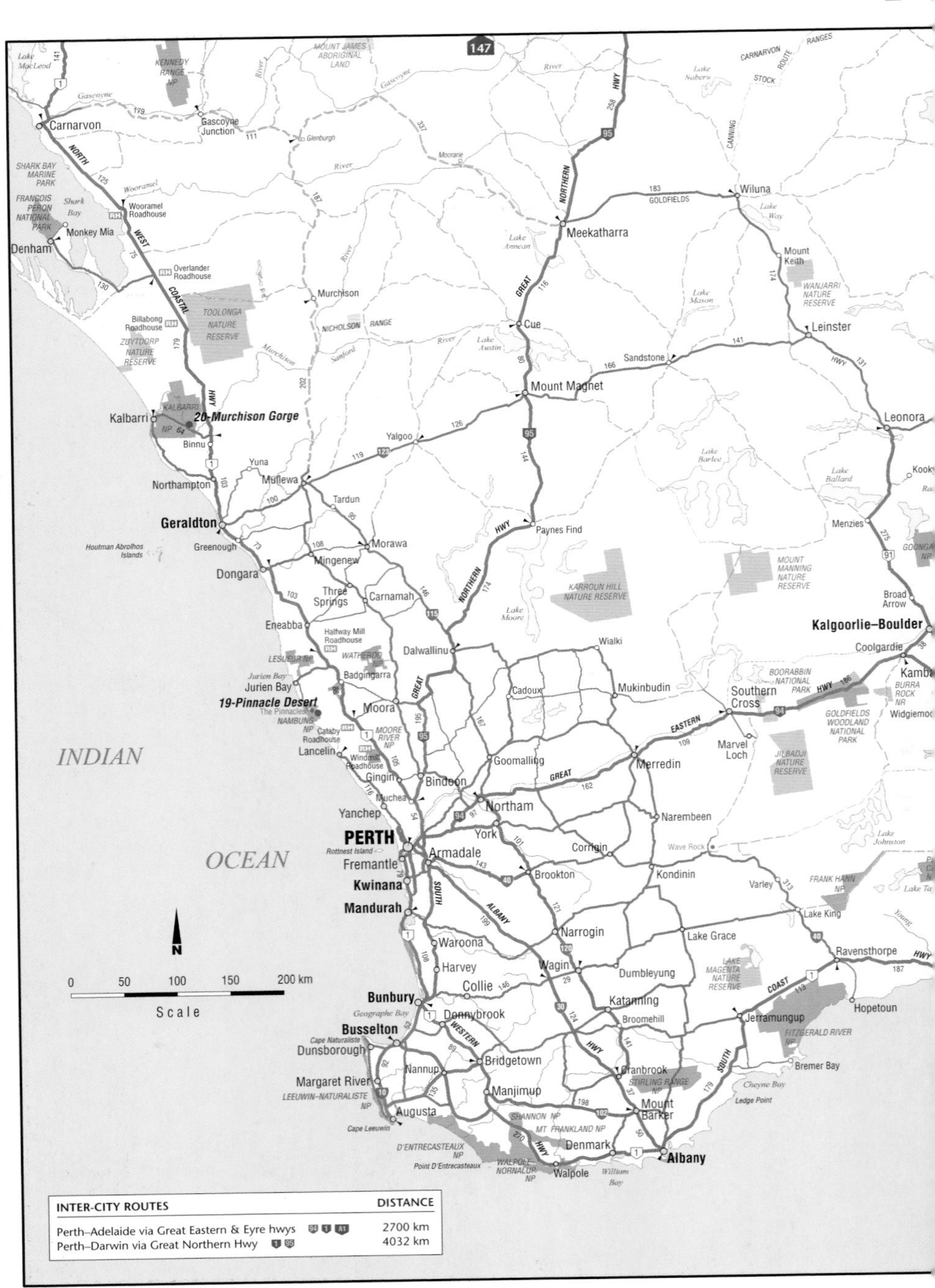

INTER-CITY ROUTES	DISTANCE
Perth–Adelaide via Great Eastern & Eyre hwys 94 1 A1	2700 km
Perth–Darwin via Great Northern Hwy 1 95	4032 km

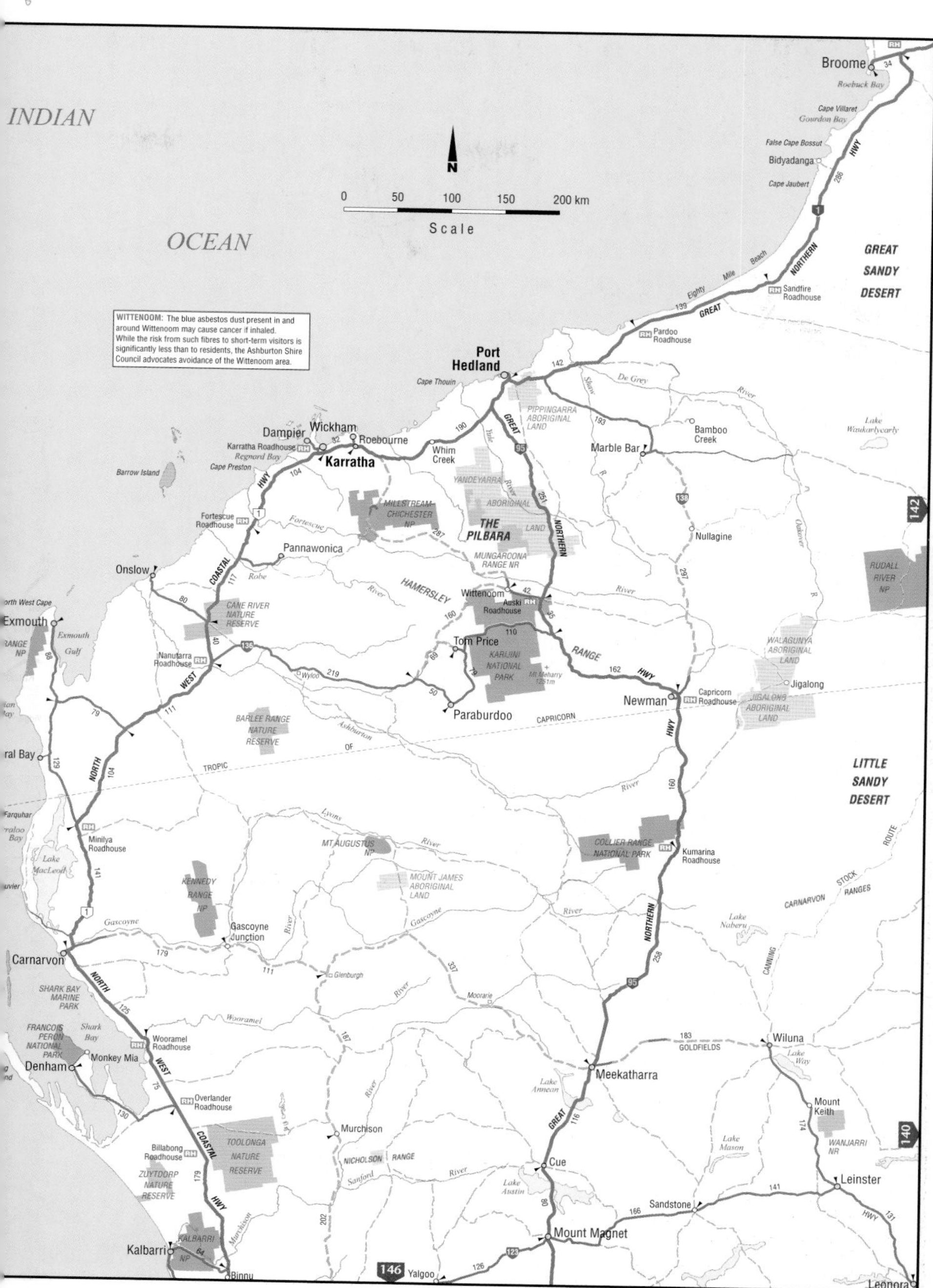

INDIAN
OCEAN
0 50 100 150 200 km
Scale
WITTENOOM: The blue asbestos dust present in and around Wittenoom may cause cancer if inhaled. While the risk from such fibres to short-term visitors is significantly less than to residents, the Ashburton Shire Council advocates avoidance of the Wittenoom area.
Broome
Roebuck Bay
Cape Villaret
Gourdon Bay
False Cape Bossut
Bidyadanga
Cape Jaubert
Eighty Mile Beach
Sandfire Roadhouse
Pardoo Roadhouse
GREAT SANDY DESERT
Port Hedland
Cape Thouin
PIPPINGARRA ABORIGINAL LAND
De Grey
Bamboo Creek
Marble Bar
Lake Waukarlycarly
Dampier
Wickham
Roebourne
Karratha Roadhouse
Regnard Bay
Karratha
Cape Preston
Whim Creek
Barrow Island
YANDEYARRA ABORIGINAL LAND
MILLSTREAM-CHICHESTER NP
THE PILBARA
Fortescue Roadhouse
Fortescue
Nullagine
MUNGAROONA RANGE NR
Pannawonica
Onslow
Robe
HAMERSLEY
Wittenoom
Auski Roadhouse
RUDALL RIVER NP
North West Cape
Exmouth
Exmouth Gulf
CANE RIVER NATURE RESERVE
Tom Price
KARIJINI NATIONAL PARK
Mt Meharry 1251m
RANGE
WALAGUNYA ABORIGINAL LAND
Nanutarra Roadhouse
Wyloo
Jigalong
Newman
Capricorn Roadhouse
JIGALONG ABORIGINAL LAND
Paraburdoo
BARLEE RANGE NATURE RESERVE
Ashburton
TROPIC OF CAPRICORN
Coral Bay
LITTLE SANDY DESERT
Lyons
Minilya Roadhouse
MT AUGUSTUS NP
COLLIER RANGE NATIONAL PARK
Kumarina Roadhouse
Lake MacLeod
KENNEDY RANGE NP
MOUNT JAMES ABORIGINAL LAND
CARNARVON STOCK ROUTE
RANGES
Gascoyne
Gascoyne Junction
Lake Nabberu
Carnarvon
Glenburgh
CANNING
SHARK BAY MARINE PARK
Moorarie
Wooramel
FRANCOIS PERON NATIONAL PARK
Shark Bay
Wooramel Roadhouse
Monkey Mia
Denham
GOLDFIELDS
Wiluna
Lake Way
Meekatharra
Lake Annean
Overlander Roadhouse
Mount Keith
WANJARRI NR
TOOLONGA NATURE RESERVE
Murchison
Lake Mason
Billabong Roadhouse
NICHOLSON RANGE
Sanford
Cue
ZUYTDORP NATURE RESERVE
Lake Austin
Leinster
Sandstone
Mount Magnet
Kalbarri
KALBARRI NP
Binnu
Yalgoo
Leonora
GREAT NORTHERN HWY
NORTH WEST COASTAL HWY

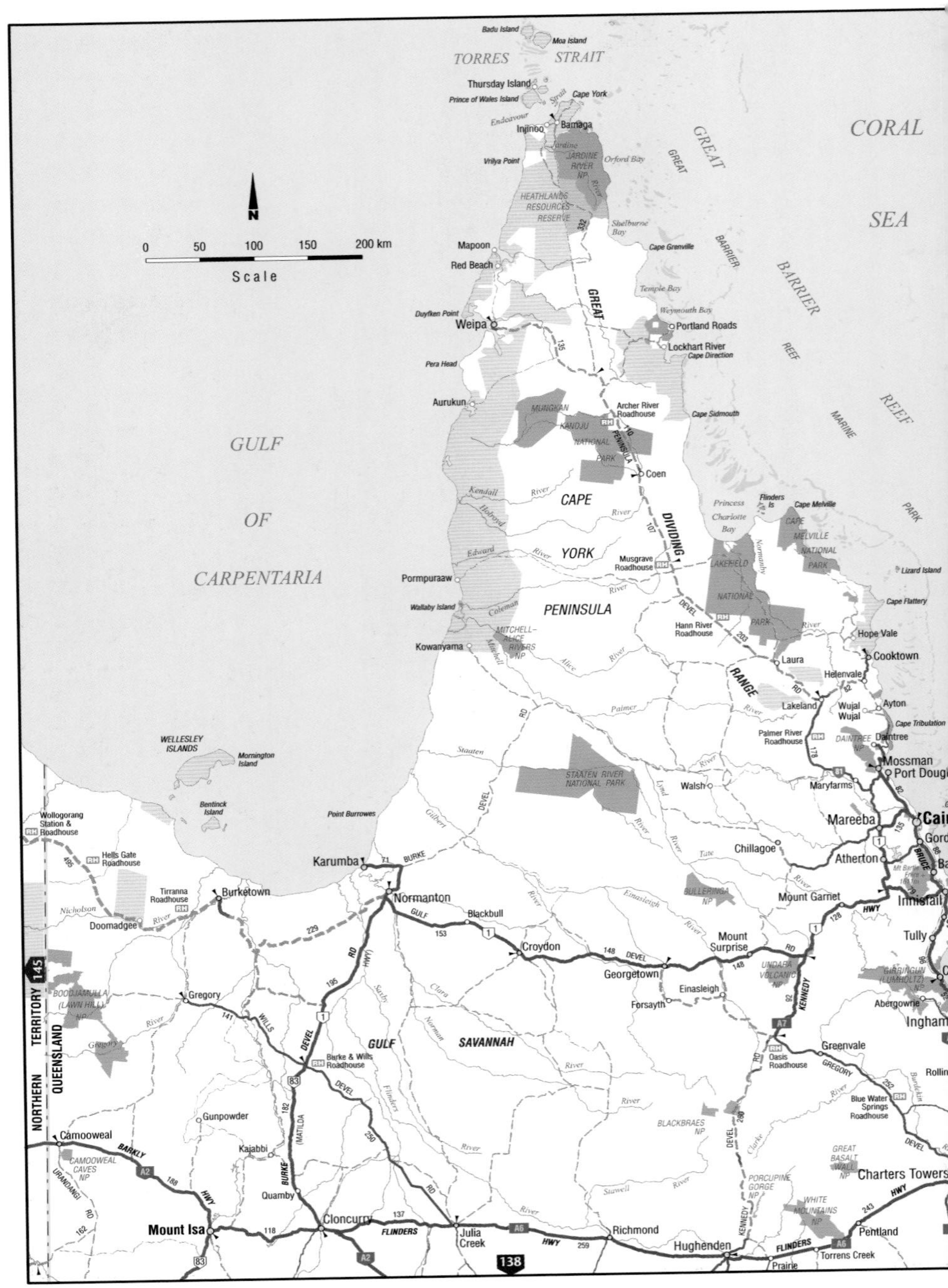
Badu Island
Moa Island
TORRES STRAIT
Thursday Island
Prince of Wales Island
Cape York
Endeavour Strait
Injinoo
Bamaga
Jardine River
JARDINE RIVER NP
Orford Bay
Vrilya Point
HEATHLANDS RESOURCES RESERVE
Shelburne Bay
CORAL SEA
GREAT BARRIER REEF MARINE PARK
0 50 100 150 200 km
Scale
N
Mapoon
Red Beach
Cape Grenville
Temple Bay
Weymouth Bay
Duyfken Point
Weipa
Portland Roads
Lockhart River
Cape Direction
Pera Head
Aurukun
Archer River Roadhouse
Cape Sidmouth
MUNGKAN KANDJU NATIONAL PARK
GULF OF CARPENTARIA
Coen
CAPE YORK PENINSULA
GREAT DIVIDING RANGE
PENINSULA DEVEL RD
Kendall River
Holroyd River
Edward River
Princess Charlotte Bay
Flinders Is
Cape Melville
CAPE MELVILLE NATIONAL PARK
Lizard Island
Musgrave Roadhouse
LAKEFIELD NATIONAL PARK
Normanby River
Pormpuraaw
Wallaby Island
Coleman River
Cape Flattery
Hann River Roadhouse
Hope Vale
MITCHELL-ALICE RIVERS NP
Kowanyama
Mitchell River
Alice River
Laura
Cooktown
Helenvale
Palmer River
Lakeland
Wujal Wujal
Ayton
Cape Tribulation
Palmer River Roadhouse
DAINTREE NP
Daintree
WELLESLEY ISLANDS
Mornington Island
Staaten River
STAATEN RIVER NATIONAL PARK
Mossman
Port Douglas
Walsh
Lynd River
Maryfarms
Bentinck Island
Point Burrowes
Wollogorang Station & Roadhouse
Gilbert River
Mareeba
Cairns
Gordonvale
Hells Gate Roadhouse
Karumba
BURKE DEVEL RD
Chillagoe
Tate River
Atherton
BRUCE HWY
Tirranna Roadhouse
Burketown
Normanton
Einasleigh River
BULLERINGA NP
Mount Garnet
Innisfail
Nicholson River
Doomadgee
GULF HWY
Blackbull
Croydon
Mount Surprise
Tully
Georgetown
UNDARA VOLCANIC NP
GIRRINGUN (LUMHOLTZ) NP
NORTHERN TERRITORY
QUEENSLAND
BOODJAMULLA (LAWN HILL) NP
Gregory
Einasleigh
Forsayth
KENNEDY
Abergowrie
Ingham
WILLS
Clara River
Norman River
Saxby River
GULF SAVANNAH
Burke & Wills Roadhouse
Oasis Roadhouse
Greenvale
GREGORY
Rollingstone
Flinders River
Blue Water Springs Roadhouse
Burdekin River
Gunpowder
BLACKBRAES NP
Camooweal
BARKLY HWY
CAMOOWEAL CAVES NP
Kajabbi
(MATILDA)
BURKE
GREAT BASALT WALL NP
Charters Towers
URANDANGI RD
PORCUPINE GORGE NP
Clarke River
Stawell River
Quamby
WHITE MOUNTAINS NP
FLINDERS HWY
Mount Isa
Cloncurry
Julia Creek
Richmond
Hughenden
Pentland
Torrens Creek
Prairie
Mt Bartle Frere 1611m
138

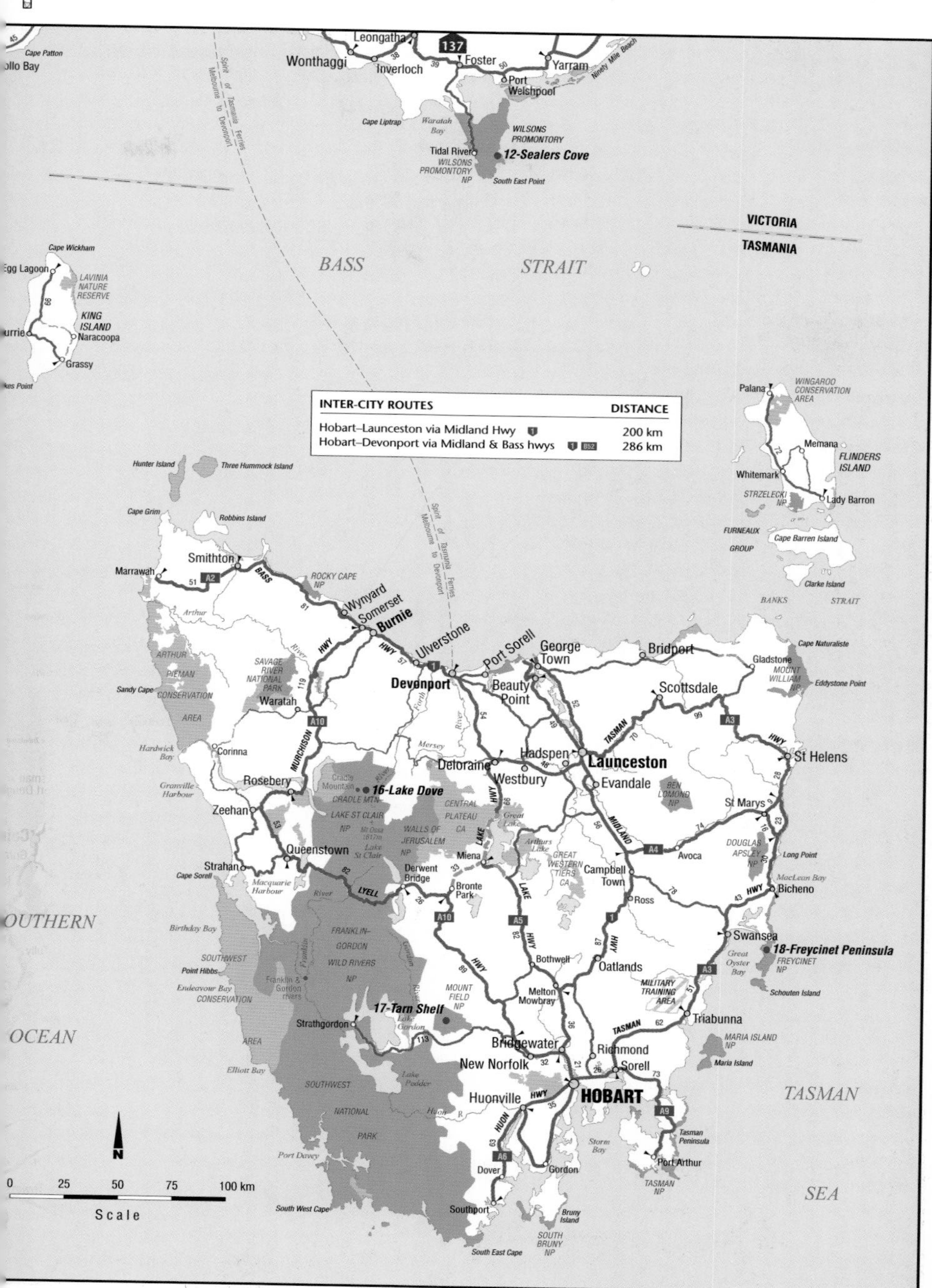
INTER-CITY ROUTES
DISTANCE
Hobart–Launceston via Midland Hwy 1 200 km
Hobart–Devonport via Midland & Bass hwys 1 B52 286 km
BASS
STRAIT
VICTORIA
TASMANIA
Leongatha
Wonthaggi
Inverloch
Foster
Yarram
Port Welshpool
Ninety Mile Beach
Cape Liptrap
Waratah Bay
WILSONS PROMONTORY
Tidal River
12-Sealers Cove
WILSONS PROMONTORY NP
South East Point
Spirit of Tasmania Ferries Melbourne to Devonport
Cape Patton
Cape Wickham
Egg Lagoon
LAVINIA NATURE RESERVE
KING ISLAND
Naracoopa
Grassy
Palana
WINGAROO CONSERVATION AREA
Memana
FLINDERS ISLAND
Whitemark
STRZELECKI NP
Lady Barron
FURNEAUX GROUP
Cape Barren Island
Clarke Island
BANKS STRAIT
Hunter Island
Three Hummock Island
Cape Grim
Robbins Island
Smithton
Marrawah
ROCKY CAPE NP
Wynyard
Somerset
Burnie
Ulverstone
Devonport
Port Sorell
George Town
Beauty Point
Bridport
Scottsdale
Gladstone
Cape Naturaliste
MOUNT WILLIAM NP
Eddystone Point
St Helens
Launceston
Hadspen
Deloraine
Westbury
Evandale
BEN LOMOND NP
St Marys
Avoca
DOUGLAS APSLEY NP
Long Point
Bicheno
MacLean Bay
Campbell Town
Ross
Swansea
18-Freycinet Peninsula
FREYCINET NP
Great Oyster Bay
Schouten Island
Oatlands
MILITARY TRAINING AREA
Triabunna
MARIA ISLAND NP
Maria Island
Bothwell
Melton Mowbray
Bridgewater
New Norfolk
Richmond
Sorell
HOBART
Huonville
Storm Bay
Gordon
Dover
Southport
Bruny Island
SOUTH BRUNY NP
South East Cape
Tasman Peninsula
Port Arthur
TASMAN NP
TASMAN SEA
ARTHUR PIEMAN CONSERVATION AREA
Sandy Cape
SAVAGE RIVER NATIONAL PARK
Waratah
Corinna
Hardwick Bay
Rosebery
Granville Harbour
Zeehan
16-Lake Dove
CRADLE MTN LAKE ST CLAIR NP
CENTRAL PLATEAU CA
WALLS OF JERUSALEM NP
Queenstown
Strahan
Cape Sorell
Macquarie Harbour
Miena
Arthurs Lake
Great Lake
GREAT WESTERN TIERS CA
Derwent Bridge
Bronte Park
FRANKLIN–GORDON WILD RIVERS NP
SOUTHWEST CONSERVATION AREA
Birthday Bay
Point Hibbs
Endeavour Bay
MOUNT FIELD NP
17-Tarn Shelf
Strathgordon
Lake Gordon
Lake Pedder
Elliott Bay
SOUTHWEST NATIONAL PARK
Port Davey
South West Cape
SOUTHERN
OCEAN
MURCHISON HWY
LYELL HWY
LAKE HWY
MIDLAND HWY
TASMAN HWY
HUON HWY
BASS HWY
0 25 50 75 100 km
Scale
N

Publisher's acknowledgements

Publications manager
Astrid Browne

Editor
Geraldine Corridon

Design
desertpony

Layout
Megan Ellis

Photography credits

Cover
Kalbarri National Park
(Thomas Schmitt/Getty Images)

Back cover
Entrance view to Wineglass Bay from Mount Amos (Andrew Close)

All other images in this book were taken in the field by the authors and are the copyright of Tyrone Thomas and Andrew Close except the following:

p. v Bushwalking in Main Range National Park. Courtesy of Tourism Queensland.
p. 3 Lord Howe Island. Courtesy Tourism NSW.
p. 27 Cunninghams Gap, Main Range National Park. Courtesy of Tourism Queensland.
p. 28 Cooktown orchid. Greg Campbell.

Other publications by Tyrone T. Thomas

40 Bushland and Park Walks in Metropolitan Melbourne

80 Walks in the Grampians

60 Walks in Victoria's Bright and Falls Creek District

120 Walks in New South Wales

70 Walks in Southern New South Wales and ACT

120 Walks in Tasmania

50 Walks in North Queensland

50 Walks: Coffs Harbour, Gold Coast Hinterland

50 Walks in South Australia

20 Best Walks in Australia

Walking in Tasmania

Tyrone Thomas: My Environmental Expose

150 Walks in Victoria (with Andrew Close)

Contact Tyrone Thomas and Andrew Close
PO Box 106
Mount Macedon, Victoria 3441

Explore Australia Publishing Pty Ltd
85 High Street
Prahran, Victoria 3181, Australia

10 9 8 7 6 5 4 3 2 1

ISBN 978 1 74117 240 9

Printed in China by SNP Leefung Printers Ltd

Publisher's Note: Every effort has been made to ensure that the information in this book is accurate at the time of going to press. The publisher welcomes information and suggestions for correction or improvement. Write to the Publications Manager, Explore Australia Publishing, 85 High Street, Prahran 3181, Australia or email explore@hardiegrant.com.au

Disclaimers: The publisher cannot accept responsibility for any errors or omissions. The representation on the maps of any road or track is not necessarily evidence of public right of way. The publisher cannot be held responsible for any injury, loss or damage incurred during travel. Travellers should be aware that conditions in remote areas change; it is vital to research any proposed trip thoroughly and seek the advice of relevant state and travel organisations before you leave.